Talking

Pictures

A Parents' Guide to Using Movies to Discuss Ethics,
Values, and Everyday Problems with Children

By Ronald J. Madison, Ed.D.
and Corey Schmidt

RUNNING PRESS
PHILADELPHIA · LONDON

Printed in the United States of America

9 8 7 6 5 4 3 2 1
Digit on the right indicates the number of this printing

Library of Congress Cataloging-in-Publication Number 00-132696

ISBN 0-7624-0803-0

Cover and interior illustrations by Cyril Cabry
Cover and interior design by Toby Schmidt
Edited by Patty Smith
Typography by Jan Greenberg

**This book may be ordered by mail from the publisher.
Please add $2.50 for shipping and handling.**
But try your bookstore first!

Running Press Book Publishers
125 South Twenty-second Street
Philadelphia, Pennsylvania 19103-4399
Visit us on the web!
www. runningpress.com

*T*o my wife, Deborah, for her continuous enthusiasm for the book, her many creative ideas and her never-ending love.

*T*o my three children, Kim, Charlie, and Emily, for making talking pictures in our home so enjoyable and insightful.

*T*o my dear parents Mary and Alfred who instilled in me the joy of life.

—Ronald J. Madison, Ed.D.

*T*o my fiancé, Alan Meizlik, for the late night drives to the video store, for letting me hog the TV, the VCR, and the computer, and for his unconditional love and support.

*T*o my mother, Toby Schachman, who helped transform this seed of an idea into a reality, combined constructive criticism with positive feedback, and always kept me focused on the end result while reciting to me her favorite mantra: "You get out of it what you put into it."

*T*o my father, Louis Schmidt, who, when I was young, instilled in me a love and appreciation for films by forcing me to watch the classics, and who still uses films to connect with me and others; you will always be my favorite movie critic.

—Corey Schmidt

ACKNOWLEDGEMENTS

Special thanks to the many individuals who took the time to complete our surveys: the faculty and staff of Hammonton Public School, Holy Family College, and the public relations staff of PNC Bank, Philadelphia/Southern New Jersey; Joel Perlmutter, Brett Rand and the employees of Perlmart ShopRite, Tom's River; as well as all our loving friends and family who participated in the process.

Also, special thanks to Paul VanVreede of Couch Potatoes Video in Medford, New Jersey, for his warmth and for giving us access to his entire movie inventory; everyone at Lil' Video in Old City; and the folks at TLA Video on 4th Street in Philadelphia.

Finally, we are extremely grateful to David Borgenicht of Book Soup Publishing, our agent and friend, who saw potential in our first proposal and helped us get a book contract; our editor, Patty Smith; and our publisher, Stuart Teacher, at Running Press Book Publishers, for giving us this wonderful opportunity.

CONTENTS

CONTENTS

CONTENTS

PREFACE

Talking Pictures offers films that are beneficial for parents and their children to watch together to discuss the important issues, problems, and concerns of today. There is one thing all of the movies in this book share: All can be used as tools to help parents communicate.

Talking Pictures is not a film guide. We did not attempt to rate, analyze, or review the quality of the films in this book. We did not critique these films for their directing, cinematography, acting, writing, or any other related component.

What we do offer is a balanced mix of movies representing different genres, eras, directors, and age groups. Many of the films in this book are critics' favorites, classics, or have received Academy Awards. Some of them may be box-office hits that were shunned by critics but loved by the general public. A few of these films may be virtually unknown, either because they were on the cutting edge, targeted to a particular subculture, or simply not seen by many people.

Obviously, each film speaks to a number of different subjects, issues, and themes and often has more than one lesson or message. Many films could have applied to several chapters, and even cross over throughout the different age groups. As you use this book, please select appropriate films to watch with your children. You need not limit yourself to a section or chapter because often, the film could easily fit into other themes and age groups.

INTRODUCTION

All over—in weekly film discussion groups, on the Internet, in coffee shops, with friends, with family, and with co-workers—people talk about movies; what we love, what we hate, who acted well, who was a disappointment, what scenes moved us, what scenes didn't work, which characters were our favorites, which ones reminded us of people we know, whether it was too long, too slow, or how we would make the movie better if we could. We've all gone to the movies, then out to dinner afterwards to discuss the issues the movie raised. It's a way for us all to relate to and communicate with each other—a way to deal with difficult subjects in a common framework.

In particular, families can use movies to get to the bottom of difficult issues with their children. Therapists and psychologists have been embracing the effectiveness of watching movies as a way to help patients address their problems. They realize that movies can provide a common ground for discussions about everything from love and friendship to family, prejudice, ethics, religion, politics, and more. This technique is effective because it allows families to talk about personal issues in relation to an outside element—the film. Discussing the topic using the objective plot and characters in the film may diffuse some tension created by discussing the sensitive topics on a directly personal level.

Movies make it easier for you to communicate with your children and for them to communicate with you. You may not be able to monitor everything they see or hear, but the more you know about their friends and their culture, the more you can prepare them for life and ensure that your voice as a parent is heard. It's better for you as a parent to be the first one to discuss or introduce an important or difficult issue than someone else; if you don't tell kids your opinion they might assume you don't have one.

Movies can be a catalyst for change. They present us with best- and worst-case scenarios and show different characters getting in and out of various problems and circumstances. Sometimes just seeing how an individual in a movie handles a situation is enough to give us a better clue of how to deal with a problem in our own lives. A teenager who watches and discusses *Good Will Hunting* may realize that she needs to forgive herself for a painful childhood and remove herself from the unhealthy patterns that hold her back, so that she can finally accept the love of others and use her skills productively.

Movies also make us feel. Sometimes emotions are locked inside and the key to unlocking them may be as easy as watching a film. Films sometimes evoke emotions that children and parents may otherwise avoid or keep buried. By eliciting this emotion, movies can offer a necessary breakthrough for your family. *Ordinary People* may uncover feelings of survivor guilt or anger towards a parent with whom we cannot connect, or it may make us aware of the signs of depression and suicide in someone else.

Films can reveal important things about your child. Children will extract scenes and issues from the movie that are important or interesting to them. In doing this, they reveal something about themselves—about their personality, their concerns, their interests, or their current problems. For example, upon watching *Searching for Bobby Fischer*, your aspiring dancer may realize her own anxiety about improving her dancing skills and performing in public.

To put things in perspective, families may find comfort in seeing the same problems with which their family is struggling played out on the screen. Children may be reassured that they are not alone when they see a character doing something they thought only they did. It is also nice to know that many families, many people, many countries and cultures, and many generations had it worse than us. For example, a child who feels like an outsider and a minority can watch *The Jackie Robinson Story* and identify with Robinson's struggle for equality. The film may help him realize that although things are not perfect, we've certainly come a long way from the time when African-Americans were not allowed to participate in professional sports leagues.

Often a movie's entertainment value is equaled by its educational value. We're not suggesting that movies should replace books or teachers, but they certainly can be a supplementary form of education. In only two hours, a film can expose the horrors of Nazi-occupied Holland (*The Diary of Anne Frank*), the self-destructive and drug-induced downfall of a rock legend (*The Doors*), or the challenge of overcoming handicaps (*The Miracle Worker*). They may teach us about a different time, place, or person.

Movies help take the spotlight off our problems. What may be so evident to a parent may be very difficult for a child to admit, understand, or address. A child may not want to admit that he is angry, sad, or sick. He may be completely unable and unwilling to even address an issue that a parent finds important. Sometimes distance helps make things clear by providing needed perspective; it is easy for children to get so caught up in their own experience that they lose objectivity. For example, by watching *The Secret Garden*, a child might become aware of his own feelings of anger, loss, and helplessness; he might learn that they are holding him back from being healthy.

Movies usually include antagonists, enemies, and villains, all of whom are cautionary examples of how not to behave. But the main characters, the heroes and heroines, can also make big mistakes, fall victim to unfortunate circumstance, or fail to make the right choices in life. Parents and children can learn from the mistakes made by characters in all different types of films. The movie *Kids* can serve as a drastic warning of what could happen when promiscuity is paired with lack of birth control.

By giving us something concrete to communicate about, movies help us communicate with each other. Sometimes words are hard to find that accurately represent the complexity of a family or parenting issue. Where words fail, films may succeed. The images shown in a movie may serve as a breakthrough for an issue to be addressed. They serve as metaphors that more effectively convey a message parents need to communicate, but have been unsuccessful at getting across. For example, by watching *Boyz N the Hood*, a parent may be able to finally communicate the importance of education in breaking away from life on the street.

Everyone remembers their first screen crush or the first time they had to cover their eyes at a movie. Movies both define and connect generations. Films can help put children in touch with the films, genres, actors, and styles that shaped their parents' generation. And they help parents get in touch with the popular stars and trends to which their children relate today. Movies define eras as well as our own personal stages in life; do you remember the first movie you saw in a theater? Who was your first screen crush or hero? What was the first movie you saw on a date? A mother might get a kick out of showing *Rebel Without A Cause* because it stars her teen crush, James Dean, while comparing him to her daughter's screen idol Leonardo DiCaprio in *Basketball Diaries* or Matt Damon in *Good Will Hunting*.

No matter how different a parent and a child are, no matter how difficult is for them to find a common ground, films can succeed at doing just that. When two people watch a movie, they might extract different meanings from it, but at least they have a starting point on which to build a discussion. For example, by watching *Stepmom*, a stepparent can come to better understand the conflicting loyalties a child experiences, while a daughter may realize how hard it is to come into an existing family unit and develop a relationship with someone who resents her presence.

Watching movies with your children is so easy! Chances are that you and your children watch movies regularly on your own or with friends together in your living room—so why not use this form of entertainment to enhance the shared time you have with your family? Important communication is so hard to squeeze into family time, but movies can make it easier to generate meaningful discussions and learning experiences between all family members.

Most importantly, *Talking Pictures* is a simple, effective, and fun way to get parents and children talking about their lives. Parents can use the book to help them solve problems, teach lessons, discuss difficult issues, or simply as an active way to communicate with their children.

The book is divided into sections based on age groups of children. Within each section are chapters centered on common themes that children from that age group may need to address. Each chapter explores the primary issues within that theme, then offers a selection of several films that explore those issues.

Each movie begins with a brief summary that is designed to provide parents with enough information about the content of the film to decide whether it may be appropriate for their children. The summary is followed by a brief analysis that explains some of the critical issues explored by the film, why it may be helpful to watch with your child, what types of questions it raises, and what types of problems it addresses.

A series of open-ended and thought-provoking discussion questions follows each film analysis. Questions are designed to stimulate communication between adults and children through inspiring a discussion about the issues raised in the film. The discussions of these movies offer the opportunities to share individual experiences, to resolve conflicts, and to further explore the meaning and messages of the film. Some questions focus more on the characters or plot of the film, while others seek to make connections between the film's content and your own family's or child's experience. There are no right or wrong answers to any of the questions listed in the discussion guide. Like books and art, films are open to interpretation and different individuals and different types of families will have various interpretations of the same scene or completely dissimilar understandings of a character's motive.

Pointers follow the discussion questions to provide a meaningful focus for conversation. They are lessons, messages, or directions that may take the film discussion to a deeper level and allow the family to communicate about an issue of relevance to their own situation. Pointers also offer an opportunity to put the focus on the parents themselves and allow them to draw parallels between the issue at hand and their own experiences.

We recommend that, before sitting down to watch a film, parents read through the discussion questions and pointers to prepare for the conversation after the film. If you prepare before watching the movie, it allows the conversation to flow more naturally after the movie because you will not be consulting the book. Don't feel pressured to address all the questions after watching a movie. Focus only on the ones that seem relevant to your child. You may want to limit the number of questions so that the conversation doesn't become tiresome to your child, particularly if she is very young. On the other hand, if your child is interested and engaged in the dialogue, offering more questions may continue to fuel the conversation.

Be cognizant of how your child will respond to *Talking Pictures*. Some children may enjoy the activity, while older children may perceive it as a lecture; still others won't think twice about it.

To take the discussion in the right direction after you have seen the film, pay close attention to your child's response to the film. If she is filled with emotion, use that powerful feeling as a starting point for discussion. If she is less open about her feelings and it is hard to get to her to open up, then focus on the film's plot as a basis for conversation.

Here are some tips for using *Talking Pictures* with more than one child:
- Make sure only one person talks at a time
- Be fully attentive—let them make their point
- Be respectful of others' opinions and direction of discussion
- Trade off directing questions at different children
- Ask what they think of others' responses; draw on what others say to get different opinions (i.e. what do you think of what Johnny said?)
- Make sure everyone gets a chance

Are you worried that your sixteen-year-old may be experimenting with drugs? Turn to Chapter 21: Drugs and Alcohol. Watching Leonardo DiCaprio in *Basketball Diaries* can help you discuss this difficult subject with him.

Is your six year old daughter having a hard time understanding the concept of "no"? Go to Chapter 3, watch *Pinocchio*, and discuss why parents set limits, and what might happen when children don't obey the rules.

Whatever the scenario, *Talking Pictures* offers suggested films and questions to address the issues, themes, or interests that are important to you and your family. Talk about an existing problem, anticipate an upcoming one, or simply watch and discuss. Sometimes just explaining why you like or dislike a film can reveal a great deal about who you are as a person.

Tips For Active Listening

The goal of *Talking Pictures* is to use films to initiate communication between parents and their children. But in order for parents to successfully communicate with their children, they need to understand what it means to be an active listener. These tips for listening actively should be applied when discussing films, but it wouldn't hurt to keep these rules in mind all the time. Too often conversations or discussions turn into one-sided lectures, which is not the point of *Talking Pictures*. The point is to promote communication, the flow of information back and forth between parent and child.

Let your child do most of the talking. You'll never get your children to openly discuss what they have seen in a movie if you occupy most of the "air time." As hard as it is, try to keep your ideas and statements short and compact. In other words, stop talking and start listening!

Ask your child "open-ended" questions. When steering conversation in a certain direction, an open-ended question that begins with what, how, why, when, or where facilitates discussion and leaves plenty of room for the child to express his or her feelings without intrusion from the adult. For example, "Why did Simba run away from Pride Rock?" tends to generate more of a response than a closed question like "Was it right for Simba to run away from Pride Rock?" which will likely lead to a simple "yes" or "no" response, preventing a wider discussion of issues. In some instances, you may not be able to avoid asking closed questions, but you can follow up with an open-ended question like "Why" or "why not."

Give your child your undivided attention. Maintain eye contact in an interested, non-judgmental manner. This lets your child know you respect what he has to say. Don't assume you know what he is going to say and don't try to finish his thoughts—let your child say it!

Paraphrase or restate key points to your child. When your child makes an interesting or complex statement or expresses an idea or opinion, it is often a good idea to paraphrase what he has just said. Make sure you do not change what he said; rather, reword it to show that you understand what he is saying. This also reinforces that you are listening to him.

No matter what, do not criticize your child's opinions or ideas. Your child may make a comment that is completely outrageous, goes against everything you believe, or simply defies the logic of the film's plot. No matter what, do not tell him he is wrong or criticize his ideas. What you can do in this situation is present him with an alternate way of looking at the film or idea, by saying something like, "A different way of looking at that character, film, etc. is . . ." In some cases, a child may be trying to frustrate or defy a parent. Break the pattern of unhealthy exchanges if that is the case.

General Questions

Regardless of what film you're watching with your children, there are general questions you can ask to assess their understanding of the film, see what characters they relate to, and tune in to what character, situation, or aspect of the film they found most interesting or entertaining. Also, feel free to make up your own questions, and more importantly, let your children make up their own questions.

The following questions can be applied to all films and age groups:
- Was there something you didn't understand about this film?
- What did you like best about this film? Why?
- What was your favorite scene in the film? Why?
- Why did [choose a character] do [select an action]?
- Is there something you would change about the plot? If so, what is it? Why would you make that change?
- Who was your favorite character in the movie? Why?
- If you could change the title of the movie, what would you change it to?
- Would you recommend this movie to someone? If so, who and why?

General Developmental Issues
Temperament...Understanding the Personality of Your Child

The more you understand the distinctive qualities of your child, the more effectively you will be able to communicate with her. All children are unique in the way they observe, react to, and discuss the things around them. Remember that your child is an individual with unique qualities.

While children of all ages are complex, dynamic, and unpredictable, labeling their personalities may be difficult and limiting, but will enable us to better understand their temperament. The more you understand your child, the better you will be able to gear the conversation toward her specific needs so that it remains productive. Research by psychologist Jerome Kazan shows that 35% of children are a mixture of all three of the following temperaments and do not fit any one type.

Easy-Going Temperament: Approximately 40% of children are "easy-going" in temperament and have predictable eating, sleeping, and bodily function routines. They demonstrate a moderate level of physical activity (as opposed to extremely lethargic or hyperactive); they are very approachable in social situations and are delighted by new stimuli. They quickly adapt to change and react moderately whether laughing or crying. They react in a relatively stable manner to frustration and are not overly reactive to loud noises, bright lights, the dark, or being hugged or pushed around. Easy going children have a consistently happy disposition and smile a lot of the time. They can stay focused on interesting stimuli, or playing with a toy, for longer periods of time.

Difficult Temperament: About 10% of children have a variable level of physical activity, sometimes being extremely lethargic and other times constantly on the go to the point of exhaustion. They have unpredictable—or have a hard time establishing—routines for eating, sleeping, and bodily functions while shying away or withdrawing from social interaction. Children with difficult temperaments do not adapt well to changes in their daily schedules and often respond intensely to loud noises, flashing or bright lights, or moderate touch. These children are

17

chronically unhappy, complain a great deal, and generally have an unfriendly or unhappy mood. Their laughing and crying responses to situations tend to be more intense than other temperaments.

Slow-to-Warm Temperament: Makes up approximately 15% of children. These children rarely display a high level of physical activity. They initially need to take time in meeting new people and need to be gradually introduced to new situations. Slow-to-warm children adapt slowly to changes in their environment and usually respond mildly when laughing or crying. Their overall quality of mood tends to be slightly on the negative side in terms of unpleasant or unfriendly behaviors.

Parental Concerns Regarding Temperament

Rather than attempting to change the temperament of their children, parents should try to work with them. For example, allow "slow-to-warm" children to pace their approach to new situations by gently encouraging them as they feel more comfortable. Difficult children need much more structure and firm limits on what they are allowed to do. Allow these children to display more intense frustration to new situations and attempts at new tasks. Even easy-going children need help from adults in deciding when they should attend to their own needs or respond to the demands of others first.

A parent should first try to identify their own temperament and how they react to movies and talk about strong feelings so they have an awareness of how they are coming across to their children. With that knowledge, parents can then decide if they can probe or ask questions about a movie more firmly or be patient and move more slowly with the slow-to-warm or difficult child.

Moral Reasoning Capabilities

All parents want to improve their children's ability to make the right choices when confronted with challenges from friends, school, and everyday life experiences. Movies can be a vehicle for observing and discussing critical choices that different people make in life.

Watching films that apply to a dilemma your child is facing and discussing the choices the characters have made is an effective way to tune into her moral reasoning abilities. Keep in mind that children develop at different rates, so while the sections are broken down into age groups, the age parameters may or may not apply to your child. Check the movie guide in the back and assess her level of maturity before watching a film with her. Psychologist Lawrence Kohlberg provides a framework to assess where children are in the development of their morality:

Pre-Conventional Level of Morality
(Part I: Early childhood)

Andy is angry with his sister, but he doesn't hit her because if he does his parents will punish him.

Reward-driven. The most basic level of a child's morality is motivated by a desire to avoid punishment or gain rewards. Children first learn that they must follow rules set by their parents or teachers because if they don't, that person will be angry with them and punish them. On the other hand, if they follow rules and do things well, they will be rewarded.

Conventional Level of Morality
(Part II: Middle child)

Andy is angry with his sister but he doesn't hit her because brothers shouldn't hit their sisters.

Approval-driven. This level of morality is characterized by a desire to maintain the values of one's family and/or culture. Conformity and approval are more valued than any specific reward.

Post-Conventional Level of Morality
(Part III: Teenagers)

Andy is angry with his sister but he doesn't hit her because he knows that hitting will not accomplish anything. Instead he talks about it with her and tells her why he's angry.

Morally-driven. The moral code within this level is based on internal values. The post-conventional child will be able to make a decision incorporating society's rules as well as her own personal situation. Less rigid than the conventional level, this particular stage emphasizes agreements made by two or more individuals, and if society may have the wrong rules for that agreement, you need to change the rule.

The three sections of this book were designed with these three different moral development levels in mind. Understanding what level of moral reasoning your child operates on will help facilitate a more fruitful discussion with her.

Gender Differences

Boys and girls differ in their approach to developing morals. Boys tend to make decisions based more on the rules or logic of an agreement, whereas girls tend to focus more on an individual's feelings and the emotional climate of the relationship between two people.

If you are wondering which approach is better for your child, try to emphasize or teach the type of moral reasoning that is less developed. For example, if your child tends to use logic when making decisions, try to develop her awareness of feelings to compliment her use of logic. Conversely, if your child is attuned to feelings in her relationships, balance her moral reasoning skills by reinforcing the logical decision-making process.

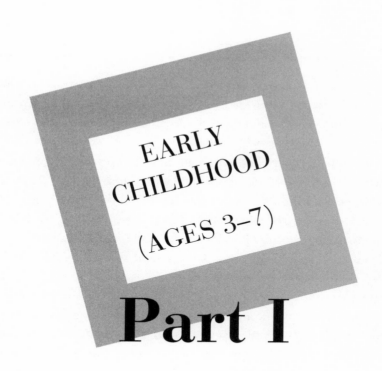

EARLY
CHILDHOOD

(AGES 3–7)

Part I

Children of this age begin to discover the biological differences between boys and girls and the different kinds of behaviors that are expected from them according to their culture. The most important need for children in preschool and elementary school is achieving a sense of personal accomplishment in performing everyday tasks, such as brushing their teeth, going to the potty without diapers, learning to count and read, or picking out and putting on their own clothes.

Because children's logic and reasoning are just beginning to form at this age, their ability to observe and formulate ideas is somewhat primitive. Their cause and effect logic makes associations between things that may not be connected at all. For example, a three-year-old child sees that it is thundering outside and believes his actions or misbehavior caused the bad weather. This preoperational thinking affects his relationship with family members, friends, and even household pets. A child may think that a stuffed animal is a living personality that interacts and coexists with him. Fantasy and reality are hard for the three- to seven-year-old to separate, creating both the joy of wonder and the fright of nightmares that seem all too real.

When talking to your children about movies, the younger child does better with specific questions about things that took place in the movie such as, "Which character did you like best?" or, "Did you like where they traveled?" Because preschoolers have a harder time recalling meaningful information, asking specific questions helps them recall more things. At about the age of six or seven, the development shifts again. Some children may be ready for the next level of discussion (found in Part II), while others may not be ready. It is very important to know your child's level of moral development and note when he is maturing and ready for the next level. The six- and seven-year-old can possibly handle more open-ended questions that ask him to remember and extract content from the film.

When children in early childhood enjoy a film, they may want to watch it several times, over and over again. They will enjoy knowing what happens in a scene before it occurs and singing along to lyrics. Repetition is important to them, as it is a primary tool for learning and offers them a sense of security when things are predictable. They may wish to have the same dialogue with you over and over again about a movie that scares them. It is perfectly normal for a child to desire reassurance more than once.

Chapter 1

"You have forgotten who you are and so have forgotten me. Look inside yourself, Simba. You are more than what you have become. You must take your place among the circle of life."

— King Mufasa, *The Lion King*

Family Life

For the preschool through early primary school years, family provides a balance of protection and nurturing, offering an environment that emphasizes safety while also recognizing that children need to explore their physical world more intimately. One of the main concerns for parents with children at this age is granting more independence to play outside with somewhat less supervision, while making sure that serious injury does not occur.

Children quickly learn which parent is more flexible about enforcing rules for safety and which parent is a tougher negotiator. They also learn which parent soothes their feelings more sensitively when they do have their inevitable falls and scrapes—and which parent has more patience responding to the never-ending questions they will ask in order to try to make sense of the world around them.

Setting Limits and Defining Parental Roles

Children probe and test their parents at an intense level at this age. They quickly find out which parent is more serious when it comes to enforcing the rules and which one is more flexible or easy-going when doling out the consequences for breaking those rules. They'll instinctively understand which parent is more even-tempered and who is more inclined to fly off the handle on certain issues such as buying or breaking toys, playing in certain areas of the house, or staying up later at bedtime. Like Simba in The Lion King, children have to learn what the rules are and what their parents expect from them, according to their capabilities.

Gender Roles for Mommy and Daddy

Parents take on different roles connected to their gender that shape the structure of how a family functions. Most studies in early childhood development indicate that fathers participate more in physical activities with their children, while mothers tend to be more communicative verbally and provide physical comfort and affection. These roles change somewhat when it comes to decision-making and disciplining, as both parents now tend to share equal power and work as a parental team. Consider watching George Banks in *Mary Poppins* or King Mufasa in *The Lion King*; fathers who were strict disciplinarians and rule enforcers while the mothers were more nurturing.

The Changing Face of the Family

While divorce rates have decreased in the nineties, what constitutes a traditional family unit has now expanded dramatically to include a variety of different kinds of family structures such as single parents, blended step-families as seen in *Lassie*, gay couples with children, unmarried single men and women having children on their own through artificial insemination and adoption. Children need to be made aware that families come in many shapes and forms so that they do not feel insecure if their family does not conform to the traditional nuclear family structure.

Sibling Relationships and the Family

Sibling relationships in early childhood are characterized by extremes: either children are very loving and caring with each other, or they are constantly quarreling like cats and dogs. One factor that contributes to sibling rivalry is closeness in age, which tends to lead to more competition. If their temperaments are similar, parents may experience more cooperation than fighting, but if two children have very different temperaments, then there will tend to be more fighting and conflict. Also, when a new child joins the hierarchy of the family, it can upset the balance between all family members. As demonstrated in *Arthur's Baby*, parents need to be sensitive to this affect on a child's status and self-esteem. To ensure that all siblings understand their unique role in the family, be sure to tell them that that there is always enough love to go around.

Mary Poppins

A serious banker puts an ad in the paper to find a proper English nanny for his two mischievous children. But instead, Mary Poppins, a nanny fitting the children's description, comes flying in on an umbrella. The children, Jane and Michael, adore her because although she is strict, she's full of magic and fantasy. She makes everything fun—an element their overly scheduled household craves. Mary Poppins stirs things up in the Banks' home and challenges the patriarch's long-held traditional beliefs about how a household should be run. A series of events finally causes Mr. Banks to realize that what his children really need are parents who can be fun and spend time with them.

This musical interspersed with animated segments is a wonderfully fun film with songs that will stay in your head after the movie is over. Mary Poppins sweeps into the Banks' lives to challenge everything they have ever known. Life is a game to her, and she finds the fun in everything. This film shows families that it's okay to be silly and have fun. Life is magical, and sometimes grownups can be so serious and focused on work and responsibility that they forget to have fun with their children. This film can provide an opportunity to discuss what makes a parent, nanny, caretaker, or babysitter good. Children will love being able to express what they like about Mary Poppins and Bert, and perhaps even their own caretakers.

Discussion Questions:

- Why did Mary Poppins come to the Banks' house?
- Would you like to have Mary Poppins as a nanny? Why or why not?
- Who do you know who is like Mary Poppins or Bert?
- What was the most fun thing that Michael and Jane did with Mary Poppins and/or Bert?
- Was Mary Poppins magical or real? Can someone really fly on an umbrella?
- How does Mary Poppins help the Banks family?
- What does a "spoonful of a sugar helps the medicine go down" mean? What kinds of chores or jobs can be turned into fun games? [Examples: cleaning their room, doing household chores, taking medicine, doing their homework, taking baths, etc.]

Pointer:

Talk with your child about what activities he would like to do with you. Even if his response is unrealistic or silly, try to think about what else you could do together to substitute for that activity. Think about the activity he suggests and how it may reflect what he is missing from his relationship with you (i.e. one-on-one time, unscheduled time, more fun activities).

The Lion King

King Mufasa, who rules over Pride Rock, teaches his son, Simba, about how it will be his responsibility to take his place among the circle of life and rule as King, just as his father had before him. But King Mufasa's evil, jealous, conniving brother, Scar, has different plans. When Mufasa is killed, Scar blames the accident on Simba, forcing him to run far away. Simba grows up in another part of the jungle where he lives a worry-free life, until his old friend Nala finds him and tells him how all the animals are starving under Scar's rule. With some help from the wise monkey Rafiki, the grown-up Simba decides to return to Pride Rock to carry out his familial obligation and take his rightful place as the Lion King.

Although it's a G-rated Disney film, The Lion King tackles some complex emotional issues: obeying parent's rules, dealing with the loss of a parent, blaming oneself for the death of a loved one, living up to familial and societal expectations, running away from conflict, and eventually taking your place among the "circle of life." This film explores the connections between two generations, deals with a problematic relative, and shows that growing up means facing your fears and taking responsibility for your actions. It provides an ideal opportunity for parents and children to discuss that what parents want for their children is in their best interest and requires bravery and discipline to achieve. As Simba learns, it is easier to run away, but it is always more rewarding to stay and face the problems that lie before you.

Discussion Questions:

- Imagine that you wanted to go somewhere, but were forbidden from doing so. Would you go anyway? Describe an experience when you behaved like Simba and did something that your parents told you not to do.
- What kind of an uncle was Scar? Do you have any family members that remind you of Scar?
- How do you think Simba handled his father's death? Did he do the right thing by running away?
- How would you feel if you lost a parent the way Simba lost his father?
- Simba is very scared of the hyenas. Describe a time when you were very scared of somebody or something. Did you face your fear or run away?
- When Simba leaves Pride Rock and moves to another part of the jungle, he learns to live by the phrase "Hakuna Matata", which means "no worries." When do you live by the phrase "Hakuna Matata"? Is it okay to live like that all the time?
- Simba ran away because he thought that his father's death was his fault. What would you do if you thought it was your fault that something bad happened?
- Scar is very jealous of Simba and Mufasa. When were you jealous of somebody? Has anyone ever been jealous of you? Why?
- King Mufasa teaches Simba about the "circle of life" and to

respect all creatures great and small. He says, "Everything you see exists together in a delicate balance. As king, you need to understand that balance and respect all creatures from the crawling ant to the leaping antelope." Do you believe in the "circle of life"? Have you ever stepped on an ant?

- Why did things get so bad at Pride Rock while Simba was away?

Pointer:

Discuss a time when your child made a mistake and upset you. Talk with her about how it is better to face up to mistakes and learn from them than to run away as Simba did. Perhaps point out a time when she did something wrong but told you about it, and praise her for taking responsibility for her actions. Share a story about a mistake you made when you were a child, and what the consequences were.

Lassie

A family moves from Baltimore to a rural farm in Virginia to make a better life for themselves. The son, Matt, is still grieving the loss of his mom, is having a hard time accepting his stepmother Laura, and is less than thrilled about their move to the country. As if this weren't enough to deal with, he has jealous neighbors who cause problems for him and his family. But with the help of his new dog Lassie, he discovers the joys the farmland has to offer, connects with his mother's childhood, and starts getting along better with his whole family.

Matt is forced to simultaneously deal with a few very difficult issues: the loss of his mother, finding ways to connect with her through learning about her childhood, a new environment, new school, and new stepmother. This loss affects his ability to accept his stepmother; although he likes her he feels like accepting her may be a betrayal to his mother. In the midst of this, he's being pulled from the urban environment he's used to and forced to adjust to a completely new culture. The family as a whole does a really good job of respecting Matt's anger, giving him his space, and then working together toward the common goal of creating a new home in the country.

Discussion Questions:

- What do you think about how the family found Lassie? Would your family have let you take the dog home?
- What do you think would be the hardest thing about moving from the city to a country farm? What would be the best part? What would you miss the most?
- Why was Matt so sad?
- How did Lassie help Matt get out of his sad mood?
- How would you handle two boys like Josh and Jim who weren't very nice?
- How did Matt change his attitude and start to enjoy the farm life?
- If Laura (the stepmother) was nice, then why didn't Matt like her?
- Do you think your family could build a sheep farm and raise sheep?
- How do you think your family would deal with a family like the Garlands?
- Do you think a dog could really be like Lassie and do the things she did to escape from the barn?
- Would you have gone into a dangerous situation to try to save someone you didn't even like, as Matt saved Josh?
- Could a dog really survive those rapids or was it magic?

Pointer:

Discuss how this family came together and helped each other through the transition of losing a mother and moving to a new environment. How can you hold on to your memory of a loved one who has passed yet still embrace the love of a new parent? Families can help someone in pain by not pushing him too hard and letting him come around in his own time.

Arthur's Baby

Arthur is an eight-year-old aardvark. He and his younger sister D.W. struggle with the arrival of their new baby sister, Kate. When baby Kate finally arrives all she does is eat, sleep, cry, and make funny smells. She certainly is not much fun to play with. D.W.

becomes jealous of all the attention her little sister is getting and runs away. D.W.'s grandmother makes her realize that Kate will need a big sister and so she goes back home. An insightful segment follows the animated story with real children commenting on their baby siblings.

This insight into a typical family can help parents prepare their children for the arrival of a new baby. It explores the frustrations that children may have with a baby sibling and allows them to identify with some of the jealousy that D.W. experiences. *Arthur's Baby* is a great film to watch to stimulate a conversation about what to expect when a new baby arrives in the house.

Discussion Questions:

- What kinds of things did Arthur find out about having a baby brother or sister?
- What are some of the good things about having a baby in the house? What are some of the bad things?
- Do you think older brothers and sisters like Arthur and D.W. should help take care of their baby sisters or brothers (help change diapers, hold the baby, read to the baby, feed the baby)?
- Why didn't D.W. like her little sister Kate?

Pointer:

The best way to help children adjust to a new sibling is by making them realize the importance of their role as a big sister or big brother. Talk about all the things for which the baby will depend on them when he or she grows up. For example, little boys may be excited about the idea of protecting their younger sibling or teaching about sports, and girls may like the idea of helping to dress and nurture a younger sibling. Stress that when the baby gets older he or she will become another playmate.

Chapter 2

"Remember: always let your conscience be your guide."
— The Blue Fairy, *Pinocchio*

Identity and Accomplishments

Young children want more control over their world and need to have a sense that they can participate and have a say in everyday experiences the way their older siblings and parents do. Temper tantrums and struggles over when to go potty, what clothes to wear, and food preferences are attempts at doing things "their way." These are a natural outgrowth of their developing sense of identity.

Children want to try everything they observe other family members doing. It is important that parents send the message that it is acceptable to attempt a task and not get it right. Parents should reward attempts at trying new things and encourage boys and girls to play and discover experiences that don't confine them to traditional roles. Boys can enjoy dolls and play house, while girls should be allowed and encouraged to participate in sports.

Dealing With "I Can Do it Myself"

Famous developmental psychologist Erik Erickson emphasized the importance of encouraging children to take the initiative and gain more control over their world. It may test your patience when you are in a rush to go somewhere and your child wants to get dressed by herself, or take apart curious objects. Parents should encourage a child's healthy exploration of the world around him, like Ariel's curiosity in *The Little Mermaid*. Parents should also respect their children's need to accomplish things on their own, as Tilly does in *The Little Engine that Could*.

Discovering Gender Differences

Boys and girls of early childhood learn the obvious physical differences between themselves by exploring their bodies and observing the adults in their world. However, it is parents, teachers, and relatives who teach what it means to be a boy or girl. Those behaviors can vary greatly, from teaching boys to cook in the kitchen to letting girls enjoy playing with trucks or playing sports, as Sister demonstrates in *The Berenstain Bears Play Ball*.

Accepting Differences in People

Children are also quick to pick up parents' beliefs about other ethnic and religious groups; they either value the positive and unique qualities of those differences or, unfortunately, begin the negative process of believing that differences between people make one superior to the other. Parents need to teach children to be kind to people who look different, like the Sneetches without stars on their bellies or Dumbo who has big ears, as well as those who act differently, like people who don't celebrate the same holiday, or speak with a different accent.

Behavioral Steps of Learning and Accomplishment

Along with letting young children explore and take the initiative in learning new things on their own, they must also learn the difference between bad behaviors and good behaviors. This is the ultimate accomplishment for Pinocchio, and one that will earn him "real boy" status. Parents can provide a model that doesn't hinder the learning process but subtly guides a child through the process of attempting something new. If a child seems frustrated while trying a new task, show her with simple steps and reinforce new attempts, whether right or wrong, by saying "nice try" or "way to go". These kinds of supportive comments set up a framework wherein children feel good about themselves and are not afraid to make mistakes.

The Little Mermaid

Ariel is a typical free-spirited adolescent girl, except that she's a mermaid who lives in a kingdom under the sea. Much to her controlling father's chagrin, she dreams of having legs and falling in love with Prince Eric. The evil seawitch Ursula will help her walk on land, under the condition that she give up her beautiful voice and, if the prince does not kiss her in three days, Ariel will be Ursula's slave forever. Despite the seawitch's plans to win Eric for herself, Ariel, with the help of her undersea friends, manages to make Eric fall in love with her.

Children love Ariel because they can relate to her: She is stubborn, imaginative, and disobedient. She follows her heart, though not always her head. She does not merely accept the world that is given to her but has hopes of something more. In achieving her dreams for feet and love, Ariel shows how oftentimes getting what you wish for comes with certain conditions or sacrifices. In the end, Ariel must give up her family and her whole world beneath the ocean to pursue a life on land. Parents can use this as an opportunity to discuss how often, getting what you want means giving up something else.

Discussion Questions:
- What do you know about mermaids? Do you think there could be a kingdom under the sea?
- Why was Ariel so curious about humans? What parts of the world would you like to know more about?

- Do you think Ariel made the right choice when she signed the contract with the seawitch? What would you have done in that situation and why?
- Did you think Prince Eric would fall in love with Ariel without her voice?
- How is King Triton like your dad or other daddies you know? Do you think he is a good daddy to Ariel?
- What do you think about Ariel's final choice to give up her world under the sea for a life with Eric and legs on land?
- What would you have done? Would have given up your family and friends for love?

Pointer:

While it is important to go after your dreams, you should never have to sacrifice who you are to do so. Ariel finds a way to live on land and maintain her beautiful voice, which is an integral part of her individuality. She couldn't have gotten there without her family and friends. Discuss a time when you or your children were so intent on pursuing a goal that you had to sacrifice something important.

Pinocchio

The Blue Fairy grants kind old Geppetto's wish by making his wooden puppet, Pinocchio, come alive. But Pinocchio isn't a "real boy" until he proves himself honest, selfless, and brave. She tells him to listen to the voice of his conscience, Jiminy Cricket, to teach him right from wrong. Pinocchio is tempted by the evil Stromboli who wants to use Pinocchio for fame and fortune, and by the conniving Honest John who sells him to Pleasure Island, where children are eventually turned into donkeys before being subjected to hard labor. Finally, Pinocchio proves his worth to the Blue Fairy in a brave and selfless act, saving Geppetto from the belly of Monstro the Whale.

This classic Disney film has a strong lesson about morality and learning to distinguish between right and wrong. Developing a conscience is a complex idea, and *Pinocchio* addresses it in a way that is understandable to children. Parents can use

Jiminy Cricket as a vehicle to show children how they should to listen to that little voice inside their head that shows them the way. Pinocchio's choices can help children learn the difference between good and bad, and show in a concrete way the bad things that happen when children disobey their parents, talk to strangers, and lie. In the end, Pinocchio learns from his mistakes and proves himself worthy of becoming a "real boy."

Discussion Questions:

- What is a conscience? What does Jiminy Cricket do for Pinocchio? When have you listened to your conscience?
- What would you do if you were on your way to school and someone tried to get you to do something else? Why didn't Pinocchio listen to Geppetto and Jiminy Cricket and continue on his way to school?
- Why does Pinocchio lie to the Blue Fairy when he is captured in the cage in Stromboli's stagecoach? How can adults tell when children are lying? What does the Blue Fairy mean when she says that a "lie keeps growing and growing until it's as clear as the nose on your face"?
- What do you think of Pleasure Island? Have you ever been to a place like that?
- Do you know anyone like Lampwick?
- How does Pinocchio prove his bravery?
- What kind of a "real boy" will Pinocchio be?

Pointer:

Pinocchio had it easy because he had Jiminy Cricket whispering in his ear. For most children, hearing that voice of conscience and then obeying it can be very difficult. Ask your child to tell you about a time when she had two choices and listened to her conscience to tell her what to do. If she can't understand, share an example from your own childhood when you followed your conscience and acted brave, self-less, or honest.

Dumbo

Circus elephant Mrs. Jumbo finally gets her wish when the stork delivers a baby to her. But the baby elephant has gigantic ears and all the other elephants make fun of him and call him Dumbo. Mrs. Jumbo loves and defends Dumbo and gets so angry with anyone who tries to mistreat him that she gets locked up. Dumbo is humiliated and made a part of the clown act until he discovers his special gift: His ears can serve as wings and allow him to fly. Dumbo eventually becomes famous, and his proud mother gets released from confinement.

This film can teach children about tolerance and empathy. By empathizing with Dumbo, children are forced to realize what it feels like to be made fun of or to be different. *Dumbo* also shows how parents have unconditional love for their children. It is also about perseverance, as is it not until Dumbo believes in himself, without the help of the "magic feather," that he really soars. Use this film to help make children aware of their own unkindness toward people who are different.

Discussion Questions:
- Why were the elephants so mean to Mrs. Jumbo and her baby? If you were there, how would you have treated Dumbo?
- If you could do anything in the circus, what would it be? What's your favorite part of the circus?
- Do you think an elephant could ever fly?
- Do you think it was really the "magic feather" that made Dumbo fly?

Pointer:
Discuss people you know who have different qualities, characteristics, or disabilities. Ask your child what kinds of things children get teased about and draw the parallel between that characteristic and Dumbo's ears. Stress the importance of being kind to people with differences (i.e. freckles, glasses, being chubby, frizzy hair, etc.).

The Berenstain Bears Play Ball

Papa has loved baseball ever since his dad taught him to play when he was little. He has big dreams about his son becoming a baseball star, but when Brother plays in the little league, it's Sister who seems more excited about the game. Though she's a girl, Sister believes that she can do anything she wants if she puts her mind to it. When Papa sees Brother playing baseball in the woods with his friends, he realizes that it's more important that both children have fun, regardless of how good they are at a sport.

This short video can be a great opportunity to discuss a child's natural interests versus the interests his parents would like him to have. This movie also presents a chance to discuss how parents reinforce gender roles instead of nurturing the natural individuality of their child. It also explores the differences between unstructured recreational activities like playing ball in the woods, and structured, supervised activities like little league baseball.

Discussion Questions:

- Were you ever forced to participate in an activity that you did not like? How did you handle that?
- Is it fair for Papa to encourage Brother to play baseball, but not Sister?
- Are there some things that are just meant for a boy and some things that are just meant for a girl to do? If so, what kinds of things?
- Why did Brother sneak away and play baseball with his friends in the woods when he didn't want to play baseball in the league?
- What was the point of Sister's song "I want it all"?
- What do you think Papa and Mama learned from this story?

Pointer:

Parents should tell their children about a time when they were forced to be involved in an activity (a sport, a musical instrument, cub scouts, etc.) when they really wanted to do something else. Or perhaps there was a time when you enjoyed an activity but didn't want to do it competitively. Discuss the difference between doing something because it's fun and doing something because your parent makes you.

The Sneetches

(included in Dr. Suess' *Sing-a-long with Green Eggs & Ham, and The Zax*)

The plain-bellied Sneetches on the beaches have an inferiority complex because the Sneetches with stars on their bellies are very mean and won't include them in any activities. Sylvester McBean arrives with a star machine that puts stars on their plain bellies. This makes the original star-bellied Sneetches angry, so they go through another machine that takes the stars off their bellies. Eventually everything gets so mixed up that none of the Sneetches know who was who. Without a physical characteristic to distinguish them from each other, all the Sneetches start to get along.

This is a wonderful, simple story about how prejudice develops in societies. The lesson is as clear as the plot: Changing physical characteristics can be as easy as using a machine, but what is inside is what really makes us unique.

Discussion Questions:

- Why were the star-bellied Sneetches so mean to the plain-bellied Sneetches?
- Can you think of anything in your world that sets people apart like the stars on the Sneetches bellies did?
- How did Sylvester McBean teach the Sneetches a lesson?
- Were the Sneetches happier in the end? Why?
- Was anyone ever mean to you because of something about your appearance? How did it make you feel?
- Did you ever leave someone out like the Sneetches did because they looked different?

Pointer:

Talk to your children about why it's better to judge people on who they are, not on what they look like. Discuss what a "status symbol" means and how the Sneetches used the stars on their bellies as status symbols. Point out why they were all so much happier when they stopped caring about the stars, and how our neighborhoods, communities, and world would be a better place if we could do the same.

The Little Engine That Could

Tilly is the smallest engine and nobody wants to let him pull the birthday train over the mountain. But Tilly really thinks he can do it. When one engine breaks down and the others pass up the job, Tilly gets his chance to prove to everyone, and most importantly, to himself, that if you believe in yourself and work hard, you can accomplish almost anything.

This "I can do it myself" story is especially popular amongst three- and four-year-olds. Tilly proves that when you believe in yourself and try hard, you can overcome great odds. Because younger children get so much satisfaction out of doing things on their own, they will particularly appreciate and relate to Tilly's success.

Discussion Questions:

- Why didn't the other engines help pull the birthday train?
- Why did Tilly want to try to pull the train up the mountain so badly?
- Have you ever said "I think I can" to yourself when you were trying to do something hard? Did it help?
- Did you think Tilly would make it?
- How could an engine that small pull the whole train up a huge mountain on its own?

Pointer:

Share with your child a time when someone said you couldn't do something and you went ahead and proved them wrong. Ask your child about a time when someone said she was too small or too young to do something and didn't even let her try. What happened? How did it make her feel? Did she ever get the chance to try it out? Did she ever prove them wrong?

Chapter 3

Beginnings of Friendship

As children begin to attend preschool programs, they are exposed to different playgroup experiences. Relationships in the three- to five-year range are more about common interests and activities than an exchange of feelings. One thing that holds true for the entire age group is that children who are too aggressive are generally disliked by most other children. Unfortunately, this makes these particular children even more hostile as a means of coping with peer rejection.

The highest form of friendship for younger children is characterized by a type of fantasy play where all feelings are made available, and the recognition of one's vulnerability and fears (i.e. fear of being left alone, fear of being physically attacked, fear of failure, etc.) is shared.

Being Ready for Friendship

Increased maturity means children will figure out how to accept differences, get through arguments, and make up, just as Lizzy Bruin and Sister do in *Berenstain Bears & The Trouble with Friends*. While the preschooler believes that an argument essentially ends a relationship with a peer, and then starts the friendship all over again the next time they meet, the four- to five-year-old learns the process of making up and forgiveness. This adds a dimension of emotional intimacy to their relationships.

Learning Empathy

The capacity to respond to someone else's feelings exists in very young children (infants and toddlers). But true empathy, the ability to perceive that someone feels differently than you and to have compassion for their feelings, is usually not present until the end of early childhood (6-7). *Charlotte's Web* demonstrates the highest level of friendship, as Charlotte empathizes so much with Wilbur that she puts all her energy into saving his life. In *Toy Story*, Woody puts aside his jealousy of Buzz in order to build up his friend's confidence.

Giving and Nurturing

Children learn how to be good friends in their interactions with pets. By learning to display loyalty, consistency, and caring, they begin to understand the reciprocal nature of friendships. In *Charlotte's Web* and *The Black Stallion*, children learn the important qualities of friendship by developing bonds with animals. Animals can teach children how to be selfless.

The Black Stallion

When Alec Ramsey's ship sinks in a storm, the young boy awakens washed up on a deserted Greek island with nothing but a wild Black Arabian stallion horse and the beauty of the natural world surrounding them. He slowly gains the trust of the horse and even teaches himself to ride the horse bareback. Eventually a Greek fisherman rescues Alec and the stallion from the island. Alec manages to bring the horse, known as "Black," to his hometown in America. Black runs away from Alec's backyard to a farm in the country, where a retired jockey trainer serves as a surrogate father to Alec and encourages him to learn to ride the horse. Alec and Henry enter Black in a big horse race against the two thoroughbred champions. Alec, as the mystery rider, triumphs with Black.

This film has beautiful cinematography and very little dialogue. It lets pictures tell the story of the remarkable bond between a little boy and a horse. Black and Alec save each other's lives, and their connection, along with the paternal guidance of horse trainer Henry, help Alec deal with the loss of his father, who died on the ship.

This films shows how animals can especially help children learn to connect after a traumatic experience; animals can have a dramatic impact on children's emotional development by teaching them to care for and love another living thing, and can make them feel needed.

Discussion Questions:

- How scared would you be in a storm like that on a boat?
- How did Black save Alec and get him to land? How did Black save Alec twice?
- Would you be able to survive on a beach alone with nothing but a horse?
- How did the horse begin to trust Alec?
- Was it fair for Alec to keep Black in his backyard? Why or why not?
- Did you think it was fair to make Black a racehorse? Did you know how hard it was to train to be a jockey?
- Did you think that Black should be set free?
- Would you like to have a pet like Black? If you could have any animal as a friend and pet, what would it be and why?

Pointer:

Discuss the connection between animals and people and whether your child has ever had a pet that depended on him. Tell your child about an animal or pet from your childhood that you loved or cared for. Ask your child if he thinks animals can love people.

Charlotte's Web

Fern stops her father from killing a pig that was the runt of the litter. To teach her a lesson, he tells Fern that the pig is now her responsibility, so Fern cares for the little pig, whom she names Wilbur. A deep bond grows between Fern and Wilbur. But when Wilbur gets bigger, he is sold to Farmer Zuckerman. Wilbur becomes friends with the other animals in the barn who tell him that he will be killed soon. Wilbur is afraid of dying, but he meets a kind spider named Charlotte who assures him she will do everything in her power to keep him alive. She spins the words "some pig" into her web, shocking everyone in the community; they believe it is a miracle. Charlotte creates more miracles by spinning "terrific," "radiant," and, finally at the county fair, "humble." Though Charlotte's life naturally comes to an end, thanks to her Wilbur will live to a ripe old age. He will never forget his friend, Charlotte—the friend who saved his life.

This film is about being a selfless, supportive, and loyal friend. It shows the lengths to which one will go to help a friend in need. It also shows the hierarchy of the farm, and the reciprocity that exists between animals and nature. Charlotte deals with her own mortality by investing in her friend Wilbur, so that after she is gone her memory will live on. As a runt, Wilbur represents the weakest of the animals, and shows how the least likely of animals can rise to greatness with the help of a true friend.

Discussion Questions:

- Was it fair for Fern's father to plan on killing Wilbur simply because he was a runt? Why do you think Fern loved Wilbur so much?
- How does Charlotte help Wilbur?
- Why does Jeffrey (the runt chicken) like Wilbur so much?
- Do you really think a spider could save a pig by spinning words in her web?
- Why did Charlotte choose the words "some pig", "terrific", "radiant", and "humble"?
- Why were people so fascinated by the words in Charlotte's web?
- What do you know about a spider's life cycle?
- Do you know anyone like Templeton the Rat who will help only if there's something in it for him?

- How does Wilbur repay Charlotte for her kindness?
- Why do you think Farmer Zuckerman decided to let Wilbur live to "a ripe old age"?

Pointer:

One of the best things to have in life is a trusted, true friend. Do you think any of your friends now are "true friends"? Parents can share who their true friends are and what qualities their friendships have that are like Charlotte and Wilbur's relationship.

The Berenstain Bears & The Trouble With Friends

Sister often plays with Brother, but they enjoy different kinds of activities, so Mama and Papa Bear are very excited when a new family moves in with a daughter who is Sister's age. Lizzy Bruin and Sister play all day, but Sister soon realizes that Lizzy is "a little bossy and a little braggy." They get into a fight when both cubs want to be the teacher when playing school. Sister goes home angry, vows never to play with Lizzy, and says she'd rather play by herself. But Mama Bear explains that perhaps Lizzy is much like Sister herself, and points out that lots of fun games require a friend.

This story illustrates a common argument that children get into and how they might resolve it by being considerate and taking turns. It also points out the importance of having same-sex friends whose interests are similar to yours. Mama Bear teaches Sister a lesson about the importance of having someone to play with, and Sister is forced to realize that perhaps Lizzy is like herself when it comes to being bossy and braggy.

Discussion Questions:

- Do you have a sibling you play with? What things can and can't you do with a sibling?
- Do you have friends like Lizzy Bruin who might be a "little bossy and little braggy"?
- What kinds of things might cause a fight between two friends?
- What kinds of things do you do that might upset a friend?
- How do you make up when you have a fight?

Pointer:

Talk about ways, like apologizing, that children can make up with their friends when they have a fight. Explain how saying they're sorry, being considerate, taking turns, and sharing are good ways friends can avoid getting into fights.

Toy Story

This computer-animated feature was a first for Disney, and works perfectly with main characters that are toys. Woody, a Western sheriff with a pull-string voice, is the leader of the other toys, and their owner Andy's favorite toy, that is until Andy receives a Buzz Lightyear space ranger for his birthday. Woody is jealous of Buzz, who has more gadgets on him and doesn't realize he's a toy. Woody develops a plan to kick Buzz out, but then feels guilty when the other toys become angry with him. Woody goes on a journey to save Buzz and prove himself to the other toys, including a Mr. Potato Head, a Tyrannosaurus Rex, a slinky, Little Bo Peep, and plastic army men. Buzz and Woody end up being held captive in the bedroom of Sid, a mean, violent little boy who tortures his toys. Woody and Buzz are forced to cooperate in order to escape and find Andy before he moves to another house.

The relationship between Woody and Buzz is similar to that of siblings who are each vying for the undivided love and attention of a parent. But they are also like jealous friends, each with unique characteristics, who don't get along at first but end up helping each other on dangerous adventures outside Andy's room. This film can help children understand the concept of jealousy. They'll learn about sharing the love or attention of a parent or friend—that there's enough to go around. *Toy Story* shows how people accomplish their goals better when they work with each other rather than against each other.

Discussion Questions:

- Why are all the toys so nervous about Andy opening his presents?
- What's your favorite toy and why?
- Why doesn't Woody like Buzz?
- Do you know any children who are mean to their toys like Sid?

- Why is Buzz so sad when he realizes that he is a toy and not a space ranger?
- How does Woody make Buzz feel better about being a toy? Describe a time when you made a friend feel better about something.
- How does Woody scare Sid? Do you think Sid learned a lesson?
- What makes Andy's toys trust Woody again?
- How do Buzz and Woody help each other get into Andy's car?

Pointer:

Parents can use the relationship between Woody and Buzz to discuss how jealousy and insecurity can affect our ability to make new friends. Stress that it's okay to be jealous of friends who are good at certain things or who have qualities we may not have, but also how feelings between friends can change over time as you get to know one another more. Ask your child if she has ever had a new person come in to her class, neighborhood, or group of friends whom she was jealous of, but then got to know and ended up befriending. Parents may want to share when they had a difficult time accepting someone new in their lives because of jealousy.

Chapter 4

"You must never rush out on the meadow. Out there we're unprotected. The meadow is wide open and there are no trees or bushes to hide us, so we have to be very careful."
— Mama, Bambi

Fantasies and Fears

Children from three to five gradually come to understand that what they see doesn't necessarily translate to what really is. For example, when a young child sees Mickey Mouse or a TeleTubbie in costume they really believe that the person inside the costume is Mickey or LaLa; that is, seeing is believing. Because their mind has a hard time picturing a person inside of a character, the outside appearance becomes the reality.

This perception of appearance as reality can wreak havoc with a child's imagination and cause him to see monsters, bogeymen, and other make-believe creatures in the dark or in his dreams. On the positive side, five- and six-year-olds still enjoy great fantasies of adventure—imagining themselves in far-off lands with powers to fly into the sky, or defeat fire-breathing dragons.

World of Extremes

Children at this age tend to perceive things in extremes—either being completely frightened by something, or reveling in the delight of something we as adults take for granted. Mother Nature, in particular, gives children a sense of awe and wonderment that adults lose as they age. Bambi's experience as a baby deer in the forest is relatable to many children who find utter enjoyment in their first snowstorm, and complete fear at the sound of thunder and sight of lightning.

Imaginative Play to Express and Control Fears

Developmental psychologists believe that when children display and express their insecurities and fears in imaginative play, they are developing coping mechanisms and gaining control of their world through drawings, imaginary friends, and make-believe with puppets or other props. In *Peter Pan*, the Darlings encounter their wildest fears, like pirates, and their favorite fantasies, like flying and swimming with mermaids. A film like *Escape to Witch Mountain* allows children to think about what it would be like to have special powers, and whether aliens could exist in the form of children.

Feeling in Control

When their limited logic can't keep up with their understanding of how things work, (i.e., lightning storms, scary dreams, or shadows in the night) young children need to feel that they can control their fears with their favorite teddy bear or a blanket. Parents can help develop their children's imaginations by reinforcing and acknowledging what they think their child is feeling. They can provide a sense of control by explaining things in logical ways, such as, "Shadows in the dark make the furniture in your room look like something scary, but when you turn on the light, you can see it is just the lamp." In *The Berenstein Bears in the Dark*, Papa teaches Sister how to take control of her imagination by giving her his night-light so she won't be scared of the dark.

Peter Pan

Michael and John Darling love to listen to their older sister Wendy tell stories about Peter Pan, the adventurous, magical boy who will never grow up. One night Peter Pan comes to their bedroom in search of his shadow, sprinkles them with pixie dust, and teaches them to fly. They fly out of their home and through the night sky to Never Never Land, where children can play all day, save an Indian princess from the evil pirate Captain Hook, see mermaids and crocodiles—all without interruption from adults. Eventually, Wendy misses her mother, and she and her brothers fly back home, never to forget the wonder of their time with Peter Pan.

Children love this film for its magic and the exotic world of Never Never Land that has no rules and no parents. It allows them to simultaneously live out their greatest fantasies and fears—a world of wonder and delight, but also one filled with danger and no parental protection or nurturing. *Peter Pan* provides a unique opportunity to discuss what it means to grow up, and what the benefits and drawbacks of maturing are.

Discussion Questions:

- Do you think your parents believe in magical things like Peter Pan?
- Would you like to be able to fly? Where would you fly?
- Are there any places like Never Never Land where you never grow up?
- What does it mean to be jealous? Why is Tinkerbell so jealous of Wendy? Have you ever been jealous?
- Would you like to go to Never Never Land where there are no parents and no rules, so that you could play all the time?
- What was the scariest part of Never Never Land? What was the best part of Never Never Land?
- Why did Michael, John, and Wendy want to go home at the end?
- What kinds of things can only a child see?
- Do you think the boys will ever go back to Never Never Land with Peter Pan again?
- Are there any places you've been that are like Never Never Land?

Pointer:

Talk to your children about the idea of Never Never Land, the place where children never grow up. Ask them what they are looking forward to about getting older (i.e. getting taller or going to bed later) and what they are afraid of (i.e. having to act too serious). Make sure you respect their fears and excitement about growing up, without trying to minimize or refute them.

Escape to Witch Mountain

Two young children, Tony and Tia, have special powers, such as the ability to move objects, read people's minds, and predict the future. They have a mysterious past and long to find out where they came from and the identity of their true family. When a strange man who claims to be their uncle adopts the children, they soon discover his millionaire employer has plans to use the children's special powers for his own benefit. Tony and Tia escape with the help of a rough but kindly older man named Jason, who leads them to their true family.

This movie has a wide appeal because its main characters are children who are empowered by special abilities, and are able to use those abilities to avoid the corrupt adults around them. *Escape to Witch Mountain* also allows children to consider whether there are life forms from other planets and if they could be on Earth and look like regular children. It also shows children the importance of discovering where you come from, and finding a secure home where you can be yourself.

Discussion Questions:

- How would you like to have special powers like Tia and Tony?
- If you could only have one special power, what would it be? (i.e. read thoughts, move things, predict the future, read the past, etc.) How would you use your powers?
- Why is Mr. Boldt so mean? What does he want to use Tina and Tony for?
- Can people talk to animals the way Tia communicated with the horse and the bear?

- What would you do if you had all those people chasing after you?
- What did the dreams or flashbacks mean to Tia?
- Do you know any people like Jason O'Day, who may seem mean at first but are nice once you get to know them?
- Do you think there are aliens out there? Can a child be an alien?

Pointer:

Have a discussion about what kind of special powers you and your child would most like to have. How would you use your special powers to help people? What would be good or bad about having powers like that?

Bambi

Bambi is the classic Disney tale that chronicles the life of a newborn deer coming of age in the forest. Bambi explores the world around him and makes friends with other animals in the forest, including Thumper the rabbit. He also learns about the dangers of man, loses his mother to a hunter, and must survive the harsh winter with little food. Finally Bambi becomes "twitterpated" and falls in love with Faline, who gives him two baby deer of his own and thereby completes the cycle.

In *Bambi,* exploring the forest is a metaphor for the unknown world outside of one's family or home. The death of Bambi's mother may be the first exposure to death for small children, and it is an opportunity to discuss one of children's ultimate fears—the loss of a parent. By pairing beautiful animation with limited dialogue, *Bambi* is a wonderful film for younger children. It shows how man can ruin nature through hunting and carelessness with campfires, and shows how animals, like children, will someday have to learn to take care of themselves.

Discussion Questions:

- Bambi was scared of some things in this film (i.e. learning to walk and jump, leaving his mother's side, lightning and thunder). What kinds of things scare you the way Bambi was scared?
- What kinds of places are like the meadow, where you have to be very careful or you could get hurt?

- Do you know what hunting is? Explain some of the reasons why man hunts animals (sport, clothes, food, safety, etc.).
- What does falling in love or getting "twitterpated" mean? Do you know anyone who got "twitterpated"? How does Bambi get "twitterpated"?

Pointer:

Children tend to personify Bambi; parents should point out that even though there are many similarities, animals are very different from humans. Discuss an animal's life cycle and how nature can be hard on animals. Dealing with basic needs like shelter and food parallels humans' needs, but is still very different. Point out differences and similarities between humans and animals in the woods.

The Berenstain Bears in the Dark

Brother and Sister enjoy reading different types of books at the library. But when Sister gets bored with her book, she listens to Brother's scary mystery story. She gets so scared that she can't sleep at night without having the bedroom lights on. Papa Bear takes Sister up to the attic to give her his night light from when he was a cub. He also teaches her how imagination can makes things seem scarier than they are, and how you must take control of your imagination so things won't be so scary.

This video illustrates how children can overcome their fears by learning to take control of their imagination. Papa does a great job of helping Sister feel less scared. He acknowledges that her fear is normal, that he was afraid of the dark himself. He gives her a physical solution like the night light, and most importantly, he explains that imagination is a wonderful quality that allows us to do great things, but that it often makes things appear that don't really exist.

Discussion Questions:

- What kinds of stories scare you? Do you like to be scared?
- How do you like to sleep—with the light on, off, or with a night light?

- Do you have a brother or sister who likes to scare you? Do you scare your brother or sister? Does it work?
- What does Papa teach Sister about how imagination makes things scary? In what ways do you take control of your imagination?

Pointer:

Share with your child what kinds of things you were scared of when you were little. Parents can help children deal with fear by telling them that it's normal to be scared, and then finding a way to help them take charge of their imagination.

The Berenstain Bears Learn About Strangers

Sister is a little too friendly when playing in the park and says "hello" to lots of strangers. Brother tells his parents how Sister talks to strangers, and Father scolds her for it, pointing out all the bad things that happen in the news. He scares Sister so much that she doesn't even want play outside anymore. Mother takes a different approach and explains that strangers are like apples; most are good but every once in a while there is a bad apple. Since you never know, it is better not to take any chances and to avoid talking to strangers.

This video provides an ideal opportunity to introduce children to the danger of talking to strangers. Parents may also want to discuss with their children the difference between a "good touch" and a "bad touch" from an adult. It is important to know that even though someone seems nice and friendly, it is still too dangerous to take a chance and talk to a stranger.

Discussion Questions:

- How friendly are you to strangers?
- When is it okay to talk to strangers and when isn't it okay?
- If Sister was just being friendly, then why did her parents get angry with her?
- What would you have done in a situation where a man who seemed nice asked you to get into his car to see something? Did

Brother do the right thing when he decided not to go with the man flying the battery-operated airplane?
- What does Mother's example about the apples mean? How are strangers like apples?

Pointer:

Parents should discuss the apple analogy and make sure children understand the comparison. Talk to your children about what kinds of things a bad stranger might do, so that children learn how to identify those behaviors and distinguish between a bad touch and good touch.

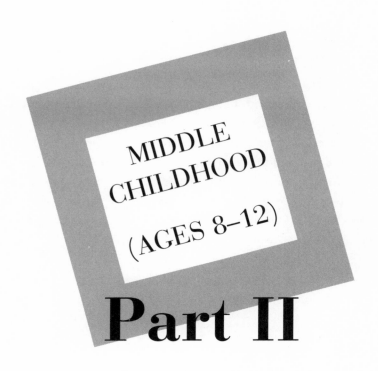

MIDDLE CHILDHOOD (AGES 8–12)

Part II

Children from the ages of eight to twelve have reasoning skills that are firmly based in reality. These skills are tested and perfected through learning and achieving within the school environment. At the same time, their physical development greatly affects their ability to relate to their peers and their inclusion in social groups. Parents can help their children develop responsible behaviors and make healthy choices by setting firm limits, communicating clear expectations, and parenting in a caring and nurturing way. Beyond the traditional family, issues such as divorce, stepparenting, and single-parenting affect the eight- to twelve-year-old in ways prior generations could not have imagined. Children in this age group begin to develop an awareness of their own strengths and weaknesses in athletics, music, writing and math skills, and, most importantly, their ability to solve everyday problems.

As far as watching and understanding films, children in middle childhood tend to prefer films with high entertainment value. They can extract meaning, morals, and lessons from the plot. However, their analysis of films will most likely occur on a very literal level, depending on their age or maturity level. Some children may have the ability to read much deeper meaning into the characters or plot of a given film. By the same token, eight-year-olds will tend to have more limited interpretive abilities than twelve-year-olds. Just as films may be appreciated on different levels, many children will appreciate the same film or scene within a film on various levels.

Chapter 5

"I won't have the children takin' after him either. Him and those dreamy ways of his I used to think were so fine. Not if I gotta cut it right out of their hearts."
— Katie Nolan, *A Tree Grows In Brooklyn*

Family Life

In this new millennium, the structure of families continues to evolve. Families may be led by two parents, one parent, stepparents, straight or gay parents, aunts, uncles, older siblings, or any combination. But what matters more than the structure of the family unit is how well any caretakers meet the physical, intellectual, and emotional needs of their children.

With grandparents, aunts, and uncles often living hours away from their relatives, the support that the nuclear family gives to the eight- to twelve-year-old child is even more critical. Creating a stable home life where conflicts are resolved effectively and morals are clearly defined is a challenge for parents. How well they deal with these complex and stressful, but very rewarding, tasks will seriously impact the well-being and growth of their children.

Obeying and Testing the Rules of the House

Parents who make an effort to explain not only what the rules of the house are, but also the reasoning behind them, will encourage in their children a healthy respect for established rules. For example, telling your child about your concern for his safety, as Ralphie's parents do in *A Christmas Story*, or providing some other practical reason, will help them accept an otherwise "annoying" punishment. Parents need to keep in mind that the maturity level of their children will affect what rules they will obey without parental monitoring. When children test or break the rules established by their parents, it is often a healthy expression of their growth, done with a sense of adventure to develop self-confidence. Even though it is healthy and normal for children to break some rules, parents do need to take action when their child breaks a more serious family rule. Be consistent in disciplinary actions, and establish consequences that correspond to the seriousness of the transgression.

Getting Along With Family Members

Getting children to be respectful of other family members usually involves two key behaviors: observing parents that treat each other respectfully, and teaching children to be accountable when they are not respectful. Children tend to copy the behaviors they see in their household, especially if they look up to the people exhibiting those behaviors. Also, contrary to what many parents believe, a little guilt can be a good thing when children are intentionally disrespectful, especially when it is discussed in a way that maintains the dignity of the child, but also lets her know that she has hurt a family member's feelings. Positive reinforcement when children do show respectful behavior will further help them display a respectful attitude toward other family members (see *The Swiss Family Robinson*).

Living up to the Family's Expectations for Achievement

Being successful in school is so important at this age that the effect on a child's self-esteem could be drastic if learning and achievement are hindered. With the exception of the learning disabled, most successful achievers in elementary school have had the stage set for them long before they started formal schooling. Parents like those in *A Tree Grows In Brooklyn* and *Sounder*, who have stressed the importance of learning very early on, reinforce a value system based on the premise that learning is an exciting and fun process, and that school is a big part of that experience. When parents read books, help with homework, and demonstrate curiosity about learning, they help develop a positive approach to achievement in school.

Respecting Roles and Personalities of Different Family Members

Children begin to develop an understanding of their role within the family as it compares to other family members' roles. They'll understand that it is their job to watch the baby while it is a sibling's job to rake the leaves. Healthy families respect the strengths of all family members and find productive ways that they can all add to the family. Perhaps the most crucial time for family members to respect each other's roles is when there is a crisis or problem. As demonstrated in *The Swiss Family Robinson*, each family member has a different but equally important role. Parents too have different jobs within the home, as in the case of *A Tree Grows In Brooklyn;* the mother is the pragmatist who takes care of things, while the father is the dreamer and storyteller.

Mr. Mom

After automotive engineer Jack Butler gets laid off from his job, his wife Caroline gets a job first and reenters the workforce, leaving him in charge of the house: the cooking, cleaning, and caring for their three young children. At first, both Jack and Caroline struggle with their new roles, but they eventually learn to master them. Caroline uses her domestic experience to develop a successful advertising campaign for tuna fish, while Jack is forced to realize that running a household is a much more challenging job than he had previously believed.

This film humorously explores the stereotypes associated with parental roles and shows how important it is to understand and value what each parent does within the family structure. The Butler family demonstrates that there is no "right" way to do things but that each family needs to find the system that works best for them. Mr. Mom also shows how children might respond to changing family dynamics. Each parent is forced to consider the challenges and rewards of his or her spouse's daily activities. Children can learn to understand the qualities and distinctions of traditional feminine and masculine roles within our culture.

Discussion Questions:

- Why are men expected to be the providers? Why are women expected to be the caretakers? Do you think men and women are "made" to do different things in the world? Why or why not?
- Do you think children behave differently around their mothers than they do around their fathers?
- Do you think acting "feminine" or "masculine" is something you are born with, or something you learn?
- Why does Jack become so competitive with Caroline when he loses his job and she suggests that she go back to work?
- Why are the advertising executives so mean to Caroline when she first starts working there? What does she add to the agency that they don't have?
- What are the problems Jack encounters when he takes on the role of Mr. Mom?
- Would you ever want to be a "housewife" or a "Mr. Mom"? Would you ever want to be a working mother? Why or why not?
- What kinds of jobs have you seen your dad do that your mom usually does? What kinds of jobs have you seen your mom do that your dad usually does?
- Why did Jack let Caroline's boss win the relay race?
- Why did Kenny have to give up his security blanket? Have you ever had to give up something like that? If so, was it a difficult thing to do?
- Do you think the children will be happier with the new set-up in which their mom is working part-time and their dad is back at work?

Pointer:

Discuss the importance of balance within the family structure and making sure everyone's needs are met. Perhaps it is important for both parents to contribute to the emotional and financial support of the family, or perhaps things work better within your family when these roles are separate. Talk about roles within the family—not just parental, but children's roles as well. It is important for every member of the family to have a distinct role, but it is also important for those roles to be flexible enough to be altered as circumstances change. Explore whether there have been any major changes in your family that have caused parents or siblings to take on different responsibilities.

Sounder

An African-American sharecropping family struggles with poverty and racism in Depression-era rural Louisiana. Frustrated with an unjust sharecropping system that exploits his family and leaves them hungry, patriarch Nathan Lee steals a ham and is sentenced to time in a hard labor camp. The oldest of the three children, David Lee, demonstrates an affinity for academics and takes on the fatherly role. During a long journey on foot, he comes across a sympathetic teacher, Ms. Camille Johnson, who instills Black pride in her students and offers to let David Lee live with her and study at her school. An injured Nathan finally returns to his family, and they collectively decide to allow David to live with Ms. Johnson, where he can use his potential to flourish in a more racially tolerant community.

This film shows a very close, supportive family that manages to overcome many hardships by depending on each other. David Lee and his siblings work together to help their mother while their father is away. Their loyalty to each other's well-being allows them to survive. They nurture the academic potential they see in David Lee, and find dignity in the face of adversity. This film introduces children to a period in American History when African-Americans were severely discriminated against, and shows how in the face of adversity, family members help each other to succeed.

Discussion Questions:

- What was the situation that led Nathan to steal the ham? Was it right for Nathan to steal ham to feed his family? Was it worth it?
- Have you ever had to take on the parental role while a parent was away, as David Lee did when his father was away at the labor camp?
- Why wouldn't the police let Rebecca see her husband in jail? Why did the police keep Nathan's whereabouts a secret?
- Do you think there are some people who are racist today?
- Why would they shoot the dog?
- Would you have been able to make such a long journey alone and on foot to a place that was so hard to find?
- What was so different and special about Camille Johnson's school?
- Was it right for David to want to leave his family to study and live at Ms. Johnson's?
- Why did David believe the boy's story about saving his sister from drowning? What was the meaning of that story?
- How does David's family help him feel good about himself?
- How difficult do you think it would be to make a decision between staying home with your family or going far away where there is more opportunity to learn and grow? What would you decide to do?

Pointer:

Discuss how hard this family worked to make sure everybody's needs were met in the worst of times, and the sacrifices they made to help their son flourish. Good parents are fair to everybody, regardless of circumstances. Perhaps this is a good opportunity to share a time in your own childhood or in your family when things were difficult and you had to come together to overcome hardships. Discuss how often, individual family members must make sacrifices for the good of another family member.

A Christmas Story

Ralphie Parker is a typical ten-year-old in a Midwestern town during the 1940s. At Christmas time, all Ralphie can think of is how much he wants a Red Ryder BB-gun. As the quirky Parker family prepares for the holidays, Ralphie struggles with academics, the bully in his town, and his longing for that Christmas present, despite the fact that all the adults keep telling him, "You'll shoot your eye out."

This is a humorous family film, a slice of Midwestern life at a time when parents still washed their children's mouths out with soap. It shows parents attempting to discipline their children in their own style, a family enjoying the stresses of the holiday season, and one little boy's realization that sometimes wishing for something can be more fun than actually getting it. The brilliance of this film is in the little pieces of every day life that many families will be able relate to.

Discussion Questions:

- Has there ever been anything you've wanted so badly that it's all you could think about? What was it?
- Do you know any bullies like Scott Farcus?
- Is there something about your neighborhood that drives your family crazy, like the dogs? What is it?
- Is there anything your parents do to get someone in your family who doesn't like to eat to finish his meals?
- Radio was the focal point for family entertainment. Is there a TV show that you watch as religiously as Ralphie listened to *Little Orphan Annie?*
- Is there anything like the leg lamp in your family—something that a family member loves but everyone else doesn't like?
- What bad words are forbidden in your family? What is the punishment for saying them? Do you think washing one's mouth out with soap is the right punishment?
- Was it right for Ralphie to blame his friend, rather than tell the truth and say that he heard it from his father?
- How did Ralphie get the guts to confront Scott and beat him up? Why was he so angry?

- Why did his mother protect him against his father by downplaying the fight and diverting his dad's attention? Has one parent ever protected you from the other parent?
- What has disappointed you the way Ralphie was disappointed with Santa?
- Have you ever been disappointed by gifts people gave you? Is there someone in your family who always gives you bad gifts? What was the worst gift you ever got?

Pointer:

When you really want something, how does your family decide whether or not you'll get it? Share with your child what types of toys you were obsessed with when you were young, and whether or not you ever got your wish. Ralphie learns that sometimes dreaming about something is better than actually getting it. Why does that happen and has it happened to you?

The Swiss Family Robinson

On their way to New Guinea after leaving their home in Switzerland, the Robinson family survives a shipwreck and finds themselves in a tropical paradise. They build a home in the trees and manage to use the island's natural resources to provide many of the comforts of home. The two oldest boys search the land and find a kidnapped young girl, for whose affections they both fight. The Robinsons then prepare for the arrival of thieving pirates by working together to build a booby trap. Eventually the Robinsons have the option of leaving the island, and must decide whether to stay on their paradise island or return to civilization.

This is an ideal film to show how a family works together and functions in a crisis. Each family member has skills and strengths to lend to the family's mutual goal. They are very respectful of one another. The film also explores sibling rivalry and shows the traditional and somewhat stereotyped gender roles associated with each parent.

Discussion Questions:
- What would be your first concern or priority if this happened to you?

- What were the different roles of the Robinson family members?
- How would you feel about living in a house up in the trees? How would you feel about being stuck on a tropical island?
- What was so significant about having all different types of animals on the island?
- Do you think you could live a fulfilling life on this island? What would you miss the most?
- What were the mother's and father's different reasons for wanting to stay or go?
- What do you know about pirates? Are there pirates today?
- If you were Roberta, which brother would you like more, Fritz or Ernst? Why?
- How hard is it for brothers who are close in age to have one be in charge? Should the oldest automatically be in charge?
- Did you think their booby trap was going to work to keep the pirates away?
- Do you think Frances had any fears, or was he seeing everything as a game?
- What would you want to do in their situation—stay on the island, go to New Guinea, or go to England to study? Why?
- Why did they all decide to stay? Why did Ernst decide to go?

Pointer:

Discuss a time when your family was in a crisis, predicament, or catastrophe. What were everyone's different roles? How did your family get through it? Were you ever without basic needs? If not, think about a possible problem and discuss how you would anticipate your family operating.

A Tree Grows in Brooklyn

The Nolans are an Irish immigrant family living in a Brooklyn tenement. The father, Johnny, is an irresponsible but affectionate dreamer who loves his children. He struggles with alcoholism, which is referred to as the "sickness." By contrast, the mother, Katie, is a hard pragmatist, who wants her children to be educated even if she has to "turn into granite rock to make 'em". Aunt Sissy is promiscuous, impetuous, and has been married several times. Their sensitive daughter, Francie Nolan, is a good student who adores her father and has a hard time relating to her practical mother. She dreams of going to a school where she will have a teacher who understands her and will nurture her creativity and love of writing the way her father does. When Katie gets pregnant, she decides Francie should leave school. Francie's feelings toward her mother are further complicated when her father dies. Francie finally learns to love both her parents for their strengths.

This film shows a family struggling to meet their basic needs while learning to deal with and respect the different philosophies and personalities of each family member. *A Tree Grows in Brooklyn* shows how sometimes the differences that may have drawn two people together are the same qualities that cause them to fight. This family has a lot of love, but has a difficult time communicating with each other. The differences between family members get in the way. This film can provide an opportunity to discuss several topics: how difficult it is to get along with family members who may be very different, how a family member's alcoholism or death can affect the family, and how the birth of a new baby or the remarriage of a parent changes the family dynamic.

Discussion Questions:

- What is your impression of the Nolans?
- Who do you like most? Why does Francie seem to like her father so much more than her mother?
- What do you think of Aunt Sissy? Do you think it was right for the mother to tell her sister not to come around anymore?
- Why is reading every night from Shakespeare and the Bible so important to the Nolans?
- What does the tree outside their window represent to Francie and Neeley? What does the title *A Tree Grows in Brooklyn* mean?
- How does Johnny's drinking affect the family?
- Johnny is a dreamer, and Katie is more practical and hardworking. Are your parents like Francie's parents in any way?
- Do you think opposites attract, just like the more practical Katie was once attracted to the dreaminess and imagination of Johnny? Are your parents opposites or similar?

- Do you think Johnny helps Francie realize her dream better than Katie?
- Do you think it was right for the Nolans to lie about Francie living with an aunt so that she could go to a better school?
- Communities were much tighter then. Would you like to have everyone close by—neighbors, family, police, etc.? How are things different today?
- What do you think would be the best solution for this family? How should they have resolved the issue with the baby on its way?
- What did Francie learn from both her parents?
- How do you think this family will change with a new baby and a new father figure?

Pointer:

It is so important for family members to accept each other's differences. Each sibling and each parent has something special to offer. Discuss the different qualities and personalities of your family members. Which parent is the disciplinarian? Which one is the dreamer? Which child is more studious and which is more creative? How do your different personalities affect how you get along? Try to discuss how everyone in the family can be more in tune with the different needs of each person, and how the family benefits from having different types of personalities in it.

Chapter 6

Friends, Bullies, and Social Life

For children in this age group, feelings of acceptance from same-gender peers, as well as belonging to a social group, is critical to the building of social skills and friendships. Affiliations with sports teams, drama groups, or boy or girl scouts can make a child feel connected and part of a group. What these affiliations do is let the child know that simply being themselves is acceptable, and that their behaviors can lead to friendships outside their families.

Children learn from each other how to relate to new and different personalities and how to handle decisions that they would not necessarily discuss with their parents. These experiences also teach children the boundaries between playfulness and hostile comments or teasing. Ongoing verbal hostility, quick retaliation at perceived wrongdoing, and overzealous physical aggression are usually interpreted by peers to mean "I don't like or respect you." This behavior can damage or even end friendships. Being able to sympathize and empathize, negotiate compromises when disagreements develop, and a willingness to share with peers are the most important skills in maintaining friends over time.

Discovering Behaviors That Create and Maintain Committed Friendships

As in all human relationships, when someone shows an interest in you, focuses their attention on you, and is willing to share their most prized possessions or deepest feelings with you, the message is that the person likes you and wants to spend time with you. Like the four boys in *Stand By Me*, good friends know how to support each other and what type of teasing is acceptable. Children who have been pampered by their parents or over-indulged will only relate to others to satisfy their own needs. These children will find it extremely difficult to sustain true friendships because other children will grow tired and uninterested in someone who consistently does not show interest in them. It is human nature to reciprocate when someone is reaching out to you for friendship.

Growing from Fantasy to Group Cooperative Play

As children mature socially, their solitary imaginary play begins to include other children in adventures and activities. Girls tend to initiate these forms of play earlier with dollhouse figures, tea parties, and make-believe storytelling *(The Little Princess)*. The content of their games involves etiquette, setting social rules, and the exchange of positive feelings. Boys develop group fantasy play a little later and usually involve playful expressions of aggression, with toys like action figures or soldiers to share in imaginative cooperative play. Competition also seems to be more of a theme for boys at this age level.

Expressing Anger and Resolving Conflict

With an advanced ability to problem-solve in middle childhood, children handle arguments with their friends differently than their younger peers. Being able to express frustration and anger—as Tom and Huck do when they argue over what do to about Muff Potter's trial—without dissolving the friendship is a true sign of social maturation. Unlike the preschooler who quickly says "I don't like you" or "you are not my friend" at the first sign of conflict, the older child should be willing to work out problems, be more flexible, and reach a compromise when differences of opinion arise. The use of humor to deal with angry feelings is also a sign of maturity, especially if the joke is perceived as gentle chiding and not teasing.

Evolving from Mixed-Gender to Same-Gender Play

It appears to be a normal process of practicing newly established gender awareness to want to play primarily with same-sex friends. Children role-play getting married, kissing, and relating to the opposite sex by establishing the "boys only" or "girls only" rules and ascribing things like "cooties" to the other gender. Like Harriet and Sport in *Harriet the Spy*, from time to time one-to-one mixed-gender play occurs, especially if there are limited numbers of children with which to play. A need and preference for same-gender play is usually a healthy expression at this age, before the hormones of the preadolescent take control.

Harriet The Spy

Harriet Welsch, a.k.a. Harriet the Spy, is a creative, passionate, and curious but often misunderstood eleven year old girl. Rejected by the "in crowd," she spends her time spying on people around her and writing notes in her journal about everything she sees as practice for her career as a writer. But when her longtime nanny Golly decides it's time to leave, Harriet's problems begin. Snooty Maryanne finds her sacred journal, and reveals her observations—not all of them nice—about everyone in her class, even her best friends Sport and Janie. Suddenly, Harriet is without her journal, her best friends, and even her beloved Golly to guide her. She is forced to learn some lessons about the meaning of friendship, the power of words, and how to use her writing for a better cause.

This film can help parents talk to their children about the value of friendship. In trying to pursue her own goals, Harriet loses sight of what's important: friendship. She is so focused on trying to be accurate and write down the truth that she is unaware of how many people she is hurting. Holding on to friends requires being sensitive to their needs, being able to say you're sorry, and realizing that without friends, your own personal successes don't mean as much. Harriet struggles between her need to be true to her own values and her need to have friends. This film also shows the value of having an older mentor, teacher, or babysitter who isn't a parent, like Golly. It can help children understand that you can be an honest person without always telling the exact truth. When it comes to saving people's feelings, a little white lie can often do more good than harm.

Discussion Questions:

- What do you think about how Harriet observes different people in very private situations and then writes it all down in her journal?
- Why didn't Harriet keep her journal more private?
- Is your class at school like Harriet's at all? Is there someone with whom you really don't get along the way Harriet and Maryanne don't?
- What is it about Harriet, Janie, and Sport that makes them such great friends?
- Why were Janie and Sport so mad at Harriet when they found out what she had been writing in her journal? What would you have done if you found out that one of your best friends was writing negative things about everybody, including you, in her journal?
- Why did Golly think it was time for her to leave and stop being Harriet's nanny? Was it fair for her to leave like that?
- What do you think of Harriet's parents? Do you think they're helping Harriet grow up?
- Have you ever felt like Harriet did—that everyone was against you? How did you handle it?
- Was it fair for Harriet to get back at her class by saying nasty things about all of them? What would you have done?
- Was it fair for Harriet's parents to take away her notebook when they have their own "unhealthy obsessions," like drinking martinis

or going to fancy parties? Do any of your friends or family members have "unhealthy obsessions"?

- Have your parents ever made you get rid of something that you really loved? What was it?
- Does it make things better when Harriet gets back at all her friends? What does Golly tell her about how she's been misusing her journal?
- What are white lies? Do you think it's okay to lie when it makes people feel better? When is it bad to tell the truth?
- How does being the editor of her sixth-grade newspaper allow Harriet to clear things up with her friends?

Pointer:

Emphasize the importance of friendships and maintaining them even when things get tough. Share times when you may have gone too far and said things that were hurtful to your friends. Discuss the difference between lying and being sensitive to people's feelings. It's a fine line between the two, but a line that needs to be understood in order to maintain lasting friendships.

Stand By Me

After learning about the tragic death of his childhood best friend Chris Chambers, writer Gordon Lachance reflects on a journey he and Chris took along with two other friends. On the brink of adolescence, Gordon and his three friends set out to find the body of a missing boy their age. Gordon is the one who comes from the most respectable family. Chris is a tough guy from the wrong side of the tracks with a bad reputation and a heart of gold. Teddy is the crazy son of an even crazier father, and Vern is the slow, chubby butt of all the jokes. In their search for a dead body, these four boys find friendship so strong and pure that for the moment they forget the way their small town or their fathers view them, and celebrate who they are as individuals.

This film deals with so many issues relevant to young teens, including the strong bonds of friendship that characterize that age. These friends serve as a surrogate family, lending support and encouragement when it is lacking in their families. *Stand By Me* shows the ways in which friends can come together, even if it's just to get through teasing from older bullies and brothers. Children will no doubt relate to the four friends, and adults may view it with the same nostalgic longing that the narrator expresses.

Discussion Questions:

- How does your group of friends compare to this group of boys? If you had to be one of them, which one would you be and why?
- Do you think you would have gone searching for the dead body?
- Why are the older boys so mean to the younger ones?
- How do these boys' family lives affect their friendships?
- These friends tease each other a lot. What kind of teasing can you tolerate from your friends and what kind is just mean?
- Why do you think these boys' friendships will change so much once they start junior high school?
- What makes the friendship between Chris and Gordon so special? How do they make each other feel better about their home lives?
- What do you think it was like for them to finally see the dead body? Do you think you would have challenged the older boys the way Gordon did?
- Why did the boys decide to make an anonymous phone call instead of getting credit and having their pictures in the paper as they had planned? What would you and your friends have done in that situation?
- Why didn't these friends remain close as they got older? What friends do you have now that you think you'll remain friends with no matter what? Are there any that you think you might grow apart from?
- What do these four friends get from each other that they don't get from their parents?

Pointer:

Talk about why friendships at that age tend to be so strong, and share your friendships. Why do you think things will change for these four boys when they get to junior high?

Parents can share stories about best friends they had at this age and whether or not they still keep in touch with them. You may want to address the idea that friends are a reflection of you, and when you change and grow, your friends do too. It may be difficult for a pre-pubescent child to understand that they may grow apart from some of their best friends over the years into adulthood, but that it doesn't devalue what they have now.

Tom and Huck

This is an updated film version of Mark Twain's classic tale *The Adventures of Tom Sawyer.* Tom is a precocious boy who always gets in trouble and upsets his worried Aunt Polly. Huck Finn is an uncivilized boy without a home who lives in the woods and does as he pleases. Tom and Huck witness Injun Joe stab someone to death in the graveyard, and they make a blood oath never to tell anyone what they saw. But when Muff Potter, the town's lovable drunk, gets blamed for the murder, the boys face a moral dilemma: keep quiet and let an innocent man be condemned, or risk their safety, break their vow of silence, and save Muff Potter.

This film addresses the conflicting longing for the security of parents and the desire to run away from parental discipline. It sets up a contrast between the home life of Tom, who has a stable home with his aunt and cousins but always tries to run away, and that of Huck, who lives on his own in the woods with no structure, but secretly craves a strong parental figure in his life. This film also reinforces the importance of making the right moral decisions and the consequences that might follow when one doesn't do the right thing. Tom and Huck are friends from different backgrounds whose common ground is their affinity for adventure and ability to help each other out of dangerous situations.

Discussion Questions:

- What do you think of Tom and Huck? How are they alike and different?
- Why does Tom always get in trouble with Aunt Polly?
- What does the blood oath mean to the boys? Have you ever made

an oath or pact to seal your friendship with someone?

- What would you have done in Tom's situation, if you had seen a crime but promised your best friend you wouldn't say anything? Would you have kept the promise or let an innocent man hang for a crime he didn't commit?
- Do you ever feel like you're caught between your loyalty to your friends and your loyalty to your family?
- What makes Tom and Huck such good friends?
- How do Tom and Huck save each other?
- What made Huck come back? How do you think he will do living with Widow Douglas?

Pointer:

Discuss how far you would go to help a friend. Share with your child how your friends have saved you in either a literal or figurative way. Ask them if any of their friends have ever saved them or helped them in a difficult situation.

A Little Princess

Based on the book by Frances Hodgson Burnett, A Little Princess is about an imaginative and kind little girl named Sara Crewe, who was raised in India by her wealthy and adoring father. When Sara's father goes off to fight in World War I, he sends her to a respected boarding school in New York. Sara quickly becomes popular at school, where her brilliant imagination and gift for telling stories help her survive the culture shock and the mean Ms. Minchin. When Sara's father is presumed dead and she is left poor, she is banished to the maid's quarters with Becky, a little Black girl who cleans the school. Sara's kindness, imagination, and her friends save her from the evil Ms. Minchin and lead her back to the love of her father.

This film shows how one good friend and a lot of imagination can make even the worst situation tolerable. More importantly, through the character of Sara Crewe, it illustrates the very qualities that make someone a good friend: sensitivity to others' needs, kindness, a sense of adventure, and an unbiased heart that is open to giving and receiving friendship from all types of people. Sara uses her father's love to instill a sense of pride in all the little girls at the boarding school, showing them that in her way, each girl really is a little princess.

Discussion Questions:

- What do you think it would be like to move from a country like India to a big American city like New York? What would it be like to be the new girl where you didn't know anyone and your parent was far away? Would you ever want to go to boarding school?
- What it is about Sara that draws all the girls to her? What is so likeable about her?
- What kinds of things does Sara do to make friends? What things does she do to earn the loyalty of the girls?
- What does Sara mean when she tells the girls that they are all princesses?
- How does Becky help Sara when she's sad?
- Was it magic when Becky and Sara woke to a feast and beautiful clothes, or was it real?
- Why did Sara encourage Amelia to run off with the milkman?
- Why doesn't Sara's father recognize her at first?

Pointer:

Discuss how good friends can get people through the most difficult of situations. What are the qualities that make someone a good friend? What kinds of things can a friend do to make you feel better about yourself?

Chapter 7

"Sometimes you really can't listen to what anyone else says. You just gotta listen inside. You're not supposed to end up in those mines. You know why? 'Cause I think you made other plans. And I want you to know something. I'm proud of you. I am. Whatever you choose."
— **Miss Riley, _October Sky_**

Gender and Self Identity

Children in middle childhood quickly get a sense from their experiences in school and their families of what comes naturally to them and what is more difficult. Academic achievement may be their strength, or perhaps skills such as playing a musical instrument or working with tools come easier. For some children, sports provide a forum for emotional and social esteem, while others who are more physically attractive and developed get a head start on their peers as leaders of their friends.

Today's children experience changes in their bodies earlier than their parents' generation. As preadolescents start to respond to sexual impulses and feelings, they often suffer confusion about what bodily changes mean, and how they may affect relationships with close friends and peers.

It is at this point that preteens look for reasons for the many things that are happening to them and want to experience life beyond their immediate families. Parents need to find a balance between allowing their children to explore the world and make mistakes, while being careful to protect them from detrimental early decisions regarding sex, substance abuse, and peer relationships.

Sorting Out Behaviors for Gender Identity

Children in this age group have to be comfortable matching their personalities with their own understanding of how males and females behave differently. If a boy is less aggressive, prefers solitary activities, and is sensitive, he should be made to feel good about choosing activities that are compatible with those traits. The same holds true for a tomboy like Vada in *My Girl,* whose best friend is a boy and who always wears jeans. Girls who are more physically competitive, enjoy group sports, and can handle rough-and-tumble play should be made to feel that it is okay to participate is such activities. It is important for parents to be aware of how culture affects those gender differences. A film like *Yentl* shows the limitations culture can place on females. It is very important that parents emphasize individual achievement and improving a child's own skills, rather than comparing her with others.

Exploring One's World Within the Expectations of the Family

It is parents' job to communicate, and then monitor their children's attempts to participate in experiences beyond the boundaries of the home. Understand that these experiences are healthy opportunities for growth and allow your children to make some mistakes. This can be very difficult for parents, especially when witnessing the frustration and disappointment on children's faces in initial attempts with life's challenges. Films like *Searching for Bobby Fischer* and *October Sky* show children struggling to become their own people and using their natural talents outside the family structure, and the consequences this journey can have on the whole family.

Beginning of Sexual Feelings and Physical Changes

Discussions with children about experiencing pleasure from their bodies can, and often should, occur much earlier than adolescence. Addressing this topic earlier rather than later can make the transition into puberty much less awkward. Parents who are openly affectionate with their spouses are modeling healthy behaviors that can lead to informal talks about how adult bodies react to touch and respond to certain feelings of intimacy. Obviously, choosing an appropriate time and place to have such a discussion is important. Perhaps instead of having "The Talk" about sex, it may be more effective and more natural to have several little talks as issues arise.

October Sky

In 1950s Coalwood, West Virginia, boys were destined to become coal miners, unless they were good enough athletes to win athletic scholarships; this was the ticket out of their small town. Homer Hickam is the younger son of a proud coal miner, whose interest in rocket science is stirred when the Soviet Union's *Sputnik* satellite flies over the United States. A natural leader like his father, who supervises coal mining in their town, Homer enlists the help of the class geek and two of his friends, who eventually become known throughout their small town as the Rocket Boys. Homer's determination to build a successful rocket, enter the state science competition, and eventually the national competition, is so strong that he overcomes initial sneers from his community and resistance from his father. The town eventually rallies around the Rocket Boys, but it takes much longer for Homer's father to get past his disappointment that his son does not want to follow in his footsteps.

This film is a wonderful example of how one person's determination and focus can enable him to overcome odds. While Homer seems to be so different from his father, we see throughout the film that his values, dedication to hard work, and natural leadership skills are qualities modeled by his father. This film also shows how little steps forward can accumulate into a giant leap. Miss Riley is a wonderful example of a supportive teacher who nurtures the best in her students and never stops believing in them, even when their goals seem close to impossible. Many children in middle childhood may feel they have nothing in common with a parent, but often similar qualities manifest themselves in very different ways. In order for the children in this story to become adults, they must break away from their parents to pursue their own dreams, rather than those of their parents.

Discussion Questions:

- What do you think it was like to have our country's archenemy at that time, the Soviet Union, put the first satellite into space?
- How is Coalwood, West Virginia, different from or similar to your hometown? What would it be like to live in a town where your only choice was to become a coal miner or a football player?
- Why do you think Homer is so interested in building a rocket?
- What kind of person is Homer? What does it show about his personality that he would befriend a "geek" like Quentin?
- What do you think of the father's attitude towards his sons? Why is Homer's father so opposed to his interest in rocketry?
- How does Miss Riley encourage and motivate the boys?
- Why does the coal mine seem so important to Mr. Hickam? Why is it such a source of pride for him?
- Do you think you could have set up a launch pad like these boys?
- Why was the science fair such a big deal to the Rocket Boys?
- Have you ever had a goal like Homer's?
- How does the town of Coalwood support these boys?
- How are Homer and his dad alike?
- The whole town of Coalwood comes together to help Homer rebuild his rocket when it is stolen at the Indianapolis science fair. Do you think something like this could happen today?
- What does he mean when Homer tells his father that he's his hero?
- How important is it to fully respect your father and still follow your own dreams?

Pointer:

Ask your child what she thinks your expectations for her are. Discuss the importance of following through with your dreams even when you are discouraged. Try sharing with your child a time when you reached an important goal. What kind of support did you have from your parents? Ask your child what her dreams are. Remember to be supportive of her whatever they might be, even if it is not something you can relate to.

The Wizard of Oz

Dorothy Gale is a small-town Kansas girl who can't seem to get any attention from the people around her; they are all too busy to listen to her problems. Feeling under-appreciated and misunderstood, Dorothy runs away, literally and figuratively, to the magical Land of Oz. There, she is made a national hero after accidentally murdering the Wicked Witch of the East. In her search to find the Wizard of Oz, the only person who can get her home, she meets up with the Scarecrow who longs for a brain, the Tin Man who longs for a heart, and the Cowardly Lion, who longs for courage. The foursome and Dorothy's dog, Toto, finally find the Wizard only to learn that he is not what they think, and that the answers are to be found within themselves.

Each of the main characters in this film—Dorothy, the Tin Man, the Scarecrow, and the Cowardly Lion—struggle with their need to be recognized a certain way. They look toward authority for approval and answers, until they finally learn that they themselves have had the answers all along.

This film is about appreciating what you have and learning to recognize the gifts that are within you. Often, the answers we seek exist right before our own eyes, but it isn't until we are taken out of our current situation that we are able to recognize their true value.

Discussion Questions:

- Why is it so important to Dorothy to have someone understand her predicament with Miss Gulch?
- Have you ever been in a situation where you just needed someone to listen to you?
- How does Dorothy's home life contribute to her experience in Oz?
- Why does the Scarecrow think that he doesn't have a brain?
- Why does the Tin Man want a heart so badly? What could the heart symbolize?

- Why does Dorothy feel as though she knows the Tin Man and the Scarecrow?
- How could a lion—the King of the Forest—be such a sissy?
- Why won't the gatekeeper allow Dorothy and her friends see the Wizard? Why does he finally give in?
- What do you think of the Wizard?
- What do you think of the Tin Man, the Cowardly Lion, the Scarecrow, and Dorothy? In what ways does each demonstrate the quality they are searching for?
- The Wizard says, "I'm really a nice person. I'm just a bad wizard." What does he mean by that? Why does the Wizard pretend to be what he's not?
- What does the Wizard mean when he says to the Tin Man, "A heart is not judged by how much you love but by how much you are loved by others"?
- What did Dorothy learn from her experience in Oz? How will she be different in Kansas now?

Pointer:

It may help your child to realize that, although the grass always seems greener in other pastures, most of the time the answers you are looking for are inside. Sometimes you have to lose what you have in order to appreciate its value. Discuss a situation that made you or your child appreciate home or see things differently.

Yentl

Yentl is a young woman who was raised in Eastern Europe by her father, a religious scholar, who instilled in her an unquenchable thirst for knowledge. This upbringing was unheard of in the early 1900s, and unacceptable in a society where a woman's domain was domestic and where females were literally forbidden to study the Talmud. When her father passes away, Yentl cuts her long hair and sets off to a yeshiva, where she pretends to be a man named Anshel. At the yeshiva, Anshel meets Avigdor, who is her intellectual equal and satisfies her hunger for knowledge. Anshel begins to fall in love with Avigdor. When Avigdor's engagement to his fiancée, Hadass, is broken, he decides the next best thing would be to have his best friend Anshel marry her instead. This love triangle is finally broken when Avigdor learns the shocking truth that Anshel is really Yentl. In the end, Avigdor and Hadass are reunited and Yentl goes off to find a place where she can be both a woman and a scholar.

This film raises interesting questions about the roles of women and the advances that women have made over the years. Yentl represents an individual so passionate about pursuing her dreams that she is willing to hide her gender to do so. Though hiding one's true identity for the sake of pursuing a goal may be an extreme measure, this film can initiate an important discussion about being true to one's identity and following one's own path, despite the obstacles that lay ahead or the expectations of one's society.

Discussion Questions:

- What do you think of the roles and responsibilities of women and men in this society? How does Yentl's father allow her to pursue her dreams?
- Why did Yentl want to pose as a man?
- How would you feel if you were a woman "in a time when the world of study belonged only to men"?
- Would you like a lifestyle that centered on questioning and studying the laws of the Talmud, the Bible, or another religious doctrine?
- Could you ever pass for a member of the opposite sex? Have you ever wished that you were the opposite gender so that you could do something different?
- How are Yentl and Hadass different? Who are you more like? Who do you like better?
- Was it right for Yentl to lie to Avigdor and the rabbis about her sex?
- Was it fair for Hadass' family to cancel her wedding to Avigdor because his brother committed suicide?
- How far would you go to be near someone you love? Would you ever lie about your gender if it meant being able to pursue your dreams?
- How does Anshel make Hadass feel comfortable on her wedding

night and still avoid revealing her secret?
- If you were Avigdor, how would you have reacted to Yentl's secret?
- Why didn't Yentl want to marry Avigdor?
- Do you think Avigdor had feelings for Yentl/Anshel?
- Why did Yentl decide to go to America? How will it be different there?

Pointer:

Discuss how a person's passion and individuality can be stifled by cultural or societal expectations. Share sacrifices you have made to reach a personal goal. When have your dreams or aspirations been in conflict with those of your culture? Share with your child a personal example about how you may have gone against the grain of your community or culture to achieve your goals.

Searching for Bobby Fischer

Seven-year-old Josh Waitzkin is a normal child growing up in New York, until his parents discover that he has an unusual gift for playing chess. His father, sportswriter Fred Waitzkin, hires Bruce Pandolfini, a former chess champion, to improve Josh's chess game. The film sets up a contrast between Josh's two mentors, the strategic and intellectual methods of Bruce and the instinctual, street-wise style of Vinnie, whom Josh plays chess with in Washington Square. Josh becomes so immersed in the world of chess tournaments that the meaning of the game begins to change for him as the pressure from his coach and his father make it less fun and more about winning. Josh's mom, in contrast to his father, wants to protect her sensitive son. Eventually his parents must decide how to nurture his talent without ruining their son's love of the game and compromising his childhood.

This film explores how a young child comes to realize a great skill, how that skill is fostered by those around him, and the possible dangers associated with being so competitive at such a young age. Ultimately, what makes Josh such a great child is not just his skill in chess, but his whole personality, his sensitivity to others, his kindness, and his interest in non chess-related activities like baseball. This film also explores one of the central conflicts of parenthood: How can you encourage and take pride in your child's accomplishments without making them your own; how can you support their special skills without making them feel they are loved for their talents alone? It is this delicate balance that is the most challenging to achieve. In this film, Josh's father becomes so immersed in the chess scene that he loses sight of the huge pressure he is putting on his young son. He takes the chance that his pride in his son's talent may be misconstrued for love and acceptance. Conversely, Josh learns that in order to be successful in the game of chess, he must uncover his own competitive nature and balance that with his sensitive side. Any child involved with musical instruments, athletics, dancing, or academic pursuits will relate to the film, which explores both the difficulties and joys of success at a young age.

Discussion Questions:

- Do you know anything about chess? What do you think about how Josh picked up the game?
- Why does Bruce decide to teach Josh after he sees him play chess in the park?
- What do you think of Bruce's teaching style? Could you handle this kind of coach? What is the difference between Bruce's teaching style and Vinnie's? Who do you like better? Who do you think is a better teacher?
- Why do you think Josh's mom wants him to continue playing chess in the park?
- What do you think of the chess tournament environment? Should parents be allowed in the room or not?
- Have you ever been in a high-pressure situation like this competitive one where you had to perform well?
- How was Jonathan Poe different from Josh?
- Why does Bruce tell Josh that he should have contempt for his opponent? Do you agree? Do you have to hate your opponent to win an intense game like chess?
- Why did Josh lose in the first tournament? Was it a fluke, an accident, or did he do it on purpose? Do you think his dad had the right attitude toward his loss?
- What is the difference between Fred's approach and Bonnie's to Josh's chess-playing? Which approach do you like better and why?

- What did it reveal about Fred when he moved all the chess trophies back to Josh's room?
- Why do you think Josh's dad took him fishing and forbid any talk about chess right before the National Chess Finals?
- How does Josh win the finals? How does he incorporate the strategies from each of his chess teachers to win the game?

Pointer:

Discuss the extent to which parents should encourage or be involved in a child's interests and accomplishments. What should a parent do if a child has a gift—should they encourage it or let the child pursue it on his own? Discuss what interests and skills your child has and what your role is. Do you push him too hard or not hard enough?

My Girl

Vada Sultenfuss is a pretty typical eleven-year-old girl with an atypical life; her mother died while giving birth to her, so she was raised by her father—who runs a funeral home—and her senile grandmother. She's a hypochondriac who runs to the family doctor complaining of imaginary ailments (i.e. one breast is developing at a significantly higher rate than the other). She has no girlfriends and spends most of her time with a highly allergic little boy named Thomas J. Things get even more complicated when her father falls in love with Shelly, a cosmetologist who works for him. Vada is torn because she likes Shelly and craves a mother figure, but feels jealous of her father's attention, and loyalty to the mother she never knew. The unexpected death of her best friend Thomas J. makes matters worse.

This film explores so many issues common to middle childhood—insecurities about changing bodies, jealousy when a parent remarries, confusion about death. At the start of the film, Vada is a tomboy, but soon becomes more concerned with her physical appearance. She gets her first period, marking her physical development as a woman, though her mental development has not yet reached the point where she can appreciate the cultural implications of womanhood. By the end of the film, she is wearing a dress and her new best friend is a girl.

Discussion Questions:

- What do you think it would be like if your father was a mortician? What kind of a father is Harry Sultenfuss?
- How do you think Vada's father's profession and living in a funeral home affects her sickness/problems?
- Why doesn't Vada have any girlfriends?
- Have you ever had a crush on a teacher or an older person?
- Why does Vada think she killed her mother?
- How does Shelly help Vada become more comfortable with her body's changes?
- Why do Vada's feelings towards Shelly change? If Vada likes Shelly, then why does she give her such a hard time?
- What makes Thomas J. and Vada such good friends? Do you have any good friends of the opposite sex?
- How hard do you think it would be to lose your best friend?
- Do you think Vada and Thomas J. have romantic feelings toward one another or are they just experimenting to see what it's like to kiss someone?
- How has Vada changed by the end of the film?

Pointer:

Be aware of a child's concerns, questions, or fears about the changes in her body. It is also important for pre-adolescent children to have someone of the same gender with whom they can discuss these things.

Chapter 8

"You never really understand a person until you consider things from his point of view, until you climb inside his skin and walk around in it."
— Atticus Finch, To Kill A Mockingbird

Values, Morals, and Ethics

With families so aware of the difficulty instilling children with morals and values, parents are more than ever looking for opportunities to inspire a sense of caring about others that seems to be missing in today's world. In middle childhood, it is important for parents to talk about situations with their children that promote a sense of fairness and empathy for others' feelings. As children mature, their ability to reason and problem-solve also leads to the development of empathy for others and giving of oneself, along with a more advanced sense of right and wrong.

There are such conflicting messages in our world today, on one hand, thinking of our own needs first and venting our anger freely without concern for whomever is the target of our frustrations, while the other extreme emphasizes a strict sense of following rules and obeying authority. Because many parents are preoccupied with making ends meet or satisfying their own needs, they do not make time to be role models or teach those values in order to achieve a balance between the conflicting messages our children are exposed to on television and in the movies. Think of films as examples of how different types of people play out their morality, and use the movies to show your children right and wrong moral or ethical choices. Don't worry if characters in a film go against everything you believe; use that as an opportunity to explain why you disagree with the characters' actions in the film.

Transition from Early Childhood to Middle Childhood Morality

Lawrence Kohlberg's research in the development of morality found that children in middle childhood become less focused on being rewarded for good behavior and punished for bad behavior. They become more morally driven, begin to feel empathy for others, and can attempt to understand the feelings of others. Examples are Belle's sensitivity toward the beast in *Beauty and the Beast*, and Charlie's more advanced level of morality than the other children in *Willy Wonka & the Chocolate Factory*.

Living Up to the Expectations of Authority Figures

Children in this age group want to be seen as obedient and respectful by following parents' rules. For example, they remind Mom and Dad to put seatbelts on or to obey traffic rules because these are society's expectations. *Pollyanna* shows a little girl who is so tuned in to the needs of others that she actually demands adults to live up to her moral standards.

Shifting from External to Intrinsic Values

A parent's goal in teaching important values should always be to emphasize a sense of inner satisfaction and to downplay the expectation of getting something from someone for doing a good deed. In *To Kill a Mockingbird*, Scout and Jem take on the values of their ethical father Atticus Finch. While it is good to acknowledge a child's attempt at improving a skill or displaying caring behavior, the ultimate goal should be for the children to reward themselves by thinking, "It really feels good to help someone," or "I'm glad I tried that. I can do that pretty well."

To Kill A Mockingbird

Based on the novel by Harper Lee, this is a film about a widowed man in 1932 rural Alabama named Atticus Finch, and his two children, Jean Louis (Scout) and her older brother Jem. Atticus is a lawyer and is regarded as a moral pillar of his community, which is filled with prejudice. Atticus takes on a controversial case defending a Black man who is accused of raping and beating a White girl. Meanwhile, Jem and Scout are fascinated by their neighbor, Arthur "Boo" Radley, the town's bogeyman, who ends up saving them in the woods one night. In this film, nothing is what it seems, as Atticus makes clear to his children.

This film is about the problems that occur when we judge both people and situations on appearances rather than truth. By appearance, Boo Radley is a scary, violent, crazy man. In reality, he is an innately good, harmless, mentally disabled young man who has been isolated from society. According to Atticus, Tom Robinson is an innocent man who has been wrongly accused by a promiscuous young White woman. Atticus Finch makes an effort to teach Scout and Jem about the world around them so that they may make important moral decisions on their own. No amount of teaching can come close to the actual experience of things; that is what happens at the end of the film, when Boo saves Scout and Jem's lives. In the end, Scout looks at her town from Boo's porch and his perspective.

Discussion Questions:
- What is the Finch family like? Why do you think they call their dad by his first name?
- Do you know what the Depression was like?
- What do Scout and Jem think about Boo? Was there anyone in your neighborhood or community that children were scared of? Are their any scary stories about a house or family that you know?
- How is Atticus Finch different from other people in the town?
- What does Atticus' story about the mockingbird mean?

- What kind of lessons does Atticus try to teach his children by bringing them with him all the time? Do you think he's a good father?
- Why do you think Boo leaves gifts in the tree for Scout and Jem?
- What does Atticus mean when he says that if he didn't defend Tom Robinson, he couldn't hold his head up around town?
- Why is Atticus such a moral person? Who do you know that has strong moral character like Atticus?
- Why did the jury find Tom Robinson guilty of rape even though Atticus made a better argument for his innocence?
- Why did Mr. Ewell spit on Atticus when he won the trial? Do you know of any cases or situations where people's prejudices or beliefs have gotten in the way of their moral judgement?
- What did Scout learn after Boo saved her in the woods? What did that show her?
- Would you have wanted to tell people in the town who saved you? Why did the Finches decide to keep it a secret and say that Mr. Ewell fell on his own knife?

Pointer:

How hard is it to go against the standard of the era, culture, or society? Share a situation in which doing the right thing according to one's own moral standards contradicted the rules of one's society. Try to think of someone you know who seems to live her life according to a higher moral standard, even when her opinions are not the most popular.

Pollyanna

Pollyanna Harrington is an eleven-year-old orphan from the West Indies who is sent to live with her unmarried aunt Polly, who, through family inheritance, literally owns the town. Pollyanna is so likeable and has such a positive way of looking at things that she slowly charms all the grumpy people in her small town. She is the force behind a town-wide effort to organize a bazaar to raise money for the orphanage. However, her aunt Polly, who owns the old orphanage, would rather maintain her sense of control and superiority by paying for the restorations herself. It isn't until Pollyanna falls out of a tree while sneaking back into the house from the bazaar that Aunt Polly finally realizes how cold and hard she has been.

Pollyanna as both an individual and a film is best characterized by the search for good in every situation. The Glad Game symbolizes the way in which Polly is able to find the positive in even the most negative of situations. This optimism is a special quality, as finding the good in things comes much easier for some than for others. Pollyanna expects the best from people and eventually is able to break through to those hardened by years of pain and fear. Her joy is contagious. Her heart is unbiased. When she is the one who is hurt and discouraged, the whole town finds a way to return the joy she has given them.

Discussion Questions:

- What do you think it would be like to live in this town?
- What's Aunt Polly like?
- What do you think of Reverend Ford's sermons? How would you feel about Sundays if you had to go to sermons like his? What type of sermon do you think is more effective: teaching people to fear God or teaching people to love God?
- What's the Glad Game? How does it work? Do you think you could ever play the Glad Game and turn a bad thing into something good?
- What is it about Pollyanna that makes everyone trust her and tell her things?
- Why doesn't Aunt Polly want everyone to raise money to build a new orphanage?
- How does Pollyanna change the reverend's approach to delivering his Sunday sermons?
- What are the Happy Texts?
- Do you know anyone like Mrs. Snow who is cranky and old and thinks she is about to die? How does Pollyanna help Mrs. Snow?
- Who's to blame for Pollyanna's accident? Do you think it was right for her to sneak out and go to the bazaar that she helped organize,

even though her aunt forbade her to do so?
- The town changes their sign to read "Harrington: The Glad Town." What does that show about the town's transformation?
- Who were the most moral characters in this town?

Pointer:

Many people believe that the most moral people are able to see what people need and give back to them. Talk about special people you may know who are caring, giving, and able to bring out the best in others. Discuss a person, a public figure, a relative, or someone in your neighborhood who is similar to Pollyanna. In what ways does this person turn situations around and find the good? Try to be like Pollyanna: Think of a somewhat negative situation and try to find a positive angle to it.

Willy Wonka & The Chocolate Factory

Charlie is an honest and sensitive but poor eleven-year-old boy who lives with his mom and four bedridden grandparents in England. His luck changes when he wins one of five golden tickets found in a chocolate bar. Each ticket-winner and a guest are allowed to tour Willy Wonka's Chocolate Factory and receive a lifetime supply of chocolate. Charlie and Grandpa Joe tour the factory, a funhouse of sweets, led by a very eccentric Willy Wonka, who loves children but not gluttons, spoiled brats, gum chewers, or TV addicts—all of whom get thrown off the tour due to bad behavior. In addition to breaking the rules of the factory, each child commits the ultimate crime when they agree to give the never-ending gobstopper to a man that poses as Slugworth, Willy Wonka's scheming competitor. In the end, Charlie's honesty and goodness win him much more than a lifetime supply of chocolate.

This film contrasts Charlie with the other four winners, all of whom are spoiled brats who have been overindulged and raised poorly by their parents. With the Oompa Loompas singing their moral commentary throughout, it is clear that good children who are honest, follow the rules, and aren't greedy will do well. This movie can generate a discussion about how being honest and moral may not be the easiest route, but in the end is the one that proves the most satisfying.

Discussion Questions:

- How is Charlie different from the other winners?
- Why are these children so obsessed with Wonka bars? Have you or your friends ever been really into a candy, special toy, treat, or prize?
- Do you think it's fair that children who come from poor families don't have the same chance of winning golden tickets because they can't afford as many chocolate bars?
- What do you think of the other children who won the golden tickets? Do any of them remind you of children you know?
- Who is Slugworth and what is he asking the children to do? Do you think it's wrong?
- How was Charlie's method of getting the golden ticket different from the actions of the other children?
- What do you think of Willy Wonka and his chocolate factory? What kind of game is he playing with the children and their parents?
- What is the purpose of the Oompa Loompas? What do they sing about?
- What do all the children do wrong that makes them get dropped from the tour?
- Was it right for Charlie and Grandpa Joe to drink the soda pop that makes you fly? What kind of lesson did they learn from that experience?
- What is so significant about Charlie giving the gobstopper back to Willy? What did that prove to Willy Wonka about Charlie's character?

Pointer:

The most important things a parent can give a child are not material possessions, but the values of honesty, kindness, and a respect for rules and discipline, not overindulgence. Discuss what was wrong with the other golden ticket winners, whether your child shares any of the winners' bad traits, or if he is more like Charlie.

Beauty and the Beast

Belle is beautiful, but she is also a thinker who loves reading and yearns for more than her small town can provide. She refuses a marriage proposal from the brutish Gaston, the object of every girl's desire. When her absent-minded father gets lost in the woods and is captured by a beast, Belle switches places with him, saving her father and putting her own life at risk. While held in captivity by the Beast, Belle discovers that the ugly, angry beast is really a gentle man inside and that years of loneliness have made him forget how to treat people. As she begins to see him for what's inside, Belle eventually falls in love with the Beast, thereby breaking the evil spell and turning the Beast into the handsome Prince that he once was.

Beauty and the Beast is a classic fairytale with a simple but important lesson that all children can understand: Don't judge people by their physical appearance, but by what they are like on the inside. This movie also reinforces the idea that by sticking to your values and giving of yourself, you can yield tremendous returns. The idea that beauty is in the eye of the beholder is also a lesson of this tale, as Belle is attracted to the inner beauty of the Beast, rather the physical beauty of Gaston. This film also stresses intelligence, creativity, and individuality over superficiality, materialism, and conformity.

Discussion Questions:

- What is this town like? Why do they think Belle is so peculiar?
- Why do they idolize Gaston? Why is Belle so frustrated with her life in the village? Have you ever felt out of sync with your community?
- What does Gaston want from Belle? Why isn't Belle interested in Gaston? Do you know any boys who are like Gaston?
- How would you feel about meeting the Beast? Why does he have such a bad temper?
- How does Belle make the Beast change?
- What does Belle see in the Beast?
- Why does the Beast let her go if he loves her?
- Belle sees Gaston as more of a beast than the Beast himself. How can that be?
- How could Belle love someone who is so ugly?

Pointer:

Share an experience where you misjudged someone because of his appearance, or discuss someone whose insides make him a beautiful person even if his outsides aren't so beautiful. Who do you know who is beautiful on the outside but is an ugly person inside? The Beast turns into a handsome prince when Belle falls in love with him. Discuss with your child how someone's appearance really can change when you love him.

Chapter 9

"Obedience without understanding is a blindness, too."
— **Annie Sullivan, *The Miracle Worker***

Handicaps, Sickness, and Loss

Handicaps, sickness, death, loss…All of these issues are interrelated in that the process of dealing psychologically with them is very similar. During this period, the concept of mortality begins to be fully understood by a child. If your family experiences a permanent loss or handicap, the realization that it is a lifetime issue that will not go away has to be dealt with directly. This way, the child can mourn the loss and the expectation that she will always have a limitation, and then turn to developing other capabilities.

A strong spiritual or religious belief system can help children deal with the many feelings that they may experience, because they can draw on inner strength, faith, and family support to move on from their loss.

Children will look to their parents for education and guidance in developing their own personal beliefs and emotional support systems. Perhaps more important than anything is respecting what your child is thinking and giving her the space to mourn, heal, and move on.

Developing Behaviors to Deal with These Issues

Communication is critical to alleviating any guilt that might be experienced by a child. To tell a child that an illness, handicap, or death is not her fault takes a lot of the emotional burden off her mind and allows for the mourning process to begin. Behaving as if nothing has happened—as Manny Singer does in the beginning of *Corrina, Corrina* —and avoiding loss will lead to more anxiety and other destructive feelings. As we will see in a number of films for this age group, animals provide a great deal of emotional stability for younger children who may be experiencing unsettling feelings or a life crisis in their family. Being responsible for an animal is an effective tool that helps children lift their mood by forcing them to dwell less on their sadness. If even for a moment, it can give direction and purpose to their life again. In addition, when children focus their energies on something concrete, they are able to see the fruits of their labor. In nurturing someone or something else back to life, as the children do in *The Secret Garden,* children inadvertently nurture themselves back to life.

Fear of Loss

Because an understanding about the finality of death is first processed in this age group, children tend to worry that they may lose their remaining parent, the way Molly worries in *Corrina, Corrina.* They will fear being left alone in the world. Also, specifically for the six- to eight-year-olds, they may maintain the illogical notion that their actions and words somehow caused the death of their parent or sibling.

Adjusting Emotionally to Death

In middle childhood, death brings the first awareness that someone whom the child cares about is never coming back. Parents should try to acknowledge feelings of vulnerability or anger that life is this way, and allow for either behavior to be acted out, depending on the temperament of their child. A child may be easily frustrated by simple tasks, or be more withdrawn or quiet than usual while trying to make sense of this newly learned aspect of life.

Coping with Sickness and Handicaps

Aside from terminal illness and severely debilitating physical or cognitive handicaps, the critical component in a child returning to healthy functioning has a lot to do with the attitude of the parents. A child should be educated as to the nature of their disability, acknowledging the frustration and limitation it brings. Then, encourage the child to attempt to return to normalcy. What a parent does not want to do is enable their child to wallow in self-pity over having a disability, as Colin does in *The Secret Garden*, thereby not challenging him to compensate and grow in stronger areas of his capabilities.

The Miracle Worker

The Miracle Worker is the story of the early life of Helen Keller. Blind, deaf, and mute from the age of six months, she is treated like the family pet until her teacher, Annie Sullivan, saves her. The Kellers have a difficult time accepting Annie, who is inexperienced and vision-impaired. She has a rather abrasive personality and an aggressive teaching approach. Annie initially focuses on disciplining Helen, and then begins to teach her vocabulary through symbolic communication. Helen mimics Annie's expressions and hand motions through sign language, but lacks an understanding of their conceptual relationship to objects in the world. Annie isolates Helen from her family in a small cabin on the Keller's property. There she has a real breakthrough—or a miracle takes place: Helen finally understands that the hand motions represent words and those words are connected to actions, meanings, and objects in the world.

This film shows the feelings of helplessness associated with having a handicapped child at a time when people thought the deaf or the blind were dumb or simply incapable of learning. On the contrary, Helen Keller is an extremely intelligent woman who went on to write books and lead a very accomplished life. As the title implies, this film is just as much about Annie Sullivan as it is about Helen. It is Annie's strength, stamina, intelligence, and belief in Helen that lead to her breakthrough. This film also explores the concepts of symbolic communication and sign language, as well as the importance of maintaining consistency when teaching someone who is handicapped.

Discussion Questions:

- How would it feel to learn that your baby was both blind and deaf?
- How does the Keller family perceive Helen? How do they treat her?
- Do you think putting her into an asylum might be good for her?
- What is the problem between Annie and the Keller family? Why don't they like her? Do you think Annie is too harsh with Helen?
- Do you think it's right that the family has been tolerating Helen's bad behavior?
- What do you think about a parent spoiling their handicapped child in order to get some peace?
- Do you think you would be able to last very long as Helen's teacher?
- Why does Annie feel that she needs to remove Helen from the family environment in order to teach her?
- Why was Kate Keller so happy when Helen learned to fold her napkin?

Pointer:

People perceive the handicapped as being less intelligent, but they may have equal or greater intelligence. Discuss people you know who have a physical handicap. How have they managed? How do their families treat them? How far have we come from the time when Helen Keller was a child? Discuss how advances in the field of psychology and medicine have benefited those with disabilities. For example, sign language is much more common nowadays than it was in Helen Keller's time. Discuss the amazing accomplishments of Helen Keller, and how your perceptions of her changed from the beginning of the film to the end.

The Secret Garden

Ten-year-old Mary Lennox's wealthy parents are killed in an earthquake in India. Emotionally crippled by the loss, she is an angry, spoiled child who goes to live in a gloomy estate with an uncle she's never met. The head housekeeper, Mrs. Medlock, is less than hospitable. Though confined to her room, Mary occasionally explores the mansion and comes across her sickly cousin Colin, who is confined to a wheelchair and insists that he's dying. Then Mary discovers a secret garden that has been unattended since the death of her aunt. The garden is a magical place where she, the local farm boy Dicken, and her cousin can play, imagine, and, most importantly, heal. Mary begins to feel emotion for the first time, while Colin discovers that he can walk and that he is not dying any more than the secret garden is dead. The three children form deep bonds of friendship and cast a spell on the master of the house to bring him back to the manor to reunite with his now walking and healthy son.

This film shows how nurturing life in someone else, as Mary does with her cousin, and something else, as they both do with the garden, can make you happy and help you to flourish. The garden is a metaphor for change. When you invest care, work, and energy into something that's alive, it rarely disappoints. Like caring for animals, the garden is alive and grows when cared for properly. The garden is resurrected from a mess of overgrown weeds to a place of beauty and joy, just as Mary and her cousin are transformed from sickly, angry, and sad children to laughing, playing, and healthy children.

Discussion Questions:
- How did Mary and Colin each deal with the loss of their parents?
- How sick do you think Colin is? Was he really paralyzed, just weak, or was he pretending?
- What did the garden mean to Mary?
- How did Dicken help her to be happy at the mansion?
- Do you think Mrs. Medlock and the servants treat Colin like an invalid? Do they help him get better or hold him back?
- How does Mary help Colin get better?
- Why was the father so unwilling to love his son and his niece?
- What do you think it was like for the father to see his son running around like a healthy boy after all those years of being confined

to a wheelchair?

- What kinds of things other than a garden could help get someone through their loss?
- What type of project or activity might you do to get through the pain of losing someone?

Pointer:

A concrete activity with cause and effect reinforces our power over things and the value of life. Giving to something or someone who will give back is the best way to affirm our own presence in this world. Discuss what kinds of projects might be good for helping people get over loss.

Simon Birch

Loosely based on the book, *A Prayer for Owen Meany* by John Irving, this film centers on Joe Wenteworth, a boy who is raised by his mother and grandmother in New England. He doesn't know who his father is, and his mother refuses to tell him. His best friend, Simon Birch, is a small, squeaky-voiced dwarf who is ignored by his own family. What Simon lacks in physical stature he makes up for in intelligence, inner strength, and faith. Simon believes that God has a special plan for him, though his views often come into conflict with the traditional organized religion of the town minister, Reverend Russell. When Mrs. Wenteworth is accidentally killed by a foul baseball hit by Simon, Joe becomes even more set on finding out the identity of his father. At the end of the film, Simon achieves heroic status. By saving a sinking bus full of young children, he proves that God does indeed have a special plan for him.

This film deals with many issues, from handicaps and the loss of loved ones, to single parent families and friendship. Simon, like many people who are born with physical handicaps, has tremendous courage and inner strength. His faith is an individual one, not ruled by town ministers or Sunday sermons, but by his own belief that he is part of God's plan. Throughout the film, Joe must deal with the loss of his mother, and eventually his best friend. When Joe finally finds out who is father is, he realizes that he was right in front of him the entire time.

Discussion Questions:

- What do you think of Simon?
- What does Miss Leavey mean when she says, "God doesn't have a special plan for you"?
- Simon accidentally kills Mrs. Wenteworth when he hits a foul ball. How do you think you would feel if your best friend accidentally killed someone you loved?
- Why do you think Joe didn't like Ben even though he seemed like a nice guy?
- What do you think it would feel like to have no parents and no one looking out for you in the world?
- How could someone as small and sickly as Simon Birch be a hero?
- How does Joe help Simon deal with being different?
- What does Joe see in Simon?
- How did Joe get through the loss of his mother?
- Who do you know who is like Simon Birch?

Pointer:

Discuss how some people perceive the disabled or handicapped. Explore together how to maintain a child's self esteem when she is faced with a physical or intellectual handicap. Talk about how much disabled people crave normalcy and want to be viewed and treated like others. Discuss how disabled people have strengths in other areas.

Corrina, Corrina

When seven-year-old Molly Singer's mother dies, she retreats into silence, where neither her grandparents nor her father can reach her. Her dad, jingle songwriter Manny Singer, hires an educated Black nanny who connects well with Molly by simply respecting her need for silence, and slowly easing her back to reality. Molly and Corrina quickly develop a close bond. Manny also seems comfortable with Corrina taking on a maternal role in their family. Molly is set on having Corrina be her new mommy. Although Manny and

Corrina are attracted to each other physically and connected by their common love of music, there are social implications for an interracial couple in 1959 suburbia.

This film deals with many issues such as race, death, love, and friendship, and does so with sensitivity. It shows the grieving process from the perspective of both husband and daughter. Molly goes through a period of denial in which she is silent, and then angry. With the help of Corrina, she is able to express her anger in a healthy way. She then turns to faith and concepts of angels and heaven for comfort. Her atheist father is not very pleased with her newfound faith. Manny, too, has a hard time accepting the repercussions of his loss. Both he and Molly struggle to get back to their lives, urged by friends and family who are eager to see them stop grieving, perhaps before they are ready. The sassy, intuitive Corrina demonstrates the things a family member or friend can do to help those who are dealing with loss.

Discussion Questions:

- Why was Molly silent for so long after her mother died?
- Why did her father tell the furniture deliveryman that his wife was in the bathtub? How did that affect Molly?
- How does Corrina get Molly to come out of her silence?
- Do you know what an atheist is?
- Which approach—Manny's or Corrina's—is better at helping Molly deal with the death of her mommy? Why does believing people go to heaven make it easier for people to get through a death?
- What is the significance of Corrina teaching Molly how to play the rest of the song on the piano?
- How long do you think it takes someone to get over the loss of a loved one? How long should a child stay out of school when a parent dies?
- Was it right for Corrina to let Molly stay out of school without telling her father?
- Discuss faith, the concept of believing in something that may not be explainable but may make you feel better. What kinds of things do people believe in to make themselves feel better about death or sad things?

Pointer:

Use Corrina as a model of how to help someone get through the grieving process, particularly children. What different stages of pain have you or your family members gone through in the past? Corrina allows Molly to hold onto her memory of the person, validates Molly's feelings, assuring her that anger is healthy and should be expressed; she also respects her boundaries, lets her take her time, uses pet therapy, and encourages her to believe in things that may not be real.

Chapter 10

"...Sometimes they get back together, and sometimes they don't dear, and if they don't—don't blame yourself. Just because they don't love each other anymore, doesn't mean that they don't love you. There are all sorts of different families, Katie."

— Mrs. Doubtfire, *Mrs. Doubtfire*

Divorce and Single Parents

The ways in which children in middle childhood react to and deal with divorce and single parenting are distinctly different from their older and younger counterparts. They tend to use less fantasy and denial than pre-schoolers in dealing with their sadness, and they experience their emotional pain in a very direct way. Often near tears at the thought of one parent moving out, children from eight to twelve years old turn their sadness into intense anger at both parents, or the one believed to be most at fault for the breakup.

Gender may also affect the reaction a child has to a breakup or separation, as boys tend to have a harder time adjusting. Less or limited visitation by the father may cause failing academic performance, grief, and feelings of rejection. The mother may perceive her son to be aligned with his father, and therefore may be inadvertently less sensitive to the losses these children experience. Boys often suffer the most from a reduced amount of time spent with their father.

Losing the Traditional Family Dream

Losing the consistent physical closeness of parents dramatically alters the assumption that one's family will always stay the way it is. As shown in *The Parent Trap*, long after parents separate, divorce, and even remarry, the wish for parents to resolve their differences and get back together remains with children. They cling to such fantasies well into middle childhood and even through their teenage years. In *Bye Bye, Love*, Donny's daughter resents her new family situation, and runs away to the house where she lived with her pre-divorce family.

Resolving the Blame Issue

If the anger level and blame for the breakup of a family does not subside and forgiveness does not replace negative feelings, the child builds an emotional wall. This wall keeps the perceived wrongdoer at a distance, further damaging the relationship between parent and child. For example, In *Mrs. Doubtfire*, Daniel Hillard's oldest daughter blames him for messing up his marriage to her mother, and therefore resents the limited time she does have with him.

Avoiding Anger Between Parents

Children at this age are very good at becoming allies of one parent in a fight between their mother and father. Often one parent or both try to lure their children into an alliance to get back at the other. This ploy creates further distance between the family members and often pits them against one another. Parents should be careful not to express their anger about their ex-spouses to their children, because regardless of how bad a husband or wife he or she may have been, a child is better off having two parents rather than one. Children shouldn't feel that by loving one parent they are betraying the other. Both Miranda in

Mrs. Doubtfire and Ivan in *Author! Author!* start out expressing anger toward their ex-spouses, but eventually realize that it only hurts the children further by doing so.

Custody and Visitation Issues

Because alliances are often in place by the time custody and visitation schedules have been set, a child will sometimes refuse to cooperate and stay angry the entire time he is with the secondary-care parent. The parent with less contact or visitation time may try to compensate by indulging the children with toys or unwarranted privileges to win their affections, which undermines the parent-child relationship. Custody and visitation are a major cause of stress and pain in divorced families. In *Author! Author!*, we see the stepchildren running away from their biological father in order to be with their stepfather, to whom they feel more connected. In *The Parent Trap,* the parents were so caught up in their own anger that they completely deprived their daughters of knowing each other.

Single-Parent and Blended Family Issues

The single parent carries an emotional and financial burden that greatly impacts children. The parent often becomes the target for all the frustrations and feelings as a result of those burdens. If the other parent has totally withdrawn from seeing the children, the resentment directed at the single parent is even more intense, because the children have no one else with whom to vent their feelings. In blended families, if anger and loyalty issues from the separation or divorce have not subsided or been resolved, the eight to twelve year old child will continue to act out their feelings at the new stepparent or companion, as Annie and Hallie do to their father's fiancée in *The Parent Trap.* It takes a highly patient, mature, and sensitive adult to cope with an angry stepchild, and this behavior can obviously strain a new relationship or marriage.

Mrs. Doubtfire

After his practical wife Miranda leaves him and his silly, immature ways, Daniel Hillard loses custody of his three children until he can sustain a regular job and find a residence suitable for them. But Daniel cannot wait three months to be with his children, who are the light of his life, so he dresses up as a slightly overweight British grandmother and interviews for the job of his children's nanny. He gets the job, which provides him with the perfect opportunity to spend quality time with his children, meddle in his soon-to-be ex-wife's love life, and finally gain an understanding of what it's like to run a household and be the day-to-day caretaker.

This film is about the hysterical—though not very realistic—extremes that one man will go to be with his adoring children. It is also about divorce and how, even though it is complicated, messy, confusing, and filled with anger and pain, when it comes down to it, all that matters is love. Daniel's love leads him to dress like a woman, and it is pure. Surely many families will be able to relate to this longing to be together. In the end, the family structure may never resemble what it was before, but it can still be strong in its new form. Children will connect with these children's frustration at their new living situation and custody set-up, while parents will relate to the contrasting roles Miranda and Daniel take on in their parenting. Some may identify with the resentment of one parent having to always be the serious one, and the jealousy that occurs when one parent starts to date.

Discussion Questions:

- What kind of father is Daniel? How is he a different kind of parent than the mother? Why do you think Miranda wants to divorce Daniel?
- Do you think the court's decision to allow Daniel to see his children only one night a week is fair?
- Do you think it was okay for Miranda to start seeing someone so soon after the breakup? What is the right amount of time? Why?
- What do you think of Daniel interviewing for the nanny job? Was it fair to lie to the children about his identity?
- If you were the child in that situation would you have kept the secret or would you have told your mother?

- What did being Mrs. Doubtfire teach Daniel about being a parent?
- If Daniel was so angry with Miranda, then why was he so jealous of her relationship with Stu?
- How would you feel if your father was dressing up as a woman to be with you?
- Was it fair for Daniel to put pepper in Stu's food if he was allergic?
- What do you think of the second court ruling, after Daniel's secret was discovered?
- What made Miranda get over her anger and allow Daniel to take care of his children every day?
- What do you think will happen between Miranda and Daniel?

Pointer:

Sometimes good things can come from divorce. Parents may be forced to come to terms with their own weaknesses. They may learn to develop a stronger and more one-on-one relationship with their children. Emphasize that divorce does not mean the end of family. It can actually mean the beginning of stronger parent-child relationships. Despite problems with custody arrangements, new spouses, new siblings, or new stepsiblings, what ultimately matters is the love of a parent. Just as the Hillards' father came in the form of an English nanny, families come in many shapes. Discuss what fears your children have about divorce, and the positive and negative things they have seen come from divorce, either in your family or in other peoples' families.

Bye Bye, Love

A trio of best friends helps each other through the ups and downs of being divorced, single fathers. Donny is a sensitive father, who still has feelings for his ex-wife and problems with his adolescent daughter, Emma. Dave is the studly father who cheated on his first wife, dates a different woman every week, and gets his buddies to cover for him. He has two young children who are less then thrilled about his newest girlfriend, Kim. Then there's Vic, a father of three who is full of animosity toward his ex-wife for her spending habits and her relationship with her new boyfriend. The three men despise a conde-scending talk-radio host who makes the divorced family situation seem like a breeze.

This film takes a comic look at the problems associated with single parenthood from the less-common perspective of the fathers. It also shows some of the very real obstacles that divorced or separated parents must face when sharing custody: the awkward exchange of custody, meeting your ex-spouse's new lover, having to say goodbye to the children, seeing changes in the house you built but no longer live in, and having to be both a mom and a dad at once. The biggest challenge for these three fathers is respecting their children's pain, and meeting their basic needs, while also maintaining some semblance of their own social life. This film doesn't provide divorced parents with answers. It simply reinforces the idea that the most important thing is to love your children.

Discussion Questions:

- Which family situation reminds you the most of your family and why? What father reminds you the most of your own dad? What arrangement do you think is the best?
- What do you do when your parents fight? How do you stay out of the fighting?
- Have you ever felt that you were caught in the middle between your parents?
- How hard is it to handle two different family expectations? In what ways is your mother's parenting style different from your father's?
- Why was Emma so angry at her father? Why couldn't she just talk with him about what was bothering her?
- Why were all three fathers so annoyed with Dr. David's talk radio segment on divorce?
- How hard is it to remain good parents when going through a difficult time, like a divorce?
- How hard do you think it would be to see your ex-spouse with a new romantic partner or spouse, living in your old house?

Pointer:

This film offers an opportunity for parents to share with their children the difficulties of divorce from a parent's perspective. Have a talk with your child about the problems a parent faces, especially a single parent. Remember to make sure that your child knows that whatever happens with your marriage, it has absolutely nothing to do with her. Remind her that although the family has changed, your presence in her life is a constant. Also, make sure your child knows to stay out of your personal problems, because no matter how mature she is, she should not be involved with problems in your relationship with your ex-spouse. She should not think that it is her responsibility to make things work between divorced parents.

The Parent Trap

About ten years after their parents fell in love and married, two identical twins who have never met find themselves at the same summer camp. Annie is without a father and has been raised by her mother, a fashion designer in England, while Hallie is without a mother and had been raised on a vineyard in Napa Valley, California, by her father. The sisters devise a plan to switch places to get to know their long lost parent, find out why they got divorced, and get them back together again. At first their plan seems to be working until Annie, pretending to be Hallie, realizes her father intends to marry a young, wicked publicist named Meredith Blake, who secretly plans to ship Hallie off to boarding school. Eventually the twins' true identities are discovered. Annie and her mother take a trip to California to sort things out, and the twins manage to show Meredith's true colors so that the engagement is broken. After comic mischief and plans gone awry, Nick and Elizabeth eventually get back together, and the twins are reunited as sisters.

This film is appealing to most children of divorce because it centers on their common fantasy to have their parents get back together someday. Instead of using this film as a realistic model for divorced family functioning, use it as a starting point for discussion about why your child may wish you would get back together someday, and as an opening for you to communicate why that probably will never happen. The film also explores a custody arrangement so extreme that there is a complete disregard for the well-being of the twins. The soon-to-be stepmother in this film may seem ridiculously evil, but certainly many children will have the same contempt for their parents' new love interests.

Discussion Questions:

- What would it feel like to discover at the age of ten that you had an identical twin?
- Do you think it was fair that these girls knew so little about their other parent and their twin? Is it right to split up identical twins at birth? What about splitting up other siblings who are not twins?
- Would you have wanted to secretly switch places like Hallie and Annie or would you have wanted to confront your parents?
- Do you know any identical twins? Fraternal twins?
- Do you think your family would have been able to tell if you had switched places with your identical twin?
- What would have been a better way for the twins to meet their estranged parent?
- How hard do you think it would be to grow up with only one parent and not know anything about the other?
- Why didn't Annie and Hallie like Meredith? Why wouldn't she have made a good stepmother?
- Why did Elizabeth and Nick decide to go back to their lives? Was it fair for the twins to have to go back to this kind of arrangement after having just been exposed to another half of their family?
- Was it right for the girls to trick Meredith on the camping trip? How did it show Nick what kind of person Meredith really was?
- What do you think of this ending? How successful will they be as a married couple? Where do you think they'll live, London or Napa Valley?

Pointer:

Discuss with your child that it is natural for him to want to see his parents back together, that it is the ideal family for most people. Wishing for something and expecting it to happen are two very different things. His desire for this family dream may never go away, nor does it have to, as long as your child knows that this may never become a reality. This film plays out many children's fantasies, but the happy ending in *The Parent Trap* is unlikely to occur in your family. Use the film as a stimulus to discuss what they miss most about the intact nuclear family. Let them express their pain or fantasies without trying to fix or negate them.

Author! Author!

Ivan Travalian is a Broadway playwright whose flaky wife Gloria walks out on him, his son, and her four children from previous marriages. Ivan's stepchildren have become very close to each other and to him, but are forced to go and live with their biological fathers. While Ivan struggles with his play, a relationship with his leading actress, and his own anger towards his soon-to-be-ex-wife, his stepchildren eventually make their way back, forcing him to finally come to terms with the fact that a family is what you make it. Often the ties that bind people together are based on love and consistency, not biology.

This film shows a family dealing with divorce, remarriages, stepparenting, stepsiblings, custody issues, and single parent-run households. The basic message is that parents should ultimately put their own needs aside and do what's in the best interest of their children, something that Gloria clearly does not understand. The casualties of divorce are the children, who crave consistency and stability but unfortunately are subject to the whims of their mother. *Author! Author!* illustrates that there are many different family types—in this case a family with five siblings, all with different fathers, have an affection for and commitment to each other that transcends biological connections. This movie proves that often, what makes a family is love and loyalty, not child support or biology.

Discussion Questions:

- What do you think of this family? Can you imagine a family having five children all with different fathers?
- How does Ivan hold this family together? How does he make it all work?
- Is it fair for these children to be in this situation? Can you imagine how many times they have had to move around and get settled in different schools and neighborhoods?
- Is it fair to break up stepsiblings, who are used to being together, when their parents divorce?
- Was it too soon after breaking up with Gloria for Ivan to have

Alice Detroit move into his house?
- Do you know any families where there are a lot of stepsiblings? Do they get along as well as these children?
- What did Ivan have to finally accept about Gloria as a mother?
- What is a parent's responsibility to her child? How common are parents like Gloria today? Are there too many divorces because of irresponsible parents who act on their impulses?
- In what ways are these children more mature than their own mother?
- What should parents do when their dreams and passions come into conflict with their ability to be good parents and provide a stable environment?

Pointer:

Discuss different divorced families you know and whether or not their situations are civil. Do the parents get along? Do they put their children's best interests before their own anger? What makes for a good parent in the throes of a divorce? Let your child make comments freely about other families without disagreeing.

Chapter 11

"I still believe, in spite of everything, that people really are good at heart."

— Anne Frank, *The Diary of Anne Frank*

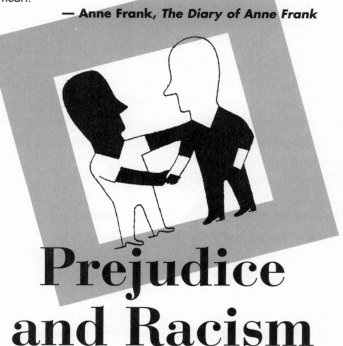

Prejudice and Racism

While racism and prejudice are approached together in this chapter, they are certainly not the same. Prejudice is a learned negative attitude toward a person, place, or thing, which results in a desire to avoid, dominate, or eliminate the target object. Racism is a more severe form of prejudice, based on a person's race, religion, or ethnic heritage. Children ages eight to twelve begin to experience and understand prejudice and racism on a very personal level. They may be the targets of discrimination, or hear things from friends that make them feel excluded from holidays and celebrations other than their own.

Because ethnic and religious education usually starts in middle childhood, it is very important that parents ensure that religious education is about valuing one's own faith without putting down others. It is at this age that prejudices begin. Understand and scrutinize the kinds of religious experiences and education you provide your children with, so that misunderstandings or prejudices are not fostered in the name of ethnic pride or religious beliefs.

Films can both introduce the concept of prejudice to children and help educate them about a culture or race with which they are not familiar. It can show them how to positively treat people of different races, religions, or ethnicities, as well as how not to treat them. It can make them sensitive to the racism or prejudice that exists toward a minority, and perhaps positively affect their own behavior for the better.

Awareness of Being in a Majority or Minority Group

Unfortunately, some children have felt the pain of prejudice early in their lives. It is very confusing for children when hurtful things are stated directly about something over which they have no control, like the color of their skin or their religious affiliation. Children who make prejudicial comments without understanding their full impact must be taught a constructive lesson about what it means to be a minority, and how comments—even unintentional ones—can hurt someone. *The Diary of Anne Frank* shows the extreme hate to which minorities—in this case, the Jews—were subjected to in the name of ethnic pride.

Appreciating Differences and Taking Pride in One's Own Uniqueness

Children in middle childhood can be taught to tolerate differences as well as to be proud of their own background, traditions, and culture. Parents should make children aware that while the customs and practices of ethnic or religious groups may differ, they usually all share very common values. Highlighting the special rituals, dress, religious ceremonies, and customs that make people unique can be a great learning experience for children. *Babe* shows how an animal at the bottom of the farm's hierarchy is able to use his own qualities to rise to greatness and win the sheepdog competition.

Reacting to Prejudice in Ourselves and Others

It is a natural reaction to strike back when one is confronted with ignorance and hatred. If your child understands that people who do not feel good about themselves sometimes try to put other people down to make themselves feel better, he might be less inclined to create a cycle of negativity by striking back physically or verbally. It is also important to recognize that we are all capable of discriminating against others when we are in a more privileged or majority position. We need to monitor our own reactions and behaviors to avoid hurting others. Both *The Jackie Robinson Story* and *Pocahontas* show real life individuals in the minority who were able to transcend their race, rise above the hatred, and take the first step at overcoming prejudice in their societies.

Babe

As the film opens, the narrator tells us that this is the tale of Babe, an "unprejudiced heart," who was raised on Farmer Hoggett's farm by a sheepdog named Fly. Fly mothers Babe and tries to teach Babe the ways of the farm—that each animal has its own place and its own function. It quickly becomes clear that Babe is not a typical pig, but a special one who excels at herding sheep. Other characters in this film are Farmer and Mrs. Hoggett, Ferdinand the Duck, the cat, and the herd of sheep. Babe, unlike the aggressive, threatening sheepdogs, uses his sweetness and manners to control the sheep, win the big sheepdog competition, and show the community not to judge an animal simply by what kind of animal it is.

In *Babe*, the hierarchy of the farm is not unlike the socio-economic systems in human societies. Each animal has its own place, its own function, its own stereotypes, and its own characteristics. Animals, like people, make judgments based on learned prejudices connected to class, race, or physical characteristics. *Babe* is the story of a born underachiever rising to greatness and overcoming odds simply by being true to his inherent gifts.

Discussion Questions:

- What do you think of pigs as animals? If you had to be an animal which one would you be and why?

- Do you think animals have feelings? Can the pig feel loss when its parents are taken away? Can the dog feel sadness when its babies are taken away?
- How is Babe different from the other animals?
- Why was Ferdinand so concerned with getting rid of Farmer Hoggett's alarm clock? Why was it so important to be "indispensable" on the farm?
- How do you think the dogs felt when the puppies were given away? How did that affect Fly's relationship with Babe?
- How does Babe help save the farm? Why is Rex so hostile towards Babe?
- Babe's politeness in communicating with the sheep proves to be very successful, although it is different from the sheepdog's approach. Is there a situation where you took a different approach to a problem and got better results than everyone else? How hard was that to do?
- How did Farmer Hoggett come to realize that Babe was special? Why did he believe that Babe could win the sheepdog contest?
- Do you think it's fair that some animals on the farm will be used for meat and others won't? What is an animal's purpose—is it just to serve man, or do animals have their own rights?
- Do you think it was fair for Babe to participate in the sheepdog competition?
- What did Babe teach both the animals and humans? How will the farm be different now?
- Do you know anyone like Babe who has a pure heart and doesn't judge people?

Pointer:

Some individuals have to believe in themselves in order to change destiny and overcome the prejudices that exist in the culture. Babe was one of these unique creatures. What people are like Babe? What kinds of prejudices and obstacles have they overcome?

Pocahontas

In the early 17th Century, the first English settlers arrived in the New World looking for gold and riches. What they found were American Indians, whom they perceived as savages and a hindrance to their goals. In this film, Captain John Smith is a strong and respected leader and, unlike the other men from his ship, he is curious about the American Indian culture. When he meets Pocahontas, the beautiful, free-spirited daughter of the Chief, the two form a bond and manage to communicate and connect emotionally despite their language barrier and cultural differences. The Englishmen and American Indians don't have an easy time accepting their union, but as Pocahontas' grandmother Willow says, they represent the first thrown stone that will create a ripple with repercussions throughout the whole river.

This film introduces children to the history of the American Indians, how they were treated by the English settlers, and how they were later treated by the Americans. Pocahontas builds a bridge between the two cultures. She teaches John Smith the beauty of her culture, the connection to nature and the earth. This film deals with cultural stereotypes and biases, showing how they lead to miscommunication and violence. Although the story is not an accurate representation of the true story of Pocahontas, it can serve as a starting point for discussions about what really happened when the Europeans began to populate this country. This film creates an opportunity to discuss how individuals can make a difference in fighting racism.

Discussion Questions:

- What are the explorers' perceptions of the American Indians? What are the Indians' perceptions of the White men?
- What's the difference between how the Indians live and how the White men live?
- What do you think of Grandmother Willow? Is she really Pocahontas' grandmother or is she just in her imagination?
- What kind of a young woman is Pocahontas? How is she different from the other American Indian girls?
- Why is it so scary to meet people who are different?
- Is it a good thing for Pocahontas and John Smith to fall in love?
- What does Grandmother Willow's advice about listening to your

heart and following the signs in nature mean?
- What does Grandmother Willow's advice mean about throwing the first stone to create a ripple?
- What are the prejudices on each side?
- How does Pocahontas create a bridge between the two cultures?
- If you were Pocahontas, would you have gone back to England with John Smith or would you have stayed with your people?

Pointer:

This film shows how prejudice develops between different groups. Differences lead to fear that can lead to hatred. We make generalizations based on stereotypes. Point out that appreciating someone's differences can make you a better person. Discuss what the American Indians could have learned from the explorers to improve their culture, and what the explorers could have learned from the American Indian culture. Talk about what kinds of prejudices your child may have toward someone who is different, or what type of prejudice someone may have toward her. How can she take Grandmother Willow's advice and throw the first stone into the river to cause the ripple effect?

The Jackie Robinson Story

This story is the autobiography of baseball great Jackie Robinson and his rise to fame. Though not a documentary, Jackie Robinson plays himself. After graduating from high school, he has a difficult time finding a job as a coach and ends up joining the army. After that he joins the Panthers, part of the Negro Baseball League, where it is clear that separate is far from equal. A courageous Branch Rickey, owner of the Brooklyn Dodgers, sees Robinson's unparalleled skill and decides to make Robinson the first African-American player to join the White minor league, and eventually the major leagues. Robinson struggles against racism and prejudice, but because of his skill on the field and inner strength, he is able to win the hearts of Americans and set a new precedent for professional sports.

This film portrays a side of American culture at a time when baseball was at the height of its popularity, while simultaneously addressing racism toward African-Americans, so prevalent at that time. *The Jackie Robinson Story* shows how the individual talent and character of one man was the first step in changing the face of American sports. Robinson has the personal courage and athletic ability necessary to overcome the bigotry and racism associated with being the first African-American to enter Major League Baseball.

Discussion Questions:

- How much do you know about discrimination against African-Americans before the Civil Rights movement?
- Did you know that until 1948, there was a separate baseball league for African-American players?
- Was it fair that African-Americans could join the army and risk their lives for their country, but they couldn't play baseball in the same league as White men?
- What do you think of the idea of "separate but equal"—is that concept a contradiction?
- What did Branch Rickey mean when he told Jackie, "No matter what, you can't fight back"? Was it fair to tell Jackie that?
- Why did the Reverend tell Jackie that what he was about to do would affect the "whole colored people"?
- Why were Jackie Robinson and Branch Rickey taking such a big risk?
- Do you think you would have been able to handle this situation? Have you ever been the "first" of your gender, race, age group, class, or ethnicity to do something? How did it feel?
- How did Branch Rickey try to stand up for Jackie? How did he try to make the other players on the team understand how their own family backgrounds related to the situation?

Pointer:

Parents should discuss how minorities are treated today. How far have we come towards equality since the time when Jackie Robinson entered baseball? How much prejudice still exists in our society today?

The Diary of Anne Frank

Based on an actual diary and published by Anne Frank's father after the liberation, this is the harrowing true story of a young girl in 1942 Nazi-occupied Holland. The Franks and the Van Daans are able to avoid the Nazis for a few years by hiding above a factory. The film documents the struggle of the Franks, the Van Daans, and Mr. Dussell to maintain a sense of hope while the world around them is being destroyed. Normal arguments and issues between family members are exaggerated for Anne, as everyone must remain silent for ten hours during the day when the factory is in operation. While in hiding, Anne experiences many normal adolescent issues: She argues with her mother, continues her academic studies, celebrates Chanukah, has her first kiss, and grows into a young woman. The fate of their neighbors and friends being taken away to concentration camps looms over everyone in this film. Eventually, it is a fate from which they cannot escape.

This film is a perfect entry into a discussion about anti-Semitism, scapegoats, prejudice, and genocide. These topics are harsh and difficult to share with children, but it is important that they know what happened, and that this horror occurred in the recent past, less than seventy years ago. More importantly, this film can help them learn to identify the racism and unacceptable behavior that is around them. Also, because Anne Frank is an adolescent, children may be more likely to identify with her fear and pain, and the frustration of growing up in such a confined and frightening environment.

Discussion Questions:

- What do you know about Anne Frank? Do you understand how this could happen?
- Do you think your family could be silent from 8 AM to 6 PM every day? What would you do to keep yourself occupied?
- Why did Mr. Kraler take these people in when others were persecuting them?
- What do you think were some of the reasons the Nazis had for hating the Jews?
- How did the Franks and the Van Daans attempt to maintain a sense of normalcy in their lives? Did it work? Why was it so important to them?
- Why was Anne problematic? What was it about her that bothered

the rest of the people in the house?
- What are the different personalities of the people in hiding?
- How would you feel about bringing in another person like Mr. Dussell, when the living quarters and food rations were already so limited? Was it the right thing to do?
- Why was Mr. Dussell's description of the outside world so different from what Mr. Kraler had been telling them?
- What was the problem between Anne and her mother?
- What was Anne trying to do by making presents for everyone at Chanukah? What does that reveal about her personality?
- Do you think it was fair for Peter to have a cat in the house? Why was the cat so important to Peter?
- How does Anne change in the two years that she's there? How does the relationship between Anne and Peter change?
- Do you think Mr. Van Daan should have been thrown out when he was caught stealing bread in the middle of the night?
- What should they have done when they stopped getting visits from the Kralers and the phone kept ringing?
- How could someone like Anne, who's going through something so horrible, still be so positive and have so much faith in the inherent goodness of mankind?

Pointer:

Discuss Anne Frank in a historical context. Why is her diary so popular and so often required reading in schools? Discuss what other situations might be similar to the Nazis' treatment of the Jews during World War II. Do things like that still happen today? Could something this awful happen again?

Chapter 12

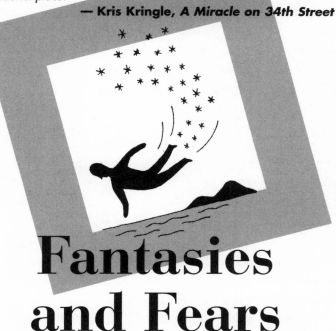

Fantasies and Fears

The stresses placed on middle childhood children are extensive. They leave the safety and protection of their homes to deal with peers who may pick on them or leave them out, and with teachers who, unlike parents, will not offer unconditional love. They feel pressure, like the need to achieve in school, and competition becomes more prominent even in play activities. With parents often becoming less available to them because of financial concerns, career advancement, or marital difficulties, children look for ways to escape from the demands of growing up.

Some children fall into a magical world of make-believe where things were simpler, people were more nurturing, and comfort was easy to find. Other children might express their worries through play that takes them to far-off lands; they may have make-believe friends with magical powers to solve their family problems. Finding the right balance between reality and the dream of a world where everything is under their control is the primary task of the eight- to twelve-year-old.

When children begin formal schooling, they are expected to understand the world more logically. Their ability to understand cause and effect allows them to organize their world with a little more complexity. They also begin not only to understand, but also to question how things are born, what is fair, and what can be proved scientifically or not.

Distinguishing Between Healthy Fantasies and Unhealthy Escapes

Most psychologists agree that children need to develop a healthy imagination in order to explore the wonders of the world that they are just beginning to understand. But when overwhelmed by negative experiences or trauma, many children retreat into fantasy play in an attempt to avoid dealing with the real world. Like Eric in *The Boy Who Could Fly*, they may prefer staying in a safe, imaginary world that will shield them from the emotional pain of reality.

Using Fantasy or Dreams to Tackle Everyday Fears

As many parents know, a child will let adults know when it is time for them to give up believing in Santa Claus or the Tooth Fairy, but many adults need to have faith in things they can't see or touch. When children and adults draw on that faith to cope with daily stresses, it should be perceived as a positive attempt to deal with a negative situation. Often our dreams allow us to visualize ourselves overcoming life's problems, and therefore provide us with the valuable idea that things will actually work out. In *E.T.*, the connection between Elliott and E.T. fulfills their mutual fear of abandonment, and *Matilda* shows how a little girl's special powers enable her to overcome the evil in the adults around her.

Finding the Limits of Magic and Fantasy

To a certain extent everyone, regardless of their age, should have a bit of fantasy or faith in their lives, and this is the main lesson Susan and her mother Doris are forced to learn in *A Miracle On 34th Street*. But when children retreat into their own make-believe world, especially the older children in middle childhood (10-12 years old), it may be a sign that life is getting too complicated for them. Parents don't necessarily have to discourage or criticize their children for using such strategies, but they should consider whether they may need to be more emotionally involved or pay more attention to their children.

E.T.: The Extra-Terrestrial

Elliott is the middle child of a recently divorced mother in a single-parent household where nobody ever seems to want to listen to him, especially when he sees an alien in the tool shed of his family's suburban home. Elliott quickly develops a bond with this creature, whose spaceship accidentally left him behind; they seemed to be linked telepathically, as they see, feel, and experience things on the same emotional and physical level. The entire film is told from a child's perspective, even when the government scientists capture E.T. In the end, Elliott's love for and connection to E.T. save his friend from the scientists, and help get him back to the spaceship so he can eventually go home.

This film explores the fear of abandonment, loss, homesickness, and friendship, all within the context of a typical suburban little boy with an atypical "friend". This film never strays from the child's perspective, and shows how children and adults have a difficult time understanding each other. Through the characters of Elliott and E.T., this film demonstrates how one's need to connect and share in pain and happiness can be so strong that it is as if there is a physical and mental connection.

Discussion Questions:

- How would it feel to be accidentally left behind and far away from home like E.T.?
- What would it be like to meet someone from another planet?
- Why does E.T. trust Elliot?
- What kind of powers does E.T. have?

- Why does Elliott feel the same thing that E.T. feels when he's in the science lab at school?
- How do the adults and the children in this film see things differently?
- Do you believe there are aliens or extra-terrestrials? If so, what do you think they are like? Are they like E.T.?
- Why does E.T. get so sick? Why does Elliott get sick when E.T. gets sick?
- Why didn't Elliott, Michael, and Gertie tell their mom about E.T.? Would you have kept it a secret from your parents?
- What made E.T. come back to life?
- How hard would it be to say goodbye to a friend like E.T.? What do you think it means when E.T. points to his head?

Pointer:

Elliott's and E.T.'s friendship fulfills their mutual desire to be needed by someone. It's a universal need for people to nurture something and to be nurtured by something. Children fulfill this need by caring for pets, stuffed animals, and sometimes even younger siblings. Discuss with your child whether she's ever had a relationship like the one E.T. and Elliott had. What is it like to be so connected with someone?

The Boy Who Could Fly

Milly, Louis, and their mom all move into a new neighborhood to start a new life after the death of their father. It's a difficult time for everybody; their mom has reentered the workforce and has to learn how to use computers, Louis can't make it around the block on his big wheel without being terrorized by bullies, and Milly has to adjust to a new school where she feels like an outsider. She befriends an autistic boy named Eric, who was traumatized by the death of his parents in a plane crash. Eric believes he can fly, and Milly becomes fascinated with trying to get Eric to connect and understand, not just merely imitate. In the end, Eric proves to Milly and the whole town that he can in fact fly, and more importantly, that he can connect with someone.

This film is about how people who have been hurt often withdraw into loneliness, but by connecting, helping others, and believing in the impossible, they can overcome their pain. Fantasy helps Eric deal with the loss of his parents, and Milly's interest in Eric helps her heal after the loss of her father. *The Boy Who Could Fly* shows how two emotionally wounded children can help to heal each other.

Discussion Questions:

- How do you think this family is managing all of their new adjustments?
- Why is Milly willing to take on so much extra responsibility with Eric, the housework, watching her younger brother, etc.?
- Why do you think Eric responds to Milly better than anyone else?
- Milly says, "I don't know if he's becoming more like me or I'm becoming more like him." Is Milly entering Eric's fantasy world or is Eric entering Milly's reality?
- What do you think really happened in the garden? Did he fly out and catch her when she reached for the flower?
- Why doesn't Milly have a lot of girlfriends?
- Why is it so important to Louis that he gets around the block on his big wheel?
- How would you have treated a person like Eric if he went to your school?
- Do you think people like Eric should be in special schools?
- What would you do to change the ending of this film?

Pointer:

This film explores how fantasy can help us deal with our pain. It is a parent's job to make sure that a child maintains a balance between fantasy and reality. Discuss what types of fantasy or imagination have helped you or your children get through a difficult time.

Matilda

Matilda is a clever little girl who is born to tacky and obnoxious parents who don't appreciate her. She practically raises herself, immersing herself in books, despite the fact that her parents force her to watch TV. Matilda finally convinces her parents, who don't see the need for education, to let her go to school. At school, the principal, Mrs. Trunchbull, is a nasty, physically abusive and brutish woman who hates children. Matilda's only hope is her teacher, Miss Honey, who is sweet, compassionate, and believes that Matilda is gifted. Matilda discovers that she has special powers which allow her to manipulate objects around her, and she uses her powers to get back at her parents and Mrs. Trunchbull. In the end, Matilda and Miss Honey make a loving family of their own.

All children at some point or another feel that everyone is out to get them: Their teacher is unfair, their siblings are rotten, and adults are just plain bad. Magic and fantasy are usually a healthy way to deal with some of this anger. Matilda is a remarkable little girl who finds the magic within herself. As a movie, *Matilda* allows children to play out their anger towards their parents, teachers, or any adults whom they feel have mistreated them. Although this film may take things to the extreme, it is a good starting point to discuss physical and emotional abuse, and to let children express some of their own fears or anger.

Discussion Questions:

- What would you do if you lived in the Wormwood family?
- Do you think there are any parents who are that mean?
- How did Matilda get to be so good at taking care of herself at such a young age?
- Do you think Matilda had the right to do mean things to her father?
- What do you think about Mrs. Trunchbull? How does your principal compare to her?
- How does your teacher compare to Miss Honey?
- What does it show about the Wormwoods that they watch so much TV? How often does your family watch TV? How does Matilda manage to turn the situation around at the school assembly when Mrs. Trunchbull is humiliating Bruce?
- What would you do if you had powers like Matilda?

- How does Matilda use her powers to save Miss Honey?
- In what ways are Matilda and Miss Honey the same? How do they help each other?

Pointer:

Using one's inner magic, as Matilda does, is a healthy way to deal with life's painful things. Talk about what kinds of special powers or skills you or your child have and how they have gotten you through difficult situations. How can you channel your anger into a more productive medium?

A Miracle on 34th Street

Doris Walker is a working mother who runs the Macy's Thanksgiving Day Parade in New York City. She hires a man named Kris Kringle to play Santa in the parade. He is such a success that he goes on to work as Santa in Macy's flagship store on 34th Street. As a result of her own experiences, Doris has taught her daughter Susan not to believe in magic, fantasy, or imagination. Kris Kringle tries to help Susan recover the power of imagination, while their friendly neighbor Fred Gailey tries to get through to Doris. Kris' belief that he really is Santa Claus causes many people, including a hostile Macy's employee, to put his sanity on trial. When Doris and Susan get exactly what they wished for on Christmas day, it seems clear that only the real Santa could have come through for them.

This film is one of the most popular Christmas stories ever told because its message is so pure: Believe in things that don't make sense, like Santa Claus. Doris' own wounds from her past causes her to deprive her little girl of the belief in magic and miracles. This movie shows that many things happen which cannot be explained, and that life is so much richer when we learn to embrace the faith within us, regardless of our age.

Discussion Questions:

- Do you think it's right for Mrs. Walker to tell her young daughter that Santa doesn't exist?
- What makes this Santa Claus different from all the others?

- How would you react if you met a man who believed that he really was Santa?
- Why does Mr. Macy want to keep Kris Kringle as Santa, even though he sends people to other stores when they don't have certain things in stock?
- Do you know anyone who reminds you of Santa Claus? If so, who is it and why?
- Why does Kris Kringle try to teach Susan the importance of imagination? What does imagination mean to you? How much imagination do you have?
- Do you think Santa ever really gets angry? Was it right for Kris Kringle to bop Mr. Sawyer on the head with his cane?
- Was it too much for Susan to ask Santa for a house?
- What makes Doris and Susan change their minds about Santa?
- Did Santa really get Susan and her mom the house or did he just lead them to it?

Pointer:

Fred Gailey tells Doris that "faith is believing in things even when common sense tells you not to." What types of things do you believe in even though you might not be able to explain or understand them? Don't act like Doris Walker at the beginning of this film! Respect your child's sense of fantasy and do not try to argue over what things are real and what things aren't. Encourage her imagination and try to understand where she developed her beliefs in things like Santa, the Tooth Fairy, and the Easter Bunny. Don't try to overexplain everything; simply listen and encourage her sense of imagination.

THE TEENAGE
YEARS

(AGES 13 & UP)

Part III

You spend years raising your child, hoping that he will grow up to be a confident, healthy, sensitive, and responsible young adult. But if you're like most parents, what you're dealing with now is a moody, emotional, rebellious, uncommunicative ball of hormones. Welcome to the teenage years! Take comfort in knowing that it is all part of the growing process, and in finding easier ways to communicate using films. As teens search for their own identity, it is only natural for them to separate themselves from their families. Don't think that they do not need you; they simply don't need you in the same way they did before. They need your support, not your speeches; your love, not your lectures. They need to be able to communicate with you and bounce ideas off you. The hardest thing parents struggle with is allowing their teenagers more freedom, while still maintaining some level of authority and involvement in their lives. While your child experiments with many issues in an attempt to learn and define who he wants to be as an adult, it is more challenging, and yet more important than ever, for parents to use active listening skills to successfully communicate with him.

Friends have a tremendous effect on how teenagers see themselves and how they cope with issues in their day-to-day lives. Teens usually trust their friends almost as much as, and often even more than, their parents; they confide their darkest fears and anxieties to them. A parent's ability to communicate with their teenager—and communicate on a level he can understand—will affect how susceptible a teen is to both the negative and positive influences of his peers. Teenagers tend to acquire values that their parents have shown them over the years at home, and that their peers have reinforced outside of the home.

Obviously, teens will see a lot of movies with their friends, from new releases at the mall to renting videos of old favorites at their friends' homes. Try to make an effort to find out what films they are watching, provide an opinion on whether the film is appropriate, and watch films with your teens as often as possible, even if they are not films you particularly enjoy. Any time spent with your teenagers—any shared experience, even if it is sitting in front of a movie screen—is valuable. It will provide you with insight into their world and show them you are trying. Use your own experience as a springboard for conversation, and perhaps some of their favorite films will give you a little look into their actions, thoughts, and emotions. Trying to talk to a teen about a serious issue sometimes feels like working your way through a minefield. Certain subjects may make them explode or shut off completely. However, they will be much more comfortable revealing their opinions, fears, and experiences by discussing characters in films than they will be discussing their lives directly.

Chapter 13

Family Life

Teenagers are caught somewhere between childhood and adulthood, dependence and independence. They may feel like they are ready to be adults, yet certain responsibilities and boundaries go along with their financial dependence on their parents. These boundaries present one of the central conflicts between adolescents and their parents. Parents want to structure adolescents' lives so that they conform to their notion of how the world operates. However, teenagers on the brink of adulthood are suddenly becoming aware of their parents' own shortcomings and weaknesses. They may want to use this new knowledge against their parents. But keep in mind that the only thing teenagers resent more than having their parents *control* their lives is having their parents ignore their lives altogether.

Communicating Expectations

Parents need to communicate their expectations—from chores around the house to curfews to academics—to all members of the family. They also need to communicate what the consequences will be when an expectation is not met. It is important to explain the reasoning behind a certain expectation or rule. The severity of the punishment should be equal and relevant to the expectation that was not met. In other words, "make the time match the crime." Most of the parents in these films, such as Helen in *Parenthood* or Ben Hood in *The Ice Storm,* are not very good at communicating their expectations and don't provide sufficient discipline for their children.

Mutual Respect

Explain and discuss with your teenager what it means to be respectful. Respect is listening when another person is talking, acknowledging what was said with some form of reply, either verbal or non-verbal, and exchanging feelings about what was said. Unlike Bull Meecham in *The Great Santini,* who dictates absolute authority over his children, treat your children with respect regardless of how combative or inappropriate you feel they are. Model for them the very behavior you would like to receive. If they sense you do not respect them, it's unlikely they'll listen. The two couples in *The Ice Storm* do not treat each other respectfully, and therefore lose credibility with their children when they demand respect themselves. And remember, it is always best to express all feelings, positive or negative, provided it is done in a respectful and constructive manner.

Establishing Boundaries

Establish both physical and emotional boundaries with your adolescent. Boundaries are the level of involvement a parent and child have in each other's lives. A parent with little or no boundaries, like Gil in *Parenthood,* does not separate his child's failures, triumphs, pain, and happiness from his own. Teenagers should stay out of all arguments between parents, regardless of the issue, unless invited to respond to something that may involve them. Respect each other's private time—talking on the telephone, reading a book, doing work that involves intense concentration—with an understanding of when it is appropriate to interrupt that activity.

Resolving Conflicts

Establish a healthy process for resolving problems that respects the feelings of everyone involved. Resolving problems begins with acknowledging that there is a problem, then identifying the feelings surrounding the problem, offering possible solutions, exploring the consequences of each solution, choosing the best workable solution, and then resolving to take action on that solution. *Ordinary People* shows what can happen when a parent is unwilling to address a problem that exists in her family. Over time, family members should discuss how effective that solution was and whether or not it needs to be renegotiated or revised.

The Great Santini

This film explores the complex relationship between Bull Meecham, a marine fighter pilot, and his teenage son in 1962. Bull is a manic, aggressive, and stubborn father who loves his family, yet clearly lacks the ability to compromise. Bull moves with his wife and four children to Beauford, South Carolina. He treats his family with the same level of authoritarian control he uses with the squadron of pilots he whips into shape. His eldest son, 18-year-old Ben, befriends a slow African-American man. Bull's aggressive personality causes conflict within the Meecham family, most obviously with his sensitive son, Ben. But the most compelling conflict is the one within himself; Bull struggles with a potential alcohol problem and fears of mortality.

This film explores the issues that arise when a father is unwilling to compromise and accept his son in spite of their differences. As an adolescent, Ben struggles with the desire to win his father's approval, while also asserting his own independence and remaining true to his own very different, more sensitive personality. Bull Meecham is the perfect example of a parent who has completely unrealistic expectations for his children, particularly for his son. He places tremendous pressure on all his children to excel in everything they do; he wants them to be the best, with little or no regard for their concerns and individuality.

Discussion Questions:

- What do you think of the father in this film?
- Do you want to follow in your parent's footsteps? Which one?
- Do either of your parents expect you to have the same career/job as them? Why or why not? Does that strengthen your relationship or does that cause problems?
- What qualities differentiate you and your parents?
- How is your relationship with your parents similar to or different from Bull and Ben's?
- Why do you think there was such competition between Bull and Ben, especially during their one-on-one basketball game? What kinds of competition exist between members of your family?
- Do you think Ben did the right thing by disobeying his father and going to help Toomer? Have you ever gone ahead and done something that you believed was right, even though it was against a parent's judgment? What were the consequences?
- What do you think will happen to the Meechams now that Bull has died?
- Do you think that Ben will serve as a better father-figure in the Meecham house than Bull did? Why or why not?
- Do you think that Bull Meecham has a drinking problem? How do you feel about Bull getting his eighteen-year-old son drunk for the first time?

Pointer:

Make sure that you allow for your teen to express some negativity; it may be difficult to hear if your teenager sees similarities between your parenting style and Bull's. Whether an adolescent is right or wrong is not as important as finding out why he thinks what he does. Exploring the differences between Ben and Bull as individuals may help you and your adolescent discuss some of your own similarities and differences.

Ordinary People

This film is a chilling slice of life about an affluent family whose relationships begin to crumble in the aftermath of a tragedy. The accidental death of one son leaves the surviving son, Conrad, distracted, unreachable, and suicidal. Conrad's parents, Beth and Calvin, are unable to relate to his pain. While his father tries to understand what he's going through, his mother perceives his grief as a personal betrayal and a distraction from their seemingly normal suburban life. In the beginning of this film, Beth lives under the pretense that everything is back to normal, but it is obvious that Conrad is still hurting and needs more time to heal. The tension between Conrad and his mother grows as her expectations for normalcy are not met.

This is a film about a family that is unable to resolve conflicts. They have not resolved the issue of their older son's death, nor have they resolved the issue of their younger son's attempt at suicide. The mother in this film is not able to admit that there is a problem, let alone allow for the healthy expression of emotional pain and begin to find solutions. Conrad and his father must come to terms with Beth's limitations and continue to heal without her involvement. This film demonstrates the importance and effectiveness of therapy in helping families and suicidal individuals through the healing process.

Discussion Questions:

- Why do you think Conrad decided to quit the swim team? Why did he lie to his mother about it? What kinds of activities, interests, or commitments have you quit and why?
- How does seeing Dr. Berger, the psychiatrist, help Conrad? Do you think therapy can help families or individuals resolve serious issues? What is the perception within your group of friends if someone sees a therapist?
- The tragedy this family undergoes affects each person individually, but also affects each relationship. What tragedy or problem has affected the members of your family? How were they affected? Were relationships between family members strengthened or weakened?
- What do you think will happen to the family in this film? The marriage between Beth and Calvin? The relationship between Conrad and his father? Conrad and his mother? Will Conrad be okay?

- Put yourself in Conrad's shoes. Would you have blamed yourself for Buddy's death?
- Do you think that Beth loved Buddy more than Conrad? What kind of favoritism exists in families you know?
- Who do you talk to when you're upset? Why?
- With whom in the film do you most identify? (Conrad? Calvin? Beth?) Why?

Pointer:

Conrad comes to the realization that his mother will never treat him the way he would like to be treated. Through therapy, he begins to accept her limitations as a parent and as a person, and does not let her prevent him from healing and ultimately finding happiness. Discuss with your teenager what people in her life have had to accept despite their limitations. Or share with your teen what person you have learned to accept in this way.

Parenthood

This insightful film comically but realistically explores different obstacles that face four adult siblings, each of whom struggles toward one common goal: to be a good parent. Susan and Nathan have extremely demanding intellectual expectations for their young daughter; their desire to turn her into a genius threatens her happiness and their marriage. Helen is a single mother trying to raise two teenagers without the help of a male role model. Her daughter Julie completely disregards her mother's rules, engaging in sex in her bedroom and even getting married behind her back, while her son Garry completely withdraws from her altogether. Gil and his wife Karen have three children and an unexpected fourth on the way. Gil's struggle to be the perfect father is hindered by problems with his job and his overly sensitive eight-year-old son.

Each family unit suffers from a lack of mutual respect, or a problem with defining boundaries and resolving conflicts. The patriarch of the family, Frank, struggles with the decision to help his irresponsible youngest son Larry or not. Susan and Nathan expect their child to be a genius, while Helen's attempts to establish boundaries with her children are unsuccessful because they do not respect her as an authority figure. Gil Buckman has not established appropriate boundaries between himself and his children. His dream to have "strong, happy, confident children" often gets in the way of his own happiness. In his quest to be unlike his uninvolved father, he goes to the other extreme and becomes overly involved in his children's problems. This film explores a great deal of humorous but relevant issues parents often struggle with, but the message seems to be to simply love your children and trust your instincts, because nothing works quite as planned.

Discussion Questions:

- What kind of father is Nathan to Patty? Do you think it is a good idea to push children intellectually, or should they just develop naturally? In what ways do you think your parents push you too hard?

- What kind of mother is Helen to Julie and Garry? How do you think she handled the situation with her daughter? Was it right to let Julie and Tod live together in her house? Why did she try to save their marriage when she clearly did not approve of it?

- Do you think it was right for the teachers to suggest pulling Kevin out of public school? Was it nature or nurture that made Kevin uptight and nervous?

- Was Gil doing the right thing by trying to push Kevin in baseball?

- Do you think Frank did the right thing by getting his youngest son Larry out of debt? Do you think it was right for Frank to agree to take care of Larry's son, Cool?

- Which set of parents did you like best? Which nuclear family reminds you the most of your family and why?

- With which conflict did you most identify?

- If you had to be a member of one of the four families in *Parenthood*, which one would it be and why?

- Garry craves the presence of a father figure in his life. Do you think that someone going through puberty needs to have an older, same-sex person to talk to? Who is the person in your life with whom you feel most comfortable talking about sex?

Pointer:

Parenthood suggests that the way our parents raise us can affect, either positively or negatively, the way we raise our own children. Discuss with your child the way your parents raised you. How was it different from or similar to the way you are raising them? Did they ever force you into any activities, push you too hard, or give you too much freedom?

The Ice Storm

This is a film about two dysfunctional families in suburban Connecticut, who all fail to connect with each other and instead drown their loneliness in sex and alcohol. The plot revolves around Ben and Elena Hood, who are having trouble with their marriage. Ben drinks a lot and is having an affair with the emotionally withdrawn Janey Carver, whose husband is always away on business. The Hoods' children are 16-year-old Paul, who goes to boarding school where he's in love with a lonely rich girl, and Wendy, a promiscuous adolescent who uses her sexuality to gain acceptance. The lives of these children parallel the corrupt behavior of their parents, who numb their pain with alcohol, have affairs, and go to "key parties" where adults swap sexual partners.

Neither set of parents in *The Ice Storm* provides boundaries for their children, nor do they serve as healthy role models. The adolescent children in this film mimic their parents, finding temporary comfort in sexual rather than emotional relationships. The desperate lack of moral adult role models mirrors the corrupt political climate tainted by the Watergate scandal and the aftermath of the Vietnam War. These parents lack respect toward their spouses, and therefore have a difficult time earning the respect of their children. This film illustrates the dangers of being distant parents and providing too much space between themselves and their children. The Hoods and the Carvers are both too uninvolved in their children's lives and totally unaware of their children's actions, a flaw that proves to be fatal at the end of the film.

Discussion Questions:

- What do you think of the two sets of parents in this film? What do you think about the children in this film?
- When Ben catches Wendy "fooling around" with Mikey, he scolds her

and then says that he's really not angry about what she was doing but rather who she was doing it with. How do you think Ben handled the situation? Why was it hypocritical for him to scold her?

- When Ben carries Wendy across the cold, wet ground, we are reminded that Wendy is just a young girl, not a seductress. Why do you think Wendy is so aggressive sexually?

- Who is the most moral person in the film? Who is the least moral person? Why?

- What do you think about the "key party" concept? Why do married adults have affairs? Do you think having an extramarital affair is forgivable?

- Why was Ben's "sex talk" with Paul so unsuccessful? Has anyone had a "sex talk" with you? Was it successful?

- As the title suggests, ice is everywhere in this film. What does it mean?

Pointer:

Talk about what could have been done to prevent this tragedy from occurring. What does it mean to be a dysfunctional family? Explore the different ways that families can be dysfunctional and how they may be helped or how their relationships may be improved. Perhaps in discussing what is wrong or problematic with the Hoods and the Carvers, you'll touch on what is wrong—or right—with your own family dynamic.

Avalon

This film highlights the triumphs and tribulations of a Russian-Jewish immigrant family in Baltimore, as they assimilate to American culture over the years. Sam Krichinsky arrives in the United States from Russia in 1914 on July 4th, as the story is told over and over to anyone willing to listen. Sam's son is a salesman who risks opening a discount store with his cousin and loses all his money when the store burns down. The precocious grandson, Michael, experiences the mix of frustration, mystery, and fun that characterizes growing up in an extended immigrant family.

Avalon celebrates the richness of having an intergenerational extended family, and how that influence becomes diluted as the family moves up the social ladder. Through holiday meals, family business openings, moves from row homes to the suburbs, birthdays, funerals, family meetings, and arguing brothers, the film shows us many of the joys and complexities of family life. Instead of dealing with one main issue, *Avalon* touches on so many of the universal, often precious, and sometimes frustrating elements of family life.

Discussion Questions:

- What did you think of this family?
- Who was familiar in this film? What situation could you relate to the most?
- How do feel about grandparents living with their children?
- How did things change in this family when they moved from the row homes to the suburbs?
- Do you think it was right for the cousins to change their names from Krichinsky to "Kay" and "Kirk"? Do you know any families whose names have changed over the years?
- How did wealth affect this family?
- Can you imagine a time when there wasn't television?
- Why was Sam's older brother Gabriel so mad when he carved the turkey without him? Do you think it was wrong?
- How do you think immigrant families like the Krichinskys are different from American-born families?

Pointer:

Share with your adolescent how things have evolved in your extended family since you were a child. Describe for them what holiday dinners were like for you growing up, or what stories were told over and over again in your family. Point out specific things that were unique to your family, what happened when your family got together for holidays, and what types of conflicts existed between different family members or even different generations. Ask your teen what she thinks will be one of her richest, fondest, or funniest family memories when she is older.

Chapter 14

"You reminded me about what the most important thing in life is: friends. Best friends."
— **Ninny Threadgoode, *Fried Green Tomatoes***

Social Life and Friends

Never underestimate the power of friendships during adolescence. Your teen is probably hanging out in co-ed groups, and the bonds between his same-sex friends are stronger and more complicated. Most teenagers report spending more time with their friends than they do with their families. Along with this increased time with their peers comes an increase in the influence those peers have. Friends will affect how your teen looks, dresses, thinks, and acts, as well as impacting his sense of self-worth.

The friends your teenager chooses may not fit your ideal standards, but be careful about expressing your disappointment. There is a very good chance that he will come to that same conclusion on his own, so he won't have to resent you for trying to control his life. Subtlety is a much more powerful tool in communicating your ideas about your teen's friends. No matter how much you disapprove of a certain individual, telling your teenager not to spend time with him is often the easiest way to ensure that he will.

Establishing New and Appropriate Friendships

As teenagers mold their identities, they'll judge whether their choices of friends are compatible with their own values and interests. As illustrated in films like *The Breakfast Club* and *The Outsiders,* teenagers will tend to be closest with peers who share similar interests, values, and often, socioeconomic background.

Trusting Friends to Provide Feedback

Adolescents begin to allow their friends to provide honest feedback in the forms of both praise and criticism. As we see in *The Outsiders,* when a teenager feels comfortable enough, he will also trust peers with his deepest fears and dreams. Friends' honest observations and criticisms of behavior are usually perceived as signs of caring; he will often reevaluate a situation or decision based on that feedback. In essence, this means that teens listen to their friends, and their friends listen to them—the basic element of a mature relationship.

Resolving Conflict with Friends

When they have misunderstandings or conflicts, most teenagers have the maturity to confront their friends with their honest feelings, instead of avoiding confrontation, withdrawing into depression, or even ending the friendship altogether. Adolescents need to learn how to resolve conflicts with their peers in a healthy, nonviolent way. As Idgie and Ruth do in *Fried Green Tomatoes,* part of this is accepting the differences between each other, and in some cases, simply agreeing to disagree is a crucial element to long-lasting friendships.

Distinguishing Platonic from Romantic Relationships

Learning to discriminate between sexual and social cues is very important, since teenagers are friends with members of the opposite sex. Changing hormones and social pressures create sexual impulses and a desire for emotional intimacy. This is often confusing or even scary for teens, as sexual feelings and fantasies complicate friendships and blur the boundaries between platonic and romantic relationships. As in *Clueless* and *Lucas,* many teens will find themselves in friendships where one person would prefer to shift from a platonic to a romantic relationship.

The Outsiders

This film is about teenagers growing up in the 1960s in Tulsa, Oklahoma, where you were either a "soc," with money, nice cars, and a promising future, or a "greaser," a poor child from the wrong side of town. This film is about two friends in particular who, despite being "greasers," overcome their social label, find beauty in the world around them, and ultimately prove that heroes come from all social classes.

Johnny and Ponyboy have a deep friendship based on trust and honesty. They are comfortable enough around each other to express their private thoughts: Johnny expresses his feelings of abandonment from his parents, and Ponyboy tells Johnny how he wanted to read *Gone With the Wind,* and how he relates to the Robert Frost poem, *Nothing Gold Can Stay.* These two "greasers" demonstrate a sensitivity and level of caring toward each other which demonstrate how the bonds of friendship can even overpower one's image. This movie shows how the connection between friends can be as strong and meaningful as the bonds between family members.

Discussion Questions:
- What do you think of the two groups—the "socs" and the "greasers"? What does each group stand for?
- Are there groups in your school that treat each other like this? Why do they put such an emphasis on fighting?
- Why aren't the parents more involved in these children's lives?
- Do you think friendships can sometimes be stronger or more valuable than family relationships?
- What did Johnny, Ponyboy, and Dallas' heroic act mean to the

town? What did it prove?

- Do you have friends or acquaintances who have done something completely unexpected or that completely goes against your opinion of them? Who, and what did they do?
- Why did Dallas shoot the store clerk? Did he want to die?
- What do you think will happen to Ponyboy? Will he overcome his social status?
- Why do you think Ponyboy and Johnny were such good friends? Why couldn't Ponyboy share with the other guys his fondness for *Gone With the Wind* and poetry by Robert Frost? What interests or aspects of your personality are you hesitant to share with certain friends?

Pointer:

It may be effective to use this film to show your teen how good friends allow us to be who we want to be and bring out the best in us. They allow us to grow and pursue our interests, even if they themselves may not be able to relate; part of the strength in Johnny and Ponyboy's friendship is their honesty and unconditional support of each other. Share how a certain friend has encouraged or inspired an interest or activity in your life.

The Breakfast Club

When five very different high school students are thrown together one Saturday morning to suffer through a day of detention, they slowly begin to realize that they have a lot more in common than their images may indicate. As the "brain," the "princess," the "basket case," the "athlete," and the "criminal" shed their masks, they learn that despite their dramatic differences, they all suffer from similar pressures from their peers and parents.

This film illustrates how easily teens get classified into neat categories, and how those labels hinder their individuality and hold them back from being who they want to be. When the five adolescents in this film begin to open up and share their fears and family problems, they see that friendship can come in many forms and can sometimes be found in the least-expected places. This film also shows how relationships can quickly change when things are shared, as two relationships in this film evolve from strangers to friendship to romance.

Discussion Questions:

- What are the cliques like at your school? What do they stand for?
- Do any of the five students in this film remind you of your friends or classmates? Which ones and why? Do you tend to only hang out with people in your group or do you have friends outside your main group of friends?
- At what point do you know that you can share a personal secret with a friend? Which friend do you share the most with?
- Why do you think Allison lied about her sexual exploits? Do you know people who lie about their sexual experiences? Is there pressure to have experienced certain sexual things at a certain age at your school?
- How realistic is it that these five students were able to break down the walls of their cliques and become friends so quickly?
- How do you feel about them smoking marijuana? Do you think drugs or alcohol can help some teens open up and reveal more about themselves?
- What do you think will happen with these characters on Monday when they are back at school? Will they remain friends or will they ignore each other?
- Do you think Andy and Allison, and Bender and Claire will be couples? How could two people from such different cliques be so attracted to each other? Do you know any couples like this?
- Do you know any teachers like Mr. Vernon? Do most of your teachers see you as part of a social group or clique, or do they see you as an individual?

Pointer:

Compare and contrast the presence of cliques or groups in their high school and at yours. Understanding what group your teen identifies with may give you a better awareness of the ways they are perceived by students and teachers. Cliques can undermine people's individuality by pigeon-holing them with certain stereotypes. This film shows us that deep down, we all have more in common than we thought. Tell your teen about the way things were when you were in school, and in which group or clique you were included. Were you friends with students outside your group of friends? Were you ever surprised to learn that you had more in common with an individual than your image would allow you to believe?

Lucas

Lucas is a gifted, quirky, precocious 14-year-old underdog who becomes friends with Maggie, the pretty 16-year-old new girl in town. To Lucas, their summer friendship is true love, but when school starts, he quickly learns that her feelings for him are merely platonic. She is actually interested in Cappie, the football team captain who defends and protects Lucas from bullies. Lucas is devastated by what he perceives as a betrayal by Maggie and Cappie. He attempts to win Maggie over by trying out for the football team, a very dangerous endeavor for someone his size. Lucas is so preoccupied with trying to prove himself to Maggie that he is completely unaware of Rina's interest in him. When the coach finally lets him in the football game, Lucas gets badly injured, but also proves to his school that his loyalty and determination make him a part of the team.

This sweet film explores all the pain and joy of high school romances, which are often defined by disappointments upon realizing that your affections are not reciprocated. Almost all of the characters in this film must endure some type of romantic rejection: Maggie tells Lucas that her dad left her mom for a much younger women; Cappie breaks up with long-time girlfriend Elise because he likes Maggie; Maggie turns Lucas down because she likes Cappie; and Lucas himself is completely unresponsive to Rina's affections. *Lucas* focuses on teenagers who don't fit the usual stereotypes, and it shows how they learn to treat each other well, in both friendship and love.

158

Discussion Questions:

- Why do you think Maggie takes such a liking to Lucas during the summer?
- What happens when your feelings toward a friend change from platonic to romantic? What happens when those feelings are not returned?
- How do you share your friends? Have you ever been upset when a friend of yours made other friends, or has a friend of yours ever been upset that you were making other friends? How do you resolve this type of problem?
- Do you think people need more than one good friend?
- What do you think about Cappie and Maggie getting together? Did they betray Lucas?
- Bruno and Cappie are both from the same social group, yet they treat Lucas very differently. Why? What makes bullies like Bruno pick on children like Lucas? Do you know people like Bruno or Cappie?
- Do you have any friends who are similar to Lucas—different, quirky, and the victim of many pranks?
- Why didn't Lucas notice that Rina liked him?
- What do you think will happen to Lucas in the end? Will he get together with Rina? Will he become a part of the football team or pursue his interest in science and etymology?

Pointer:

Allow your child to stumble through his friendships and first loves, but help pick him up if he falls. Don't try to solve anything or dictate who his friends should be. You can remain supportive of your adolescent without condoning a friendship that you think is detrimental. Rather, by acting as a springboard for conversation about his social life, you may help him clearly see the positive and negative aspects of his friends and romantic interests.

Clueless

This is a lighthearted film about Cher, a spoiled but charming Beverly Hills teenager who also happens to be extremely sensitive to those around her. While Cher's lifestyle may seem foreign to the average teen, many of the obstacles she encounters should be very familiar. She plays cupid to two teachers in the hopes of renegotiating her report card, befriends a "clueless" new girl in school named Tai, gives her a makeover, and attempts to fix her up with a popular boy, Elton. But when Elton rejects Tai, professes his interest in Cher, and Christian, the object of Cher's affection, turns out to be gay, Cher realizes that she is actually the clueless one. When it comes to matters of the heart, she is in dire need of an emotional makeover. Cher finally turns her energies inward, and becomes aware of her romantic interest in her ex-stepbrother, Josh, a socially conscious, budding lawyer who is turned off by materialism, and lifts Cher out of her own self-absorption.

This film humorously and accurately captures the terminology of the MTV generation while managing to show how human kindness really does win out. Cher is not popular solely because she is beautiful and rich, but because she is truly a kind person who brings out the best in people. Cher is a giving friend to Dionne and Tai, and she is a caretaker to her father. She appreciates the talents and uniqueness of each of her very different friends. She learns to celebrate them for who they are and see the beauty in their individuality. This film is also about relationships, and the inability to control who we're interested in romantically versus who we simply like as a friend.

Discussion Questions:

- What do you think of Cher? What do you like or dislike about her? Does she remind you of anyone you know?
- Can someone be both superficial and kind at the same time?
- How does your school and social life compare to Cher's?
- Cher's ex-stepbrother, Josh, says she only does good things when it serves her. Do you agree with him?
- What do you think about Cher ending up with Josh, her ex-stepbrother?
- Have you ever befriended someone who was new to your school, without friends or, as Cher says, "clueless"? Were your motives pure or were they self-serving? Are you still friends with that person?

- Do you know anyone who was romantically interested in someone who turned out to be gay? Did they remain friends as Cher and Christian did?
- Have you ever tried to play cupid to any of your friends? Did it work out?
- How does Cher change from the beginning of the film to the end?

Pointer:

What defines a generation? Be in tune with the terminology—the phrases, styles, and interests of your adolescent's generation. Ask her to share her high school culture and tell her about yours. What phrases did you use when you were a teenager? What were the trends, the styles, the political issues? Perhaps show her some pictures of you when you were her age, or play some music that you loved from that time of your life.

Fried Green Tomatoes

This film retraces the misadventures of two Southern friends in the 1930s—Idgie and Ruth—from the perspective of Ninny Threadgoode. Ninny is an elderly woman in a nursing home who is befriended by Evelyn Couch, a frustrated middle-aged housewife. Idgie is a liberal tomboy who has never gotten over the death of her brother, Buddy, until Ruth, her brother's old girlfriend, visits one summer and lifts her out of her misery. The two very different women eventually form a deep friendship. When Ruth gets pregnant by her physically abusive husband, Idgie saves Ruth by taking her to a small town, where the two friends go into business together, and open the Whistle Stop Café. These two friends live life on their own terms, serving African-Americans in their shop during segregation in the South. Together they raise Ruth's son on their own. Their friendship and independence is seen as a threat to their community.

This film illustrates the depth of certain bonds between two women and how those friendships are strengthened by tragedy. These women helped each other through enormous obstacles, and they also had loyalty to their African-American friends and employees, Sipsey and George. Their friendship makes them better individuals, and they refuse to conform to the ideals of their corrupt community. On two levels, in two different time periods and with two different women, this film shows us how friendships can positively impact us and change the way we live our lives, and in some cases, can actually save us.

Discussion Questions:

- How were Idgie and Ruth different as women? How did those differences help their friendship?
- How similar do friends have to be?
- What circumstances brought them together?
- How did conflict and tragedy affect their friendship through the years?
- How have painful experiences or conflicts affected your friendships? Has your friendship with anyone become stronger after a conflict or painful experience? Do you have any "fair-weather" friends?
- How did these two women handle their problems?
- What did Ruth and Idgie give each other? What did Ninnie and Evelyn give each other?
- How did hearing the story of Idgie and Ruth affect Evelyn's life? How did Evelyn change as a result of her friendship with Ninny?
- Have you ever had a friend that helped you change your life for the better?
- What do you think will happen to Evelyn and Ninny?

Pointer:

Share a story about one of your best friends. Tell your teen why you are friends with that person. Explain how a certain friend helped you through a particularly difficult time in your life, and ask him about one of his friends. You may be surprised to discover how many parallels exist between your friendships and his.

Chapter 15

"Oh, Jo. Jo, you have so many extraordinary gifts; how can you expect to lead an ordinary life? You're ready to go out and—and find a good use for your talent. Though I don't know what I shall do without my Jo. Go and embrace your liberty, and see what wonderful things come of it."

— Marmee March, *Little Women*

Coming of Age

Learning, growing, changing, maturing…There is an endless amount of films about teens going through transition, after which they are some-how transformed into more mature, complete individuals. The teenage years are a period during which your child will be challenged to live according to her own standards, undergo major life changes, and experience something that makes her more mature and changes the way she sees the world. The films in this chapter show young men and women doing just that. By discussing how the main characters in these films overcome obstacles, deal with their parents and peers, and integrate into the adult world, perhaps you and your teen can discuss some important issues she is facing as she becomes an adult.

Awareness and Acceptance of One's Abilities

Teens will become increasingly aware of their own strengths and weaknesses, recognizing whether they work well with their hands, whether they are musically or athletically inclined, whether they are drawn to creative pursuits, or if analytical skills and numbers are their expertise. Some teens will compensate for their less-developed skills by making healthy adjustments, such as accentuating their strong points, while others will turn to self-destructive outlets. In *Good Will Hunting*, Will may be aware of his gift, but he is not emotionally mature enough to use or accept it. For teens, figuring out what their strengths are and how to put them to use is an important part of growth.

Experiencing Emotional Feelings Beyond the Family

Teens are often overwhelmed by self-judgment, and believe it or not, they tend to be their own worst critics. Over-dramatizing negative things and their implications are very common. When teens try new things that have negative results, they tend to react with extreme emotion and apply exaggerated meanings because of their lack of emotional maturity.

Integrating Familial and Individual Values

When teenagers begin forming a perception of who they are, they'll hold on to some of the values stressed within the family unit and discard others. This step is natural in disengaging from the family unit. Like Tre Styles in *Boyz N the Hood* and Jo March in *Little Women*, most teens will develop into young adults by integrating some values instilled from their families with other more personal values that they have learned on their own.

Dealing with Parental Control after Leaving the Immediate Family

The many years of attempting to achieve in school, to develop a sense of self-worth, and to begin to take risks based on sound judgment and effective problem solving culminate with the teenager's need to separate herself from her childhood world into a new and scary, but exciting, adult reality. As teenagers experience more independence, teens and parents should develop an understanding and respect each other as adults, even though the teen is expected to communicate where she is going and when.

Boyz N the Hood

At the age of ten, Tre Styles goes to live with his divorced father in South Central Los Angeles, otherwise known as "the hood." Over the years, his father, a strict disciplinarian, instills in him values that will keep him off the streets. Seven years later, Tre has grown into a mature, responsible young man. He plans to attend college and get away from the violence that prevails in his neighborhood and threatens the lives of his friends. In contrast to Tre's relatively stable and nurturing home environment, are Tre's best friends, Ricky and Doughboy, fatherless half-brothers. Ricky, who has a promising future in football, is shot on the street, and Doughboy is involved with gangs, drugs, and violence. The film tells us: "One out of every twenty-one Black males will die of murder, and most of them will perish at each other's hands." Tre's ability to overcome this harsh statistic is itself an accomplishment, and a testament to his upbringing.

Although many families may not be able to relate to this film's violence, the issues facing these three boys are very real, and on many levels, quite universal. This film explores how the rules of one's peer group or gang can come into conflict with those of one's parents, and how difficult it can be to choose the right path. *Boyz N the Hood* demonstrates the hopeless cycle that occurs when an individual has little or no education, and how that cycle can be avoided with a caring, involved parent or mentor, such as Furious Styles. Even if families cannot relate to the specific cultural environment of the Styles, they will probably be able to relate to Tre's being pulled in two different directions, and his desire to please both his parents and his "boyz."

Discussion Questions:

- Why did Tre's mom send him to live with his father? Do you think she did the right thing?
- How difficult do you think it would it be to make the right decisions with so many bad things happening around you?

- What are the differences between Tre's family life and Doughboy's and Ricky's?
- Do you think you could survive in "the hood"?
- What kind of father is Furious Styles? What were his views about Blacks and gentrification?
- How hard was it for Tre to resist the gang and do his own thing?
- Why did Tre's father dislike the Black cop? What did the cop do wrong?
- How did Tre mature throughout the film?
- How do the choices that Tre made differ from those of Doughboy?
- Why do you think Tre survived all the violence when his friends didn't?
- How did Tre grow from the values he learned from his father and those he learned from the street?

Pointer:

Discuss how parenting affects a child's growth—how identifying and nurturing a teenager's strengths can help him develop into a more competent and confident adult. Let your teen know what his best qualities are—an athletic ability, an artistic gift, an intellectual skill, or an emotional intelligence. A mentor also has the responsibility of pointing out the consequences of poor choices, as Tre's dad did when he warned him about becoming one of the criminals on the street corner. Instead of merely telling a teen what to do, provide him with concrete examples of what happens when wrong decisions are made.

Good Will Hunting

Will Hunting is a wounded, stubborn, angry foster-home veteran who also happens to be a genius. While mopping floors at MIT, he solves a difficult math theorem, capturing the curiosity and respect of a professor, who bails him out of jail on the condition that he will study with him and see a therapist. After many prestigious psychologists fail to connect with Will, he ends up seeing Sean, a sensitive therapist from the same South Boston neighborhood. Will, who was abused as a child, struggles with his fear of rejection both in his romantic life, where he fails to commit to his girlfriend Skylar, and with his work, where he settles for menial jobs instead of using his gift. Sean slowly gets through to Will, helping him understand that he needs to take a chance and grow emotionally before he can even begin to utilize his genius in a productive way.

Will is an example of a 20-year-old whose emotional baggage interferes with every decision he makes. His friends are his family, and he doesn't trust anyone but them. Will fears taking chances. Although he is a genius with a photographic memory, he has absolutely no emotional intelligence. He is completely unable to use his intellect in a positive way until, with the help of Sean, he realizes that it is time to work on forgiving and accepting himself, and then he can focus on a meaningful career. Though few teens have gifts as extreme as Will's, many have special strengths, and oftentimes are not emotionally mature enough to find ways to use them in a way that is productive. This film shows how you must be comfortable with yourself and embrace your gifts before you can even attempt to make it in the world.

Discussion Questions:

- What do you think of Will? What are his strengths and weaknesses? Why was he so angry?
- Why does Will always have jobs that don't utilize his intelligence?
- Why didn't Will trust any of the therapists that Professor Lambeau made him see? What was different about Sean that allowed Will to trust him?
- What was the conflict between Professor Lambeau and Sean? What were their different opinions about how to help Will?
- Do you know anyone like Will? How are they like him?
- Why couldn't Will tell Skylar that he loved her?
- How did Skylar, Chuckie, and Sean contribute to Will's growth, and help him make the decision to go to California?
- What was the choice Will was faced with at the end of the movie?
- How did Will help Sean?
- How did Will change through the film?
- What do you think will happen to Will in California?

Pointer:

Teenagers need to learn not to blame themselves for things that are beyond their control. Talking with someone you really trust can help you learn about yourself and help you make better choices. Just as Will needed to let go of the pain and anger of growing up a foster child in an abusive household, many teens need to hear—from their parents especially—that certain things are beyond their control and not their fault. Talk about what fears have held you back. Were you ever afraid to take a chance for fear of getting hurt? Ask your child if she is embarrassed about utilizing her skills, or pursuing some of her interests for fear it will separate her from her friends.

Little Women

Set in Concord, Massachusetts, during the Civil War, this film, based on Louisa May Alcott's novel, follows the four March sisters as they learn and love. Times are hard; their father is away at war, but they find comfort in their strong mother, Marmee, who nurtures the individuality in each of her very different daughters. Meg is the oldest sister and the beauty. Beth is the good hearted sister whose health is poor after surviving scarlet fever. Amy is the baby of the family who is artistic and dreams of marrying a rich man. The protagonist of the story is Jo, a tomboy and aspiring writer who stages theatrical performances in which all of her sisters play a role. Theodore Laurie is their surrogate brother, playmate, and wealthy next-door neighbor who initially admires Meg, then befriends and falls in love with Jo, but eventually ends up marrying Amy.

This film addresses the conflict between society's notions of marriage and a young woman's own dreams of doing something special in the world. Each sister's path demonstrates how she resolves this conflict and ultimately finds love and comfort in her own individuality. Little Women shows how different teens can find a balance between their own dreams and society's expectations for them. It also demonstrates the importance of family members in nurturing individuality and helping teens to pursue the best path for their future.

Discussion Questions:

- How does the March family differ from other families during this time period?
- What did each sister want out of life? Which sister do you like the most: Meg, Jo, Beth, or Amy? Why?
- If you had to marry one of the men in this film—John, Friedrich, or Laurie—which one would you choose and why?
- What do you think of Marmee? What kind of role model was she for her daughters? What did she want to teach them?
- Why does Jo turn down Laurie's marriage proposal?
- How were things different for women in the 1860s?
- What does Jo want to accomplish by leaving her family and moving to New York?
- How does Professor Bhaer challenge Jo with her writing? Have you ever had a friend or love interest who helped you become a better person?
- How does Jo grow and change throughout the film?
- How would these sisters make out in today's world?

Pointer:

Share what your dreams were when you were younger, how those dreams compared to those of your siblings, and whether or not that posed a problem with your parents. What skills of yours did your family encourage? Teens need honest, constructive feedback about what their skills are so that they can make intelligent choices about their future.

Slums of Beverly Hills

The Abramowitzes are an eccentric family who move from one cheap condominium to another in order to maintain their Beverly Hills address and education. The film centers on Vivian, a sexually maturing fourteen-year-old who is embarrassed by her large breasts and changing body. Their father, Murray, is a single dad who can barely support his three children. In the summer of 1976, Vivian gets her first bra, loses her virginity to a neighbor, and her older cousin Rita, a pregnant rehab drop-out, lives with them while try-ing to go to nursing school. On the cusp of adolescence, Vivian is the most emotionally mature individual in this film. The arrival of her cousin Rita provides her with a much-needed female confidant, who helps her gain confidence in her sexuality. Murray's inability to provide for his children financially results in his having virtually no control over his children. Vivian eventually comes to the realization that her father's fallibility makes him all the more lovable, and she finally learns to embrace the uniqueness of her family and herself.

This film explores the ways in which a dysfunctional yet loving family can both contribute to a young woman's frustration with her sexuality, and serve as a source of comfort. It provides an opportunity to explore how understanding the limitations of one's family members and appreciating their strengths can make someone a more confident, mature individual. Vivian finally learns to judge herself on her own terms, and to appreciate the family structure inside her father's borrowed demo car where, although he may be a poor provider, at least his presence in her life is consistent and loving.

Discussion Questions:

- What do you think of the Abramowitz family? What is good about them as a family? What is not healthy about this family?
- What do you think of Vivian? Can you relate to her frustration with her changing body?
- How did Vivian's family hold her back? How did Vivian's family help her grow?
- How did Rita "mother" Vivian? How did Vivian "mother" Rita?
- Why didn't Vivian want to continue dating Eliot after they moved? How did Vivian set her own limits sexually?
- Murray tells a story about when he had his own restaurant and he caught the chef stealing meat from the kitchen. What was so ironic about this story? Was it right for him to say to his cook "I'm their father"? Was it right for Uncle Mickey to say the same thing to Murray in front of the children?
- What makes someone a good father—financial or emotional support?
- What do breasts mean in this film? How do they help and hinder situations?

Pointer:

Part of maturing is accepting a family's limitations. Vivian learns to accept the eccentricities and uniqueness of her own family members, and to see her father, her family, her breasts, and her body for what they are. Discuss what makes someone a good parent—emotional or financial support? Who is a better father, Murray or Uncle Mickey? Discuss parents who may not be good financial providers but are otherwise very loving and involved. What parents do you know who provide their family with financial but not emotional support?

Rebel Without A Cause

This film follows a day in the lives of three troubled teenagers in the 1950s who are each alienated from society in some way. Each character has had to endure a great deal of emotional pain from their families. Jim Stark is the new kid in town. He is a sensitive and frustrated teen, a troublemaker whose superficial, ineffectual parents move from town to town neglecting to understand their son's need for acceptance and stability. Judy is a pretty but insecure girl who craves attention from her cold father. Plato, the most disturbed of the three teens, suffers from extreme feelings of abandonment by his parents, who support him financially but are virtually absent from his life. When Jim is challenged by the popular kids to participate in a dangerous car game, he wants to avoid confrontation, but participates as a "matter of honor." The competition ends with the gang leader going off a cliff. Afterwards, Jim, Judy, and Plato find comfort in each other and create a surrogate family in an abandoned mansion until eventually the authorities come and find them.

   This movie was one of the first films to show an adolescent questioning authority—both his parents and the police. Considered one of Hollywood's best films of the fifties about rebellious youth, it shows how young adults can be emotionally stunted due to an unhealthy family environment. Jim, Judy, and Plato are all scarred by unhealthy family situations. Only by separating themselves from their families can they grow and heal. In this film, parent-child alienation is the ultimate reason for such prevailing teenage angst. Rebel Without A Cause provides an example of how a rebellious and lonely teenager can learn to take responsibility for his actions and choices.

171

Discussion Questions:

- What do you think of these teens—Jim, Judy and Plato? What do you think of their families?
- Why do you think Jim is always getting into trouble?
- How are Jim, Judy, and Plato similar?
- What does the title of the film mean?
- Who do you know who reminds you of Jim, Judy, or Plato?
- What tortured Jim most about his parents?
- How did the events of that night help Jim stand up to his parents?
- How did Jim's rebellious actions that night cause his parents to finally change?
- Why does Jim befriend Plato?
- Why is Judy attracted to Jim?
- Did Jim do the right thing by accepting the challenge to race in the chickie run? What else could Jim have done to maintain his honor in a situation like that? What would you have done in that situation?
- What kinds of dares do children make today that are similar to the chickie run?
- What do you think will become of the Stark family? Will they stay in this town?

Pointer:

Use the characters in this film to discuss how parental alienation can affect a teen's behavior. Discuss with your teenager what situations have made him more mature or brought him closer to being an adult. Discuss whether your teen is a "rebel without a cause" or if he has friends who are. Share with your teen whether you were rebellious during your teenage years and why.

Chapter 16

Sex and Romance

As natural as sexuality is, there probably isn't anything that feels as unnatural as discussing it with teens. But the reality is that adolescence is usually the time of sexual awakening, as well as the time when first "serious" relationships occur. By the time your child reaches the teenage years, you can probably assume that she already knows a lot. Messages about sex are everywhere—movies, friends, television, advertisements, songs, and books. But don't make the mistake of assuming she knows everything. Remember, it is better that she learn from you than from her friends.

As demonstrated in the shocking film *Kids*, now more than ever teenage pregnancy and sexually transmitted diseases (STDs) are a serious reality. Education can prevent unwanted pregnancies and the transmission of STDs, and education involves communication. Although most schools have a sex education course in junior high school, to many children it is perceived as a joke. Therefore, it is up to parents to communicate with their young teenagers the potential risks associated with sex, as well as the decision-making, values, and emotions that accompany it.

Although sexuality and love are addressed together in this chapter, they are obviously two very separate concepts. It is important that you discuss with you teen how to differentiate between sexual feelings and emotional feelings. They don't always go hand-in-hand, and assuming that they do can cause a lot of heartache. While you certainly cannot be your child's friend, you can make an effort to be accessible to her, so that she feels comfortable asking you questions and expressing her fears and frustrations.

First Time Feelings

When an adolescent experiences his first feelings of love or sexual desire, it is likely that he'll feel as though he is the only one on earth who has ever had these feelings. Often when teens try to share their emotional or sexual feelings with their parents, as Bud does in *Splendor in the Grass,* their parents minimize their feelings by labeling their very real emotions as "puppy love". Regardless of your opinions about their romantic interests, it is important that you recognize the intensity of their feelings. You may have the hindsight to know that he will recover from a break-up or that his relationship is just the first of many, but your teen's emotions can be very real and very intense, certainly deserving of your respect.

Developing Confidence

Most adults can relate to Hermie in *Summer of '42,* and the overwhelming feelings of fear and excitement associated with first love. Teens are figuring out how to approach their crushes or romantic interests. It is important to help adolescents gain confidence as they stumble through the ups and downs of their sexuality. Remember, your role should be less like a parent and more like a coach. A support system—not a superior—is what they need most as they navigate through their relationships.

Experimentation

Experimentation is a natural precursor to intercourse, and teens usually discuss with their friends "how far to go" sexually. While parents should not dictate how far a teenager should go, or when it is time to lose his virginity, it is up to parents to instill the values that will affect his actions in romantic and sexual situations. Parents should raise the issue of birth control long before they feel their adolescent is sexually active. If you believe your son or daughter is engaging in sexual intercourse, you should discuss with them what type of birth control would be best for them, as well as the importance of using condoms with all partners to prevent sexually transmitted diseases.

Giving Oneself Over to Feelings of Love

It is usually during adolescence when teens first experience mature feelings of love. While their definition of love may be different from yours, or may be experienced on quite a different level, by minimizing their feelings, parents risk further alienating their children from sharing things with them. Remember, everything is relative. Whether their feelings are reciprocated or not, they are often so powerful that it may affect other areas of their lives, and it is important to respect and empathize the intensity of their emotions.

Reality Bites

This film is about a group of Generation-X post-college young adults experiencing angst in their love lives and careers. Lelaina Pierce is an amateur documentary filmmaker employed at a local television morning show, who is forced to choose between the two very different men who are competing for her affections. Michael is a successful yuppie, who works for an MTV-like television network and wants to commercialize her documentary. Her long-time friend Troy is a philosophical, scruffy, perpetually unemployed intellectual. Lelaina's other friends are her sarcastic roommate, Vickie, who keeps a running list of the many men she's slept with, and who takes an AIDS test when she finds out one of them was HIV-positive, and Sammy, who is gay and must break this news to his family.

This film is about making choices between your emotions and your intellect, both in love and work. It explores the question of when "selling out" is the right thing to do, and what should guide us through these tough decisions—our hearts or our heads?

Reality Bites also illustrates how significant or traumatic life events, such as the death of a parent in Troy's case, can affect a relationship by serving as a wake-up call that makes someone aware of his true feelings. It shows how dating can be a valuable, often necessary learning process, and how who you chose to be with romantically is often a reflection of yourself.

Discussion Questions:

- Why wasn't Lelaina responsive to Troy the first time he kissed her? Why didn't she want to get involved with him? Have you ever been in this type of situation?
- Why was Lelaina hesitant to give her tapes to Michael to use on "In Your Face TV"? What do you think the documentary means to her?
- How hard do you think it was for Sammy to tell his parents that he was gay? How hard do you think it was for his parents to find out such a thing? Do you know anyone who is openly gay? How do their parents feel about it?
- When is it okay to date two different people at once? When isn't it okay? Have you ever dated or been interested in two people at the same time?
- Vickie says the AIDS test is a "rite of passage" for their generation. Do you agree? Do you think STD tests should become a part of a serious relationship?
- How are Troy and Michael different? How do Troy and Michael meet Lelaina's needs differently?
- Which guy do you think Lelaina should have chosen and why? Who do you know who is like Michael or Troy?
- What do you think about Lelaina choosing to be with Troy instead of Michael? What do you think their relationship will be like?

Pointer:

Know when to voice your opinions about a teenager's romantic interests and when to stay out of it. Dating is a learning process that helps teens better understand who they are by discovering what qualities they like and dislike in their romantic interests. If your teen is in a physically or emotionally abusive relationship, then you need to get involved. But if they are simply dating someone whom you do not like, then step back and give them the freedom to make their own mistakes and learn their own lessons.

Summer of '42

Hermie, Oscy, and Benjie are the "terrible trio," three fourteen-year-old friends who keep each other entertained on an East Coast island vacation during the summer of 1942. Hermie, the most mature of the three, is looking for romance. His best friend, Oscy, is pre-occupied with "getting laid," while Benjie, the least mature, is not even interested in sex yet. Armed with notes from a stolen medical journal, Oscy loses his virginity on the beach, while Hermie sets his sights on Dorothy, a lonely woman whose husband is away at war. He fantasizes about having a romantic relationship with her and struggles through the nervousness and fear that accompany first love. Hermie befriends her by helping her with household chores, and when she receives notice that her husband was killed in combat, she seeks comfort in Hermie's arms; he has his first sexual experience and a memory he'll never forget.

This film is a classic coming-of-age tale, and while the language may be somewhat dated, the film explores the universal experiences that young adolescents, particularly boys, encounter. Although today's teens may no longer have to learn about sex from stolen medical journals, many adolescents still suffer through that embarrassing first condom purchase, or the first feel of a breast at the movies. These young men express the fear, confusion, and excitement that accompany burgeoning sexuality and first love. This classic film also does a great job of showing how three young men of the same age can be at such different stages of development, both physically and mentally.

Discussion Questions:

- What do you think of these three boys? How are they different from guys your age?
- Which boy reminds you the most of yourself or your friends?
- These boys had to learn about sex from a stolen medical book. How are things different today?
- How do teenagers today get contraceptives? Is it as awkward for them as it was for Hermie in the drugstore?
- Why do you think Dorothy had sex with Hermie?
- Do you think that Hermie told his friends about his sexual encounter with Dorothy? Would you have told your friends?
- How should a guy read a girl's signals? How can a guy know when a girl wants to have sex and when she just wants to experiment or "fool around"? How should girls set limits during sexual experimentation?
- How was Hermie's first experience with Dorothy different from Oscy's with Miriam?
- Why was Hermie shaking when he was on the ladder helping Dorothy with her boxes?

Pointer:

Discuss with teenagers how important it is to respect an individual's sexual boundaries. No matter the situation, "no" means no. Let teens know that if they are ever in a situation where their boundaries are not being respected, then they should get help and get out of the relationship.

Splendor in the Grass

This film is about the high-school relationship of Deanie, a good girl in 1920s Kansas, and her handsome, rich, captain-of-the-football-team boyfriend, Bud. Passionately in love and struggling with their awakening sexuality, both Bud and Deanie receive some bad guidance from their parents. Bud satisfies his sexual curiosity with a promiscuous girl not unlike his sister, who is an embarrassment to their family. When the whole school finds out, Deanie is heartbroken, has an emotional breakdown, and is sent to a mental institution. There, with the help of a caring doctor, Deanie learns to accept that she will always be a little girl in her parents' eyes, and falls in love with another patient. Meanwhile, Bud is frustrated by pressures from his controlling father to attend Princeton and begins drinking heavily. When Bud's father commits suicide after losing his fortune, Bud leaves school, marries a waitress, and goes to live on a ranch. At the film's end, Deanie and Bud finally find happiness and learn to look back on their relationship with fondness.

This classic film is still relevant today as a beautiful tribute to that all-encompassing, passionate first love that we all may get over, but will never forget. This film also shows how poor parental advice can set teens on the wrong, often destructive, path. While part of this had to do with the values of the 1950s, when the film was made, unfortunately today's parents often give their children bad advice about sexuality. Making teenagers feel bad about their new sexual curiosity can be detrimental to their long-term emotional well-being.

Discussion Questions:

- What were Deanie's parents' expectations of her? What were Bud's parents' expectations of him?
- What kind of girls were Juanita and Ginny (Bud's sister)? Do you know any girls like that?
- What do you think about the advice that Deanie's mom gave her about her sexual feelings? What do you think about the advice Bud's father gave him about his sexual feelings?
- What happened to Deanie when she found out about Bud's sexual encounter with Juanita? What was wrong with Deanie? Who do you think was at fault for her breakdown?
- How did the doctor at the institution help Deanie get better?
- Do you think Deanie and Bud were ready to have sex? What should the level of commitment between two people be before they decide to have sex?
- What do you think of Bud and Deanie's relationship? Was it healthy?
- How did Bud and Deanie's parents get in the way of their happiness?
- Do you think Bud and Deanie were happy at the end of the

movie? How do you think their relationships with their spouses were different from their relationship with each other?

- Do you know anyone who was so devastated by a breakup with a boyfriend or girlfriend, like Deanie was?
- In what ways does the Wordsworth poem that Deanie recites relate to your life?

Pointer:

Tell your teen about your first love. By doing so, you remind your teen that you too were young once and vulnerable to the same joy and pain that accompany romance. Who was he or she, what was your relationship like, how did your parents react to the relationship, and how do you look back on that part of your life?

Kids

This shocking but realistic film, which feels more like a documentary, follows a day in the life of a group of inner-city teenagers as they skateboard, talk, party, have sex, and use drugs. The focus of the film is Telly, a sixteen-year-old sexual predator whose favorite conquest is virgins; we also meet his vulgar best friend Casper, and the more innocent Jenny, whom we learn has only had sex with one person—Telly. When Jenny accompanies her more sexually promiscuous friend to get an AIDS test, it is she who tests positive, and then sets out to find Telly. Amidst the backdrop of kids who are obsessed with sex, drugs, and skateboarding in New York City, Telly seduces his next exploit, a fourteen-year-old virgin named Darcy. By the time Jenny finds Telly, he has already conquered Darcy and unfortunately, at this point, Jenny is too drugged to care.

Despite presenting a very bleak, one-sided view of teens, this film is extremely realistic. These "kids" exist in a world entirely of their own making. Parents are rarely present, and when they are, like Telly's mom, they do not escape sexual objectification either; they are just adults from whom to steal. This film can be a harsh wake-up call, and while it may not be appropriate for many adolescents to watch, it may be just what is needed for more sexually promiscuous ones. As Jenny tells the clinic nurse, "I only did it once." This film demonstrates tragically that sometimes "once" is all it takes. The boys in this film achieve self-worth from sexual conquests, using sex as a way to give meaning to their lives, while the girls' sexual encounters reflect their desperate need for attention and acceptance of any kind. Drugs and alcohol are also prevalent, numbing these adolescents' pain, and compensating for their low self-esteem.

Discussion Questions:

- What do you think about the kids in this film? Why are they so focused on sex and drugs?
- How do the guys and girls use sex differently in this film?
- What are the guys' and girls' attitudes towards STDs and pregnancy?
- Where are the parents in this film? What will these children's futures be like?
- Why do you think these kids don't have any other interests besides sex, drugs, and skateboarding?
- Do you think children like this only come from the "inner city," or do you see the same type of problems in wealthier suburban communities?
- What do you think this film's message is? Does it glorify or show the dangers of drugs and sex?

Pointer:

When you mix drugs and sex with low self-esteem, the combination can be dangerous and in this case, deadly. Parents need to point out the serious danger of drugs and alcohol, as well as the risks associated with unprotected sex.

Chapter 17

Values, Morals, and Ethics

The ability to balance society's expectations with their own personal sense of right and wrong characterizes teens' morality. Often their cultural morality clashes with their individual needs. Also, men and women are generally inclined to different moral perspectives, as women focus more on the importance of respecting feelings and interpersonal relationships, and men focus on social agreements or contracts between people to dictate their moral reasoning. Some teenagers may have a sense of moral obligation and responsibility to their neighbors or to a social cause, whereas other teens' first impulses are to satisfy their own needs. Teens also begin to shape their morality and values separately from those of their parents and people to whom they have looked up in the past.

Internalizing Familial Values

For years, teens have watched their parents demonstrate their own values in everyday behaviors, such as how they treat each other, their parenting style, the way they relate to extended family members and neighbors, as well as the choices they make in their jobs or recreational activities. Teenagers usually internalize some of their parents' values that they feel comfortable with and use them to develop their own unique moral reasoning.

Gender Differences in Moral Development

Subtle differences exist in the type of morality society expects from each gender. Boys are encouraged to be more competitive and make moral choices based on absolutes, legal issues, and rules that affect their honesty and integrity. Because girls are taught to be more sensitive and respectful to others' feelings, their moral reasoning is based more on interpersonal relationships and empathy, rather than on social justice or laws. Girls are more likely to see the consequences of moral choices and how those decisions affect the needs of others. When those two different perspectives are taught to both genders starting in early childhood, the differences in adolescent morality between the sexes become less distinct and more integrated.

Using Moral Role Models

Culture can also set the tone for the moral issues that are explored in movies, television, and books. Parents may be the moral keepers for some teens, while in other cases it is another adult, such as a mentor, famous actor, athlete, or politician. Characters like Sister Helen Prejean in *Dead Man Walking* and Jaime Escalante in *Stand and Deliver* can serve as role models. On an individual level, teens will take on the moral values of those whom they perceive to be the most powerful, successful, and influential people in society.

Accepting Responsibility for Moral Decisions

After a teenager has made a moral decision, the process of accepting responsibility for that decision is very complex. *Quiz Show*'s Charles Van

Doren must live with the unfortunate consequences of his moral choices. Morally mature teenagers have fully considered the consequences of their actions and truly understand how those choices will affect the people in their lives. Because of past emotional pain or learned behaviors due to poor upbringing, teens may be afraid to make the right moral decisions, or may not understand what to do when they are faced with a moral dilemma in their everyday lives.

Dead Man Walking

Convicted felon Matthew Poncelet is on death row because of his involvement in the heinous rape and murder of an innocent young man and woman. Professing his innocence to the murder charge, he writes to Sister Helen Prejean, a nun who has dedicated herself to helping the poor. She agrees to help Poncelet file a last-minute appeal with the hope that if she can get him to admit his role in the crime, he can find some peace. She hopes that he may be granted forgiveness, if not by the victims' families, then perhaps by God. In addition to lending her moral courage and unconditional love to Poncelet, she also offers her support and sensitivity to the grieving families—Matthew's mother, and the parents of both victims. Sister Helen is a remarkable individual, a woman who is against capital punishment but can see the reality of the brutal crime that was committed, and simultaneously wish to comfort everyone involved.

This film's strength is in its ability to address the serious and controversial ethical issue of the death penalty from all angles, without taking a particularly definitive stance on it one way or the other. It explores the moral and psychological relationship between a convicted killer and his spiritual counselor. It addresses the conflict that can occur between an individual's moral standards and those of an institution. As side issues, this film explores grieving, forgiveness, healing, revenge, and letting go of anger. By juxtaposing the institutionalized lethal injection method of murder versus the violent civilian murder that takes place in the woods, it raises interesting questions about the death penalty. Discussing this issue with your teen and learning where she stands on the issue can help you gauge her moral reasoning.

Discussion Questions:

- What are your feelings about the death penalty?
- Have your views about the death penalty changed after seeing this film? What effect did this movie have on your views?
- Did Sister Helen do the right thing for Matthew Poncelet? Did she do the right thing for the victims' families—the Delacroixs and the Percys?
- What did Sister Helen want for Matthew? What did she want for the families?
- What kind of a moral role model was Sister Helen?
- Why did Mr. Delacroix come to Sister Helen at the funeral in the end?
- What caused Matthew to finally admit to his crime? Was it because of Sister Helen or because he was facing death?
- Why did the prison chaplain say to Sister Helen, "Do not oppose the authority of Rome"? Why were the prison chaplain and the Catholic Church threatened by Sister Helen?
- Was Sister Helen a feminist?
- Right after Matthew Poncelet was killed by lethal injection, the film showed us the reflection of Walter Delacroix and Hope Percy in the glass. What do you think that meant?

Pointer:

While it is a good idea to voice your opinion about the death penalty, make sure you don't argue it. Let your teen freely express her ideas about this controversial topic and ask her to explain her position. You need to respect her opinions even if you don't agree with them. Try to discuss recent news events and whether or not certain convicts should be killed by the death penalty.

Scent of A Woman

Charlie is a well-mannered young man who attends a New England prep school on scholarship. He accepts the job of watching a blind, retired, grumpy ex-Army Colonel in order to make some extra money. What was promised as "an easy three hundred bucks" turns out to be quite an adventure. Charlie realizes that Colonel Slade has big plans lined up for the weekend: a first-class trip to New York City, a stay at the Waldorf Astoria, as well as dancing, dining, drinking, driving, and women. As Colonel Slade warms up to Charlie, he also manages to teach him some life lessons, but it is Charlie who ends up saving Slade's life when he realizes that the weekend is a prelude to his planned suicide. When Charlie is forced to testify before his school's disciplinary committee for witnessing a crime, Slade comes to Charlie's rescue, saving Charlie from the headmaster who has attempted to bribe a confession out of him.

This film is about two people who have made very different moral choices in their lives. Charlie is an intelligent, polite, hard-working, honest young man who refuses to take the easy way out and allow the headmaster to buy his future. In contrast, Colonel Slade is an obnoxious, harsh, cynical old man who, by his own admission, has always avoided the right path, because it was "too damn hard." This film shows how integrity can win over influence, money, and politics, and how coming to grips with your own mistakes can help you grow. It explores dysfunctional family dynamics, suicide, honesty, and integrity.

Discussion Questions:

- What kind of a person is Colonel Slade? Do you think he is a moral person?
- How did Charlie and Colonel Slade help each other?
- How would you deal with someone who was depressed or threatening to kill himself?
- What is your position on the dilemma that Charlie was in at school? Do you think he was doing the right thing?
- Who was the most and least moral people in this situation— Charlie, his friend Henry, the other guys who pulled the stunt, or the headmaster, Mr. Trask?
- Have you ever witnessed a crime, or seen your friends doing

something bad? Did you ever have to rat on a friend? If you were in that situation, what would you have done and why? Would you have accepted the bribe from Mr. Trask?

- What do you think would have happened to Charlie if Colonel Slade hadn't stood up for him?
- Why was Colonel Slade so convincing in his argument to the disciplinary committee?
- How was Charlie different from the other students at Baird and how did that affect his situation?
- How did both Charlie and Colonel Slade change by the end of the film?

Pointer:

Tell your teen about a time when you had to make a tough moral choice. Perhaps you were witness to some sort of trouble, or maybe you participated in a school stunt. How did you handle it? Letting your child know that you too have made mistakes or have been forced to make difficult moral choices may make him more likely to open up to you about his own moral dilemmas.

Stand and Deliver

This true story is about a group of inner-city Hispanic students who, with the help of their determined teacher Jaime Escalante, pass the Advanced Placement test in Calculus. Mr. Escalante arrives on the first day of class at Garfield High to a zoo of a classroom filled with students who barely grasp basic arithmetic. His passion, sense of humor, and confidence in his students allow him to teach them calculus, but he also teaches them about life. He teaches them that with *ganas* (desire), people can accomplish anything. He believes that students will live up to whatever expectations their teachers set for them.

This film shows how an individual can make choices that will allow her to overcome poverty and prejudice. It also shows how with determination and dedication, people can overcome the social and familial obstacles that lie before them. A strong role model can instill lasting values in students that will stay with them their whole lives. This film presents the moral dilemma of having to retake a test on which you know you did not cheat in order to prove yourself, and challenges the morality of the Educational Testing Service in investigating the high scores of this class.

Discussion Questions:

- Have you ever had a teacher like Mr. Escalante? Who was the best teacher you had—what was he or she like?
- How did Mr. Escalante get these students excited to learn? What kind of approach did he use?
- How do you think you would have responded to a teacher like this?
- Have you ever had someone convince you that you could accomplish something you never thought possible?
- Why does working hard for something make you value it more?
- What did passing the Calculus AP test mean to these students? Is it different from what a test means to you? What in your life meant this much?
- How did these students' home lives hold them back academically? Was it right for Mr. Escalante to go his student's family to urge her father to let her attend special classes instead of working?
- What effect did Mr. Escalante have on the entire school and faculty?
- Why did the Educational Testing Service investigate these students' scores? Were their actions racially motivated?
- Should they have taken the test again? Why was Mr. Escalante originally against them taking the test again?

Pointer:

Discuss what goals you have that have been difficult to attain. Was there a mentor or teacher who helped you reach that goal? Have a discussion about what may be holding your teen back from rising to the level she would like to attain in a certain area. Perhaps there is some way you can help her overcome obstacles and better reach her goals.

Quiz Show

Based on the true story of a 1950s quiz show, this film is about congressional investigator Dick Goodwin, who turns a buried newspaper item into a national scandal when he suspects the popular show *21* is rigged. Herbert Stempel is the nerdy, Jewish contestant who is "defeated" by a handsome college professor named Charles Van Doren. As Goodwin investigates and tries to bring down the television industry, he befriends Van Doren and tries to protect him from the spotlight of the scandal. But eventually justice wins out and Goodwin must make the ultimate choice between exposing the truth or protecting his newfound friend.

Goodwin's dilemma mirrors the public's, as he is drawn to the likeable Van Doren and repulsed by Stempel. On a different level, he is guilty of the very same crime as the TV execs, holding Van Doren to a different standard than Stempel. All of the main characters in this film—Goodwin, Stempel, and Van Doren—are faced with moral dilemmas. This film shows us how often what is right is not always what is moral, and how sometimes the right choice can be hard to distinguish. The characters here must all live with the moral choices they have made, and face the repercussions those decisions have on their careers and family lives. *Quiz Show* asks whether is it ever okay to lie, and seems to take a strong stance that the answer is no. In an era where television was becoming such a popular media outlet, this scandal showed how its audience could be abused, and how the lines between fiction and fact become blurred. This film shows how media attention, fame, and glamour can affect people's moral reasoning.

Discussion Questions:

- In what ways do appearances affect people's views? To what extent did Charles Van Doren and Herbert Stempel's physical appearances help or hurt them?
- Are quiz shows still dishonest? What about other types of "real life" television programs? Are talk shows manipulated to increase their entertainment value?
- How could personal issues influence a person's desire for fame or money? What was motivating Charles Van Doren? What was motivating Herbert Stempel?
- How did Goodwin treat Van Doren and Stempel differently? How

did the way Goodwin felt towards these men parallel the public's reaction to each contestant?

- Did Charles Van Doren do the right thing? Did Herbert Stempel do the right thing? What did Van Doren learn? What motivated him to tell the truth?
- What was Goodwin's motivation for bringing out the truth about *Twenty-One*? Who did he want to expose? Who was actually exposed?
- Who ended up getting hurt the most? How did the television executives and corporate sponsor Geritol get away with everything?
- How did appearance, ethnicity, or background affect people's reaction to the two contestants?
- Do you think what happened to Stempel and Van Doren after the trial was fair?
- Who was the most moral person in this film?

Pointer:

Discuss with your teen where to draw the line between entertainment and honesty. Does television have a responsibility to accurately represent the truth? Is it okay for shows that look real to be manipulated? What kinds of issues are taking place today that relate to television's affect on society? (I.e. pro-wrestling, Jerry Springer, etc.)

Eve's Bayou

Eve is the ten-year-old middle child of the Batistes, a wealthy African-American family in a Louisiana swamp town in 1962. She, her older sister Cisely, and her mother all compete for the affection of her charming but philandering father, the town doctor. One night, Eve discovers her father making love with a married woman, but Cisely informs her that they were just telling jokes, thus rewriting her memory, a recurring theme throughout the film. The film is a layered selection of moments and memories: Cisely waits at home for her adored father, their mother is so nervous about his alleged philandering that she always cuts herself, and her aunt practices voodoo and can see everyone's future but her own. When Cisely goes into a deep depression, she tells Eve that it was because their father crossed the line when he kissed her after arriving home late one evening. Eve, in an effort to protect her mother and sister, seeks to make sense of everything and turns to the local voodoo lady to solve her family's problems. The film concludes without answering whether Dr. Batiste's tragic fate was of his own making or caused by the actions of his daughter.

This film demonstrates that there are so many ways of perceiving the same actions. Eve is confused about loyalty toward her father and her sister. How can she reconcile loving her father while knowing that he made wrong choices? Can someone be good and yet act immorally? She must also deal with feelings of guilt about being responsible for her father's death. Eve, in her own way, tries to resolve the wrongs committed by everyone in her family. *Eve's Bayou* implies that there is more than one reality, more than one way of interpreting the same event, as everything is experienced through the eye of the beholder. Therefore, it is best not to act on hunches because often, the truth is not what it seems. This movie provides an opportunity to discuss how people in your family could have different memories about the same event.

Discussion Questions:

- How did Eve's awareness of her father's affair affect her moral choices?
- How did her awareness of her father's affair change the way she felt about him?
- How hard is it to love someone in the same way when you know that they have made wrong choices?
- How did Eve's relationship with her mother and her sister change as a result of her newfound knowledge?
- What do you think of Aunt Mozelle? Do you believe people can have special powers?
- Do you think that Eve had special powers of her own?
- What led to Eve's decision to get back at her father and get the voodoo lady to kill him? Do you think she made the right moral choice?
- Was it right to go to the voodoo lady? Was it right to go to Mr. Morrow and hint to him about her father's affair with his wife?
- What—or who—really killed Louis Batiste? Was it voodoo, his

actions, the jealousy of Mr. Morrow, or Eve?

- Did Eve really want her father to die?
- Who was the most moral person in this film and why?

Pointer:

How difficult is it to make really good choices? Discuss with your child the importance of collecting the most information before making important life decisions. Eve didn't have all the information before she made her decision. She was searching for the truth, but only got the truth according to her damaged sister. Know where all your sources are coming from before you make any important decisions. Discuss a situation where different family members had very different interpretations of the same event. Why does that happen?

Chapter 18

"You think of yourself as a colored man. I think of myself as a man."
— Dr. John Prentice, *Guess Who's Coming To Dinner*

Prejudice and Diversity

Prejudice is a negative outgrowth of the normal process of learning about the similarities and differences between groups of people. Unfortunately, once we have a clear idea of who we are, the concept of who we are not often converts differences between groups into negative stereotypes. Prejudice also stems from our everyday frustrations: When negative things happen to us, we look to blame something or someone. We often rely on cultural, racial, religious, or ethnic differences to explain why something negative has occurred. Teenagers are incredibly sensitive to being different, and in the process of discovering where they fit in, strong feelings of resentment and anger may create prejudices toward certain groups.

As adolescents begin to discover, fantasize, and experiment with sexuality, their fears and frustrations over not fitting society's views about what is "feminine" or "masculine" sometimes produce displaced anger toward anyone who does not fit society's definition of "normal" sexual behavior. Spending time in the classroom, on sports teams, in summer camp, or just hanging out in the neighborhood offers situations where teens' limited beliefs are challenged, where they learn that all people are unique and that differences can actually enrich their lives. Through increased experiences with members of different groups, they will eventually come to understand that when it comes to our need for love, respect, and appreciation, all people have the same basic needs.

Unfortunately, one problem with films that address racism and prejudice is that in order to make a strong point, the character who represents the minority tends to be too perfect. For example, David in *School Ties* and Dr. John Prentice in *Guess Who's Coming To Dinner* are incredibly smart, likeable, handsome and talented individuals, almost to the point of perfection. This perfection undermines the very point that even if David weren't the perfect student, or Dr. Prentice the perfect fiancé, they should still be judged by the same standards as everyone else. As parents, you should be aware of this and inform your children accordingly.

In addition to showing how certain people handle the prejudice they encounter, such as David Greene in *School Ties,* films also introduce us to a world with which we are not familiar. By watching films, we can immerse ourselves in another culture: We learn about the plight of the American Indians in *Dances With Wolves;* we can understand the struggle of a homosexual man looking for love in *Torch Song Trilogy,* or we see the breakdown of a racially mixed neighborhood in *Do the Right Thing.*

Recognizing Prejudice in Ourselves and in Others

Gaining an understanding of our own prejudices requires the ability to monitor our thoughts and feelings when we become angry or frustrated. The nasty things we say to ourselves when someone of the opposite sex or another race or ethnicity cuts us off while driving are part of our prejudices and stereotypes. Being aware of the many ways—both insignificant and meaningful—that we stereotype others and make prejudiced assumptions, is the first step in trying to eliminate those beliefs. African-Americans, Italians, Jews, and Asians are all equally stereotyped in one of the most humorous and powerful scenes of *Do the Right Thing*.

Deciding Whether to Assimilate the Beliefs of One's Family Background

As teenagers develop their own set of values separate from those of their parents, they may feel the need to reject the religion, traditions, or culture in which they were raised. For example, teens often try to fit in by taking on the values and morals of their friends, creating conflict with parents who are more inclined to maintain their own cultural and religious practices. This is part of the growing process; it is important to respect the views and practices of your teen, even when they contradict or differ from your own cultural or religious beliefs. In *Guess Who's Coming To Dinner*, Joanna has seemingly rejected her family background by choosing to marry an African-American man. Ironically, we learn that her family considers themselves to be extremely liberal and open minded, and raised her to be who she is.

Confronting Prejudice in Constructive Ways

It is possible to unlearn distorted perceptions in order to become more intimate with other people. In *School Ties*, Jack Connors admits to believing negative stereotypes about Jews, but is also open-minded enough to realize that David Greene goes against every stereotype he has ever heard. Monitoring ourselves when we say things helps us realize how foolish or silly those comments are, especially as you spend time with people you like and respect and get to know them better. It also requires the ability to distance oneself from friends or family members who make racist comments, and to reject such behaviors.

Understanding and Respecting Alternative Lifestyles

Perhaps one of the hardest things for teenagers to deal with are differences in sexual orientation or alternative lifestyles. As a teen's sexual identity develops, her own insecurities often create fears and anxieties concerning sexual differences in others. Usually violence directed at homosexuals, such as the violence that killed Arnold's lover, Alan, in *Torch Song Trilogy*, results from people's insecurities regarding their own sexuality. The person who is relatively secure about herself sexually tends to be the most understanding and respectful toward those leading alternative lifestyles.

School Ties

David Greene, a bright, likeable Jewish teen from a small town accepts a football scholarship to the prestigious prep school St. Andrew's, where he will be the ringer quarterback for their football team. David quickly becomes part of a privileged group of seniors who all face pressures from their families to be accepted by Ivy League schools and carry on the family tradition. But in order to do so, he must remain quiet about his religion and endure racist remarks about Jews. Charlie Dillon, a friend of David's, struggles to live up to the academic and athletic standards set by his older brother. When Charlie finds out that David is Jewish and is dating his long-time girlfriend, Sally, he becomes enraged. In his anger, he turns everyone against David and frames him in a cheating scandal.

This film shows how anger and jealousy can ignite into full-fledged anti-Semitism. Like other films such as *Dead Poets Society, School Ties* explores how the enormous expectations placed on students by their parents can drive them to extreme actions like cheating, or in the case of one student terrorized by a French teacher, suffering an emotional breakdown. Most of the boys at St. Andrew's have internalized their parents' anti-Semitic views, allowing them to feel justified using David as a scapegoat. But some students— Charlie Dillon in particular—are motivated more by their own anger. Most of the boys in this film have never actually met—let alone become friends with— someone Jewish. Several of them are mature enough to confront their own prejudiced perceptions. They compare their previous notions of Jews with their experience of knowing David Greene, and they are able to see the error in their thinking. This film poses the question of whether David's end (a ticket to Harvard) justifies the means (hiding his religion).

Discussion Questions:

- Should David have told people at St. Andrew's that he was Jewish from the beginning? Was withholding his religion as bad as lying? How would you have handled yourself in David's situation?
- To what lengths would you go to be accepted if you were a minority or an outsider like David?
- Does the end justify the means? Was it worth it for him to hide his identity to go to this school?
- Was it right for the school to "buy" David as quarterback for the football team?
- How do you think you would handle a situation in which people were making negative remarks about your religion, ethnicity, etc.?
- Why did some of the boys resort to prejudice and use David as a scapegoat, while others were willing to simply see him as a person?
- Why do you think it is so difficult for people to handle racial, religious, or ethnic differences between each other?
- Why was Sally so willing to end her relationship with David upon learning that he was Jewish? Was she really angry that he had withheld his identity from her, or was she being anti-Semitic?
- Do you think the film made David too perfect? How would it have changed things if David weren't so likeable, smart, and athletic?
- Do you think Charlie Dillon will change from this experience?
- How did this experience change David? What did he learn?
- Why do you think the committee decided he cheated? Did they really think that he cheated or were they just using him as a scapegoat because he was Jewish?

Pointer:

Discuss the extent to which friends and peers can disclose their religion, ethnicity, race, or cultural background. Share with them your experience—current or past—of a time in which you were an outsider or a minority. Or perhaps there was a situation in which you were the insider and acted with prejudice toward someone. What did you learn from that experience?

Torch Song Trilogy

Arnold, known as Virginia Hamm on stage, is a quirky, homosexual entertainer searching for a somewhat traditional romantic relationship in a world that does not accept him. Based on the long-running play by Harvey Fierstein, who also wrote the screenplay and stars in the film, *Torch Song Trilogy* is divided into three separate but connected vignettes. In the first, Arnold expresses his desire for true love, and we see his difficulties trying to find that with Ed Reese, a bisexual who is not comfortable embracing the gay lifestyle or admitting to his family and friends that he likes men. In the second part, Arnold finally finds commitment, companionship, and true love in a young model named Alan. The two move in together and plan to adopt a child when Alan is killed on the street by gay bashers. In the last part, Arnold has adopted a homosexual teenage son and must simultaneously deal with Ed, who has returned to express his love, and a visit from his opinionated mother, who fails to accept her son's homosexuality.

During the course of the film, Arnold slowly becomes more comfortable with himself as a man and as a homosexual. As we follow Arnold's journey toward self-acceptance, we realize that this film is not as much about a society that doesn't accept gays as it is about a man who has trouble accepting himself. *Torch Song Trilogy* can initiate a discussion about the pre-AIDS world of gay men living in New York and educate us about its similarities with the heterosexual dating world. Arnold opposes the stereotype that homosexual men avoid commitment, are promiscuous, and don't want romantic relationships. *Torch Song Trilogy* illustrates the problems that can occur when someone doesn't adopt the lifestyle of his family and how people can come to accept alternative lifestyles by seeing universal similarities in all of our struggles.

Discussion Questions:

- What kind of relationship does Arnold want? How does being gay affect Arnold's ability to get what he wants out of a relationship?
- What was the problem between Arnold and Ed? How was Ed different from Arnold?
- What do you think of the way Ed tries to keep his homosexual and heterosexual lives separate?
- What kind of relationship do Arnold and Alan have? Do you know

any gay people who are in committed, long-term relationships? Are gay relationships different from heterosexual ones?

- Who betrayed whom up in the mountains? Did Ed betray Arnold or did Alan betray Arnold?
- How did Alan satisfy Arnold's desire for a long-term relationship?
- Why do you think it is so difficult for parents to accept a child who is gay?
- Why is Arnold's mother resistant to accepting her son's gay lifestyle? Why does Arnold's mother get so angry when he says the mourner's prayer at Alan's gravesite?
- Do Arnold and his mother resolve anything at the end of the film? How does their shared experience of losing a loved one make them closer?
- How do you think the film ends? Does Arnold get what he wants? What does the last scene mean when he gathers various items, sits down, and hugs them to himself?

Pointer:

Discuss the issue of homosexuality and how homosexual individuals are perceived in your community. Share stories about friends, family, or acquaintances who are homosexual and what types of difficulties they face from society. If you or your teen is homosexual, what kinds of problems must your family face as a result? Talk about how things have changed over the years in terms of society's tolerance of homosexuality. The most important thing to emphasize is that regardless of race, religion, or sexual orientation, all individuals should be treated with respect.

Dances With Wolves

After accidentally becoming a hero while attempting to end his life during a Civil War battle, Union army lieutenant John Dunbar requests to be stationed at the westernmost post, Fort Sedgwick, to experience the American frontier before it is gone. At first, he is awed by the beauty of nature surrounding him. Then, as Lieutenant Dunbar encounters the Indians, he slowly learns that they are not the uncivilized brutes they have been made out to be. Among the members of the nomadic Sioux tribe he befriends are Kicking Bird, a spiritual leader; Wind in His Hair, a fearless warrior; and Stands With a Fist, a White woman who was raised by the Sioux when her family was killed by the Pawnee tribe. The film follows Lieutenant John Dunbar's transformation as he assimilates into the Sioux community and becomes Dances with Wolves.

This film shows us how stereotypes and prejudices are often part of our culture; when we are alienated from that culture and immersed in another, only then can we understand and appreciate the other. Only by disassociating himself from the Union army and all that goes along with it could Lieutenant Dunbar realize the harmony, love, and resourcefulness that characterize the Sioux Indians. Just as jealousy is a breeding ground for prejudice, so is any threat to a human's basic need for food, shelter, and land. While the Union and Confederate armies fought over such issues in the Civil War, the Sioux and the Pawnee Indians were fighting for the same basic needs, demonstrating that despite such obvious differences in culture and language, deep down our common humanity surpasses ethnicity or race.

Discussion Questions:

- How did John come to understand his own culture's prejudices? What were some of the prejudices or misconceptions about American Indians? How did they develop?
- Were the Sioux prejudiced against the White man?
- What do you think about how the film portrayed the Pawnee Indians?
- How did John Dunbar and the Sioux overcome their initial prejudices toward each other?
- What was the significance of Two Socks, the wolf?
- How did conflict between the Indian tribes parallel the conflicts of the Civil War?
- What have you been taught about American Indians? Do you know any? How else could the White men have dealt with the Indians as they settled on the frontier?
- What was the symbolism of American soldiers wanting to kill the wolf?

- What is the state of American Indians today? What kinds of stereotypes still exist?

Pointer:

Discuss the ideas of genocide and ethnic cleansing. How can prejudices affect governmental policy? Compare the treatment of American Indians to the Holocaust or to slavery. What other parallels exist? What has happened in the news recently that addresses the same issues?

Do the Right Thing

This film is set in a predominantly African-American neighborhood in Brooklyn on the hottest day of the year. The action unfolds around Sal's Famous Pizzeria, a local landmark, owned and operated for twenty years by a likeable Italian-American who takes pride in his restaurant. When Buggin Out, a frequent customer and angry activist, notices that Sal's Wall of Fame features only Italian-American celebrities, he demands that Sal have some African-Americans represented on the wall. Sal refuses, and Buggin Out enlists the help of Radio Raheem to organize a boycott of the pizzeria. Mookie, a long-time pizza delivery boy for Sal's, is African-American, and is torn between his loyalty to his neighborhood pals and his need to keep his job. When Sal asks Radio Raheem to turn off his boom box, an all-out riot occurs. Anger and racial tension boil out of control, resulting in violence, police brutality, the destruction of Sal's Famous Pizzeria, and a total upset of the delicate racial balance that existed for so long in the neighborhood.

This film explores the underlying problems that exist in a racially diverse neighborhood, and how when that balance is upset, the results can be catastrophic. We are never really sure where the filmmaker, Spike Lee, stands on the issue, although it is clear that he concerned with addressing the problem. Whether the solution is to be found in the teachings of Martin Luther King, Jr., who advocated non-violent direct action and passive resistance, or of Malcolm X, who believed that violence, when performed in self-defense, was justified, is left for the audience to decide. *Do the Right Thing* explores the present-day state of race relations in this country without taking a definitive stance on the solution. Mookie must choose whether or not to assimilate the values and beliefs of his neighborhood or those of his employer in an environment where doing "the right thing" is anything but clear.

Discussion Questions:

- Do you think Buggin Out had a right to request that Sal have African-Americans represented on the wall? Do you think Sal should have done what he asked?
- How did the different races manage to coexist in the beginning of the film?
- How did Buggin Out upset the balance that existed in their neighborhood?
- Was Sal a racist? How about his son Pino? How were they different?
- What was the conflict between Pino and Mookie?
- Why was Mookie upset over Sal's feelings toward Jade?
- What did Da Mayor and Mother Sister represent to the African-American community?
- What kind of racial issues existed in Mookie's relationship with his girlfriend Tina?
- Who is to blame for Radio Raheem's death?
- What did the pizzeria mean to Sal?
- What do you think will happen to this community?
- What do Malcolm X and Martin Luther King, Jr. represent? How are they alike and different? With whom do you agree?

Pointer:

Mookie is torn between his loyalty to Sal and to his neighborhood friends. Discuss with your teen what types of situations you have been in where your loyalties were tested. Within what two groups were you struggling to maintain a balance? What choice did you make, and do you think it was the right thing? What types of situations have placed you in racially mixed arenas? What types of issues came up and how were they resolved?

Guess Who's Coming To Dinner

Joanna Drayton is the beloved 23-year-old daughter of two wealthy, liberal, socially conscious parents. But when she returns from Hawaii with an African-American fiancé, their beliefs are put to the test. Her fiancé, Dr. John Prentice, in addition to being Black, is every parent's dream: handsome, well-educated, polite, respectful, highly-successful in his career, and he makes their daughter happier than she's ever been. But it is 1967, and interracial marriage is still illegal in several states, so Joanna's and John's parents have a difficult time accepting their childrens' decisions. Everything comes to a head at dinner when Mr. Drayton must decide whether or not to give his approval for their marriage.

This film explores an issue that was especially controversial in the sixties, but is still relevant today: interracial marriage. *Guess Who's Coming To Dinner* confronts the idea of struggling with your own prejudice by showing characters who are likeable, open-minded, and relatively liberal having to live up to what they say they believe. The Draytons aren't so much distraught over their daughter's choice to marry a Black man as they are concerned about how the rest of society will react to this interracial couple. We get glimpses of this from Mrs. Drayton's nosy business partner Hilary, who reacts with shock and rudeness, and from the Drayton's long-time African-American maid and honorary family member, Tillie, who is disapproving of a "colored man tryin' to get above himself." This film shows how even the most liberal peoples' beliefs are challenged when an issue hits closer to home, and it provides an interesting opportunity to discuss racial relations today and how they have evolved from the late sixties.

Discussion Questions:

- What were the different reactions to the interracial couple?
- Tillie said she didn't care to see a man of her race "gettin' above himself." What did she mean by that?
- Why was Monsignor Ryan so accepting of the couple?
- Why did Dr. Prentice hesitate to tell his parents that Joanna was White?
- Was it noble of Dr. Prentice to ask for Joanna's parents' approval?
- What were Mr. Drayton's concerns with the two getting married? Were his concerns justified?
- How would the Draytons have reacted to a less educated, less

handsome, less prestigious African-American man?

- How did Joanna's and Dr. John Prentice's mothers' perspectives toward their engagement differ from those of the fathers?
- Did John owe his father anything for having sacrificed all those years to provide for him?
- What finally made Mr. Drayton decide to support the marriage?
- Do you think people today are more tolerant of interracial or interfaith marriages? Do you know of any interracial or interfaith marriages in your family or community?
- What is the difference between interracial and interfaith marriages? Which one is more easily accepted?
- How do you feel about marrying someone of a different race or religion? How do you think your parents would react if you were engaged to someone of a different religion, ethnicity, or race?
- What kind of problems or obstacles do you think Joanna and John will encounter during their marriage? How could they overcome them?

Pointer:

Discuss your stance on interracial or interfaith marriages. Parents need to explore and be aware of their own prejudices before having a discussion with their children, otherwise there is a danger of alienating the teen. Be respectful of differences of opinions and, if necessary, simply agree to disagree. Talk about some of the problems that could occur in interracial and mixed-religion marriages. Discuss how you feel about raising your children: Do you expect them to adopt the same religion as you, or would you be open to an interfaith marriage?

Chapter 19

"Dying's a really hard way to learn about life."
— Bob Jones, My Life

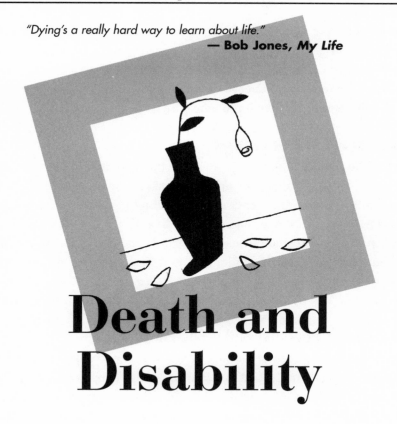

Death and Disability

The biggest mistake parents often make when it comes to discussing disability, sickness, and death with their children is that in trying to protect them, they often avoid the issues altogether. It is so important that parents encourage their teen to discuss her feelings, her fears, her anger, and her grief, whether she is coping with the death of a loved one, or with a serious illness or physical disability. Unlike other issues such as drugs or unwanted pregnancy, there is little parents can do to protect their teen from feelings of loss, but there is a great deal they can do to help her deal with it. At some point, we all must learn to accept these things as a part of our growth as human beings.

The films in this chapter show the triumph of the human spirit over adversity— people getting past their pain and anger, and somehow being stronger because of it. Try to watch some of these films and begin your dialogue about the issue at hand before it happens. The sooner your family begins to communicate with each other about these issues, the sooner your family will be able to move on in a healthy way.

Experiencing Stages of Grief

Grief is the natural response to a loss. While avoiding it postpones the inevitable sorrow, clinging to grief prolongs the pain. Although everybody's journey toward acceptance and healing is different, some of the basic elements are shock, emotional upheaval, physical distress, guilt, hostility, depression, aimlessness, hope, and finally, reaffirmation of life. It is important that each individual's pattern be respected, allowing them to move to each phase at their own pace. *Truly, Madly, Deeply* shows a woman going through many stages of grief after the death of her lover.

Developing a Personal Belief System to Cope

Teens may no longer accept at face value what their religious or cultural upbringing has taught them about why bad things happen to good people. They are likely to examine the situation more deeply and seek explanations that attempt to deal with such issues. When teens scrutinize or challenge concepts that their parents have used to bring them comfort, it can lead to conflict within the family. Parents should respect their teen's belief system and unique way of dealing with a loss or handicap.

Impact on Different Family Members and Survivor Guilt

When accidents occur that result in handicaps or death, the way parents deal with these events obviously has significant consequences for the whole family. It is important that the accident is seen as no one's fault and that no blame is assigned. The incident should be openly discussed and feelings should be vented so that healing can begin. If these processes do not take place, individual family members may carry around unnecessary feelings of blame, guilt, and anger for the rest of their lives, overshadowing all future family and life experiences.

Forgiving, Overcoming, and Growing

Forgiveness is the process of letting go and releasing painful emotional feelings like hatred, anger, or hurt. As the Chinese doctor tells Bob Jones in *My Life*, preoccupation with those negative thoughts and feelings prevents us from experiencing life to the fullest and perpetuates a feeling of helplessness or victimization. When we don't forgive, we cut people off emotionally in order to protect ourselves from future loss. Forgiveness can be a verbal, face-to-face interaction, or it can be a mental state. But after the long process of forgiving ourselves for putting ourselves in a position of vulnerability and making our own mistakes, we can move on and allow ourselves to have faith in others again. Teens must learn to forgive themselves, their friends, and their family members so that the entire family can approach the process of grieving without anger and living without unnecessary hostility.

Mask

Mask is the true story of a young man named Rocky Dennis who suffers from craniodiaphyseal dysphasia, a bone disease that leaves his face severely disfigured. Despite his physical deformity, Rocky is a remarkable, intellectually gifted, and extremely likeable high school teen. His single mother Rusty and her Harley Davidson gang serve as Rocky's surrogate family as they move from town to town. Despite a wavering drug problem, when it comes to her son, Rusty is a consistently proud and devoted mother who refuses to listen to the negative doctors who've been giving him only months to live since he was four. As an adolescent, Rocky craves emotional and physical intimacy. He becomes frustrated by the limitations associated with his physical handicap. Working at a summer camp for the blind provides him with an opportunity to find a girlfriend, Diana, and the two help each other overcome their handicaps.

This film demonstrates how an individual's character can allow him to triumph over his physical limitations. Rocky's humor, intelligence, and compassion make him likeable to everyone from the school jock to the principal to his mother's tough biker friends. He lives his life to the fullest and with the help of his mom, uses disassociation, a non-traditional approach to pain management, to manage his excruciating headaches. Concerned about his mother's drug use, Rocky demonstrates some of the common fears and behavioral patterns that exist in single-parent homes. In addition to Rocky's struggles, we also see some of the challenges faced by his blind girlfriend Diana, and his loyal motorcycle friend who does not speak. Although the disease eventually kills Rocky, the manner in which he chose to live his life shows his victory over it.

Discussion Questions:

- How difficult do you think it is for children with disabilities to adjust to new people and new situations?
- How does Rocky handle people's negative reactions to his face?
- In what ways is Rusty a good parent to Rocky? In what ways is she a bad parent?
- How do normal high school events such as the prom affect Rocky's perception of himself?
- What is revealed when Rocky brings up plastic surgery to his mom?
- Why was Rocky going away to summer camp such a significant thing to do? How did he grow and change as a result of that? How was Rusty forced to change with Rocky away?
- How do Diana and Rocky help each other deal with their physical handicaps?
- In the poem that Rocky wrote, he lists the sun as both something he likes and dislikes. What is the significance of this?
- What were Diana's parents' prejudices against Rocky? Why didn't they want their daughter to date him?
- What do you think will happen to Rusty now that Rocky is gone?

Pointer:

Have a discussion with your teen about what it must be like to raise a handicapped child and whether you think handicapped students should be mixed with mainstream students, or be in special schools that cater to their needs. Share what experiences you have each had with either physically or mentally disabled people.

One True Thing

Ellen Gulden is a Harvard-educated young reporter who lives in New York. She idolizes her father, George, a college English professor and award-winning novelist, and feels she has nothing in common with her mother, Kate, a happy homemaker, doting wife, and supportive mother to Ellen and her brother. But when Kate is diagnosed with cancer, George asks Ellen to move back to small-town suburbia to take care of her mother. As Ellen takes over her mother's role—preparing meals, cleaning the house, and planning community holiday events—she learns some harsh truths about her not-so-perfect family. As she watches her mother die, Ellen finally begins to appreciate her, and she is forced to confront the rude awakening that her father is unfaithful and flawed.

This film shows how a family member's sickness can expose the dysfunction of any family. Sickness can upset its balance by accentuating both its underlying problems and its strengths. When Ellen is forced to take care of her dying mother, for the first time she begins to identify with her, finally seeing her father's weaknesses and learning to respect her mother's strength and beauty. Her mother's imminent death forces Ellen to finally listen to her mother when she tells her that it is so much easier "to love the things that you have." This film provides an opportunity to discuss how a death in the family can change its dynamic and how each person deals differently with that loss. Kate's sickness brings Ellen closer to her and actually changes who she is as a person, and how she will live the rest of her life.

Discussion Questions:

- How would you feel about having to take care of a parent if one got really sick?
- How did having to take care of her mother bring Ellen closer to her?
- Was it fair for Ellen's father to expect her to move back home to take care of her mother? Why couldn't he help out?
- How are Ellen and her mother different? How are Ellen and her dad similar?
- What kind of a person is George, Ellen's dad? How did Ellen's view of him change when she lived at home?
- What did it indicate about Ellen when she told her boss at the magazine that she never got the interview with the politician,

when she really did speak to him?

- How did the process of caring for Kate change Ellen's priorities and values?
- How difficult do you think it is to be so close to someone while you're watching them die?
- How do you think Kate got the extra pills?
- How did George deal with his pain? How did Ellen deal with her pain? What kind of relationship do you think Ellen and her father will have now that her mother is gone?
- What would you have done in Ellen's situation—would you have assisted your parent in her own death if you knew it was imminent and she asked you to?
- How do you think this family will operate differently now that Kate has died? How do they make amends?

Pointer:

Explore the impact of death and sickness on your family relationships. How would a death change things? How would the family function? Who would take care of whom? Discuss with your child what families you know who have endured sickness or loss, and how that shed light on their relationships or upset the balance. Talk about the controversial issue of assisted suicide and whether or not you agree with this concept.

Children of a Lesser God

Children of a Lesser God is a love story between Jim Leeds, the speech and language teacher at a school for the deaf, and Sarah, an angry, intelligent young woman who works as a janitor there. Jim falls in love with Sarah and begins to break down some of the defenses she's built over years of loneliness and anger. Sarah often uses sex to connect with Jim, further complicating the difficulties in a relationship between a hearing man and a deaf woman. The recurring conflict in their relationship is that Jim feels Sarah should learn to read lips and speak phonetically, while Sarah has resigned herself to a world of sign language and silence.

This film explores the difficulty that exists between two people in a relationship where one is disabled and the other is not. In order to be truly connected, they must find a common ground on which to communicate—not in Jim's world of sound, nor in Sarah's world of silence. Part of loving someone completely requires understanding and respecting the way she experiences the world. This movie shows the difficulties that can arise in families when a child is deaf; we learn that Sarah's father was unable to accept his daughter's disability, and that Sarah's mother has always blamed her for driving him away. This film asks the question—is love enough to connect two people from such different worlds?

Discussion Questions:

- Do you think you could ever be married to a person with a disability?
- Why is Sarah hesitant to learn how to speak?
- Why is Sarah so angry in the beginning of the film?
- What attracted Jim to Sarah?
- What kind of a teacher is Jim? How does he help his students talk?
- What does Sarah think the problem with their relationship is? Why does she leave Jim?
- Why was Sarah so promiscuous with hearing boys when she was younger? What was she trying to gain?
- Why did Sarah leave her mother? Why did Sarah go back to her mother?
- What was the problem with Jim and Sarah's relationship? What happened at the party that caused the breakup?
- What was the significance of the underwater scenes?
- Do you think that Sarah should have tried to learn to speak and read lips, or do you think that she had a right to her silence and that Jim should have respected that?
- How did Sarah grow when she lived with her mother? How did their relationship change or improve?

Pointer:

Discuss how hard you think it would be to be in a relationship with someone who is deaf. Share with each other whom you know who is deaf or disabled. How does that person function in the world? What kinds of technology help him communicate or function in his day-to-day life? For example, now voice-simulated computers can help deaf people communicate with hearing people.

Truly, Madly, Deeply

Since her lover Jamie's recent death, Nina has been living alone in a new house, paralyzed by grief and virtually non-functioning at work. Nina tells her therapist that she still hears his voice reminding her to lock the door or do other mundane things. One day while playing the piano, the cello accompanies her music, and suddenly Jamie is there for Nina to see, talk to, and touch. The two of them transcend reality by hiding away in the house, and for some time Nina is happy again, although she must separate herself from reality to exist with Jamie. Eventually, her beloved's return from the dead presents problems. She must chose between the love of her past and the possibilities of life that lie before her.

This film is about the process of loss and grieving. Willed by Nina's pain and longing, Jamie's return permits her to experience the stages of grief. As a ghost, Jamie allows Nina to be with him again, to express her love for him, even remember some things about him that annoyed her, and finally, actually grants her mental permission to love another and move on with her life. *Truly, Madly, Deeply* is the quintessential film about the grieving process, and provokes a discussion about loss on many different levels.

Discussion Questions:

- How healthy is Nina at the beginning of the film? Can you relate to how Nina feels?
- Is Jamie a figment of her imagination or is he real? Did he come back on his own or did Nina will him back?
- How is Nina affected by witnessing the birth of her friend's baby?
- What is the purpose of Jamie's dead friends? Why is Jamie always too cold and Nina always too hot?
- What triggered Nina's reemergence into the world of the living?
- What is the significance of the title *Truly, Madly, Deeply*?

- How does Nina finally come to the decision to put Jamie to rest?
- How does meeting Mark make her choose between her past and her present?

Pointer:

Discuss the grieving process with your teenager. What happens to people when they have lost their loved ones? Have a discussion about loss, whether it's the loss of a pet, a grandparent, or a close family member. While people typically take six months to a year to grieve, everyone's timeline for grieving is different, and that process needs to be respected. Share stories about people you know who have had to grow through the grieving process and the different ways in which they handled it.

My Life

Bob Jones is a successful public relations professional in Los Angeles, whose beautiful wife Gail is four months pregnant. Unfortunately, he has also been diagnosed with inoperable cancer and has been given only a few months to live. In anticipation of the birth of his son, Bob begins the process of videotaping his life, trying to introduce his unborn son to the father he'll never know. Using his camera as a conduit for communication, Bob gains a better understanding of who he was, where he came from, and who he is now. A Chinese healer advises Bob to let go of his anger and fear so that he can find peace. In doing this, Bob resolves important issues with his estranged family in Detroit and becomes closer to his wife. As he tells his baby boy once he is born, the process of dying has taught him about the value of living.

This film explores the growth and appreciation for life that can result from a person's anticipation of his own death. Bob Jones finds comfort in the healer's prescription to let go of his anger and embrace forgiveness toward his family and himself. Bob goes through the four stages of dying, first denying his sickness, becoming angry, learning to accept his situation, and then finally finding peace and comfort in the birth of his son and the unconditional support of his family.

Discussion Questions:

- How do you think it would feel to be told you have only three months to live? What would you want to do?
- In the beginning of the film, how does Bob handle his sickness? How does he feel about his wife's pregnancy?
- What did the interviews with Bob's coworkers tell him about himself and how they perceived him?
- What do you think about healers or other alternative and experimental types of medicine? How can they help you cope effectively?
- Why couldn't Bob work through his feelings with his parents when he went to visit them?
- What did outliving the doctor's predictions mean to him?
- What kinds of things would you want to resolve or forgive if you knew you were dying?
- What is the significance of the circus wish Bob made when he was little?
- How does Bob change throughout the film?
- How does making the videos help his emotional/mental state?
- What did the healer mean about letting go of his anger? Do you believe in alternative medicine? Do you know anybody who has gotten help or been treated from acupuncture, hypnotism, etc.?
- How does letting go of his anger affect his relationship with his wife, his brother, and his parents?

Pointer:

Discuss the issue of forgiveness. Holding on to anger and pain is the biggest obstacle in getting through loss. What issues does your family need to forgive each other for? Share with your child what it feels like to lose someone. Have you ever had to forgive someone who died? How did forgiving help you?

Chapter 20

"I'd like to know what law it is that says that a woman is a better parent simply by virtue of her sex . . . .that says that a woman has a corner on that market, that a man has any less of those emotions than a woman does."

— Ted Kramer, *Kramer Vs. Kramer*

Divorce and Single Parents

In the biggest study of the effects of divorce on children, Wallerstein and Kelly (1980) found that the vast majority of children did not want to see their parents live apart from each other, even in homes where there was extreme fighting and violence. With this in mind, dealing with a divorce or a single-parent situation can present a lot of problems. Children of separated or divorced parents tend to feel a pervasive sense of loss over the split of their once-intact nuclear family, anxiety that their basic needs will not be attended to, rejection by one or both parents, loneliness, and a belief that the world has become uncertain and unpredictable. Two-thirds of the children longed for the absent father, had anger directed at the absent father, and experienced conflicting loyalties. Two-thirds of the parents studied competed for the children's affection and allegiance.

Teenagers tended to express anger when their parents began dating, as it triggered feelings of jealousy and competition, and tested their loyalties to the other parent. They also felt anxiety about whether the breakup foreshadowed failure in their own relationships. Like the youngest children, many adolescents experienced a deep sense of loss. They reported feelings of emptiness, troubled dreams, difficulty concentrating, and chronic fatigue. These symptoms of mourning reflect grief experienced as a result of the lost family of childhood.

Despite all the negative things associated with divorce, there are some positive things that can come from it, too. It can serve as a catalyst for a child's maturity, causing them to take on more household responsibilities, such as helping with the care of younger siblings and displaying increased sensitivity in their relationships. As in the case of Ted Kramer and his son Billy in *Kramer Vs. Kramer*, divorce may also help a relationship by creating more quality time between a parent and child.

Preventing Triangulation

Every child has a separate level of emotional intimacy with each parent that contributes to his or her identity and value system. Divorce challenges that intimacy, affecting how loyal or intimate a child remains with each parent. In *Stepmom*, Anna's loyalties toward her mother are challenged when she has to accept her father's new wife in her family. It is critical that parents do not triangulate their children by attempting to "win" more of their emotional intimacy. As demonstrated in *Irreconcilable Differences*, parents will often put down their ex-spouse and his or her new romantic partner in front of their children, causing the other parent to feel less important in their child's life and exposing their child to unnecessary hostility. Parents should never pull their children in different directions.

Cutting Off Emotionally From One or Both Parents

If one parent starts to feel a child pull away from her emotionally, it may cause that parent to have less contact with that child and send the misleading or unwanted message that a relationship is no longer wanted or valued. This can cause children to emotionally "cut off" parents in order to protect their own self-esteem. Unfortunately, this process is very damaging to all involved because of the constant anger and hurt it generates within the family. In *Irreconcilable Differences*, both of Casey's parents take turns essentially neglecting her needs, causing her to cut off both parents emotionally in an effort to protect herself from future hurt.

Single-Parent Issues

Whether caused by separation, divorce, or the death of a spouse, a single-parent household often does not have the financial resources or emotional energy to maintain the same standard of living that the family was accustomed to. As seen in *Men Don't Leave*, a parent's financial and emotional resources may be so drained that she becomes severely depressed, has no time for her own social life, and loosens her discipline. Out of guilt for not being able to sustain the same quality of family life, single parents tend to loosen their discipline, causing behavioral or academic difficulties for their children.

Kramer Vs. Kramer

Ted Kramer is a busy advertising executive who barely has time for his wife and five-year-old son, Billy. When his wife Joanna walks out on them, he is forced to care for his son alone, and transforms from a distant, insensitive father to a loving, patient one. He finally realizes that fatherhood is a more important, more challenging, and more rewarding job than any job he could have in advertising. After a year, two problems arise: Ted, whose priorities have clearly changed, loses his job, and his ex-wife returns, fighting to regain custody of their son. The Kramers go through a nasty custody trial and the judge chooses Joanna over Ted. Eventually, the Kramers reach a different decision on their own for the good of their son.

This film explores both the positive and negative aspects of divorce, and demonstrates the dramatic effect it has on the parent-child relationship. Being a single parent forces Ted to become a better father, as he becomes more involved in his son's life and more sensitive to his needs. He also begins to reassess his values and realizes that his job as a parent is more important to him than his job in advertising. This film was one of the first to realistically address the issue of divorce and show a single-father custody arrangement rather than a single-mother one. It challenged the long-held belief amongst lawmakers and psychologists that a mother was always the best parent to raise a child or have custody. It also shows that despite anger, hurt, and negative feelings between spouses, the most important thing is keeping the child's best interests in mind. Billy's parents do not triangulate by putting him in the middle or turning him against a parent. The Kramers eventually put their problems aside, and make decisions based on what they believe will be best for their son.

Discussion Questions:

- Why did Joanna leave her son and husband? Do you know any parents who have been in similar situations?
- How did Ted feel about taking care of Billy in the beginning of the film? What kind of a father was he?
- Do you know any children who were raised by their fathers, or whose fathers had sole custody of them growing up?
- What was good about Ted's explanation to Billy of why his Mommy left?
- How does divorce upset the balance between work and family? How does Ted become more sensitive to Billy's needs throughout the film?
- How do Billy and Ted work through their problems?
- Why do children blame themselves for causing their parents to break up?
- What would you have done if you were the judge? What kind of alternative would there have been in this situation?
- Why does Joanna come back? Does she have the right to expect to get her son back?
- What do you think about the decision Ted and Joanna came to at the end of the film?

Pointer:

Discuss various custody options; if you are a divorced family, how does your teen feel about his custody situation? What would he do to change it? If you are not divorced, what kind of custody arrangement would he prefer? What do you think works best—single-parent custody or joint custody? Share what you think are the problems and benefits of each arrangement.

Men Don't Leave

When Beth's husband dies in a work-related accident, she is left alone to raise her two sons, seventeen-year-old Chris and ten-year-old Matt. The flood of debts and expenses forces her to sell their truck and suburban house. They have to move to a middle-class apartment complex in downtown Baltimore, where Beth gets a job in a gourmet food shop. Chris starts dating an older woman in their building and moves in with her, while Matt, determined to get money so that his family can move back home, starts stealing and selling VCRs, using the proceeds to buy lottery tickets. Beth dates an artsy, sensitive musician who is also a divorced father. When Beth realizes that she can no longer keep her family together, she delves into a deep depression, but emerges from her breakdown whole and healthy, aware that her family, though altered, is still there for her.

Men Don't Leave explores the difficulties that exist when a death or divorce forces a parent to reorganize the family situation. It shows the problems that many families face when there is a single mother who must keep her family running smoothly, make a living, and maintain some type of social life. Chris' resistance and hostility toward his new surroundings and his mother's boyfriend are indicative of many teenagers, especially boys, who have a difficult time respecting the new authority of their single mom and accepting their new social lives. Matt's jealousy of his friend whose parents are married and his longing to return to his old home where his own family was still intact is indicative of children from divorced or single-parent families. This film can open up a discussion about a single parent's attempt to reemerge from a tragedy as a whole, independent, competent parent who demands respect from her children. Beth's plea to her sons, "I need you guys to have faith in me," is a noble one, and by the film's conclusion, we see that she has regained their respect and that they do indeed have faith in her.

Discussion Questions:

- What would it be like to have your world turned around by the death of a parent?
- What kinds of struggles does the family have to face as a result of the father's death?
- What is Beth's new role and why does that pose problems in the family?
- How difficult is it for a single parent to balance their parental responsibilities with their responsibilities to be a provider?
- Why was Chris so angry about Charles coming into his life?
- What was Chris accomplishing by moving in with an older woman?
- Do you think Chris should have been allowed to move in with Jody?
- What caused Beth's breakdown? What was Beth trying to accomplish with "Family Night"? Does your family have anything like this and if so, does it work?
- How does Jody help pull Beth out of her self-destructive cycle?
- What was Matt trying to accomplish by running away to the club-house at his old house in Bingham?
- In what ways is Beth a new person at the end of the film?

Pointer:

Discuss how families often have to reorganize when one parent is no longer present. Talk about families you know that have had to function without one parent and what kinds of stress they have to face as a result of that. What are the difficulties for a single parent in maintaining authority, discipline, and also in pursuing her own interests or social life?

Stepmom

Jackie is a divorced, single mother to precocious, 12-year-old Anna and mischievous, seven-year-old Ben. She lives in the suburbs and her children adore her. They are less than thrilled about their father's girlfriend and soon-to-be-wife, Isabel, a young, successful, Manhattan photographer. Jackie is the perfect mother and despises Isabel, whom she thinks is irresponsible and selfish. But when Jackie is diagnosed with an untreatable form of cancer, she is forced to rely on Isabel to help her out with the children. She slowly gives her children permission to accept and like Isabel, as she comes to realize that Isabel will be the one to care for her children after she passes away. Isabel and Jackie slowly begin to respect each other, realizing that each one of them has something valuable and unique to offer the children.

This film shows the difficulties that arise with blended families. Anna and Ben don't like Isabel at first, partly because she is so different from their mother, and partly because they feel obligated to dislike her out of loyalty to their mother. Despite difficulties with the newly mixed family, the children' father, Luke, and Jackie do a pretty good job at communicating with each other and remaining an intact parental unit for their children, even though they are no longer married. Luke recognizes that in order to gain the children's approval of his marriage to Isabel, his ex-wife Jackie will need to lead the way. They also work together when it is time to tell the children about Jackie's cancer. Jackie struggles with the realization that after she is gone, Isabel will be the one raising her children. Jackie has to slowly learn to trust and accept Isabel, while Isabel has to endure tormenting from her stepchildren and respect the natural affinity and loyalty that they have for their mother. This film shows a divorced family in the process of incorporating a new person into the family structure, and discovering what the role of a stepmother should be; in this case it should be somewhere in between that of a birth mother and that of an older friend.

Discussion Questions:

- How do the children feel about Isabel in the beginning? How do Jackie's feelings toward Isabel affect her children's feelings toward Isabel?
- How hard is it to witness the relationship between a parent and his new romantic interest?
- Would you have been able to maintain your own opinion about a parent's spouse or would you look toward the other parent for validation?
- Why is it so difficult for Jackie to learn that her ex-husband is going to remarry?
- Why does Isabel take the blame for Jackie's being late to pick up the children?

- Why do you think Jackie tells Isabel she can't take Anna to the Pearl Jam concert, and then goes ahead and takes Anna herself?
- Why does Luke need Jackie's approval before telling the children that he's marrying Isabel?
- Why does Jackie begin to trust Isabel? How does her sickness affect their family situation?
- Was it right for Jackie to wait so long to tell the children that she had cancer?
- What are the differences in the ways Isabel and Jackie parent the children? Think about the advice that Jackie and Isabel give Anna about how to handle the boy at school. Which one do you think gave her better advice?
- Do you think Isabel is a good stepmother?
- What does the last scene show about the family?

Pointer:

Discuss whether you think Jackie's death will make it easier or more difficult for the children to accept their stepparent. Talk about whether it is possible for children to accept and develop a close relationship with their stepparent without betraying their love or commitment to their biological parent. Ask your children if any of their friends have "evil" stepparents, or if any of their friends are particularly close with a stepparent. If you are divorced, make sure your children understand that getting along and bonding with a stepparent does not mean they are being disloyal to the other parent.

Irreconcilable Differences

The film opens at the start of a court hearing, where nine-year-old Casey Brodsky is the youngest minor to divorce her parents on the grounds of "irreconcilable differences." The film traces the marriage of Lucy and Albert, who fell in love while driving across the country to pursue their dreams in California, but found that as their careers took off, their marriage began to crumble. Albert leaves Lucy for Blake, the young star of their hit film, and becomes an even bigger success while Lucy suffers as a single mom, gains weight, becomes depressed and struggles financially. It doesn't take long before the tables turn: Albert's third film flops, Blake leaves him, and he's forced to sell his mansion to Lucy, whose autobiographical book about her marriage is a bestseller. In the midst of all this, their daughter Casey is either used or simply neglected. Her loving housekeeper Maria, who is the only consistent parental figure she has, basically raises her.

This film is about adults who are so immersed in the anger and pain caused by their divorce, careers, and remarriage that they barely remember their role as parents. Lucy's and Albert's needs overshadow the needs of Casey. The Brodskys do everything divorced parents should avoid: They put their daughter in the middle of their anger; use her to communicate between them; complain about their financial and romantic problems openly in front of her; use her to get back at each other; ignore her when they're doing well; and use her when they're in pain. It isn't until their daughter makes the dramatic move to "divorce" them and live with Maria that Lucy and Albert realize the damage they've done and how self-absorbed they've been.

Discussion Questions:

- How could a child want to divorce her own parents?
- What do you think about how Lucy and Albert met? Did they fall in love too quickly? Do you know the story of how your parents met? How did your parents start their careers?
- How do Lucy's and Albert's careers affect their marriage? Their relationship with Casey?
- How do your parents balance their jobs and raising their children? Have you ever felt like your parent's career came before being a parent?
- What did Albert see in Blake? Why was he so willing to have a complete stranger move into the house and give up on his marriage to Lucy?
- What should a child like Casey do when parents aren't speaking to each other and put her in the middle?
- Is it fair for parents to be so angry with each other that they stop communicating?
- Who would you turn to in this type of a situation?

- Why does Casey spend so much time with Maria? Do you think Maria could be a better parental figure to Casey than her own parents?
- Why is it that when Lucy and Albert went through bad times they paid more attention to their daughter? How did they treat Casey like a pet?
- What are the positives and negatives about having money, success, and fame?
- Is it fair for divorced parents to use their children to communicate between each other? Why or why not? Have your parents ever done this to you? How did you feel? Did you ever feel like your parents were pulling you in two different directions?
- What do you think the judge should have done? If you could come up with an alternative solution, what would it be?
- What do you think of the judge's decision to give Maria custody of Casey? What do you think will happen to the Brodskys now? Will they ever get back together? Will they be better parents to their daughter?

Pointer:

Have a discussion about whether you think a child has a right to divorce her parents. Discuss what a child should do in this type of a situation. Use this film as a vehicle to discuss the best- and worst-case scenarios between divorced parents. What divorced parents do you know who are unfair to their children by putting them in the middle of their anger? What divorced parents do you know who get along well for the sake of their children?

Chapter 21

"I am not your problem to solve. It was so much more fun in the old days, wasn't it, Michael? I'd get drunk. I'd pass out, and you'd put me back together. That was the best, huh? That made you feel good. And that's what hurts."

— Alice, When a Man Loves A Woman

Drugs and Alcohol

According to statistics, the average child starts drinking at the age of thirteen, and starts smoking marijuana at fourteen, but pressure to experiment with drugs may become an issue earlier in adolescence. The ability to go against the actions of peers is usually related to your teen's self-esteem. Almost all children will think about what it is like to smoke a cigarette or drink beer, and wonder what it feels like to get high. The danger in prolonged experimentation with any substance is that it may become associated with a means to deal with feelings or emotional pain, and as a mechanism to cope with negative things that occur in everyday life.

Obviously, you can't always be with your children to prevent them from experimenting with drugs, but the lessons you teach them, both directly and through your example, can be. Listen carefully to what your teen communicates to you about their use, knowledge of, or curiosity about drugs and alcohol. Encourage your children to act independently of their friends in other capacities, like after-school interests or even how to dress, because the more comfortable they are being independent thinkers, the more comfortable they will be saying no. Provide your teen with accurate, thorough information on drugs; don't make the mistake of relying on school or others to do it for you. The more facts and information your teen has about the negative and dangerous effects of alcohol, tobacco, marijuana, cocaine, and others drugs, the better prepared they will be to make their own educated decisions. Keeping the lines of communication open and creating an atmosphere of trust is the best way to ensure a drug-free child.

Deciding Whether or Not to Experiment

Most early adolescents go through a period of curiosity and want to appear "cool" about the use of substances like cigarettes or wine. It is important to recognize that experimentation is a relatively normal and healthy process. Asking yourself the following questions may help you determine whether your child's experimenting is healthy or dangerous:

- How well is your teenager functioning in everyday life?
- How well is your teenager functioning academically?
- Has his relationship with his family changed?
- Has his relationship with his friends changed?

Resisting Cultural and Peer Pressure to Use

American society has only recently become aware of the degree to which the tobacco industry influences adolescents' initial motivation to smoke cigarettes. Most experts agree that smoking cigarettes can be a "gateway" to other drugs like alcohol, marijuana, or cocaine. The use of alcoholic drinks such as beer and wine has become such a common peer experience at social gatherings on weekends from middle school through college that it takes a very mature, self-assured adolescent to step back and resist those damaging substances. If your children don't hear your opinion on the subject of drugs, they may think you don't have one.

Familial Values' Effect on the Use of Drugs and Alcohol

Teenagers have observed their parents' relationship with drugs and alcohol over many years, whether it's using prescription drugs for medicinal purposes, drinking wine with dinner, or smoking cigarettes when under stress. As demonstrated in *When a Man Loves a Woman*, children, even young ones like Jess and Casey, are very astute at knowing that their parents may have a problem with substances. Remember that you should be a role model, and be aware of what kind of message you're sending to your children about drugs and alcohol. What do you do if your children ask if you tried drugs, and you don't want to sound like a hypocrite? It's better to be honest but not offer more information than necessary; children will tend to respect your honesty and will listen better to a parent who has "been there and done that." Draw on real-life experiences that you have had and tell them stories about people you know.

Use of Drugs and Alcohol to Cope

Whether your teen's relationship with drugs and alcohol is experimental or abusive depends on a number of variables, including the level of stress in her life, friends who influence her in either negative or constructive ways, and of course, parents who can recognize that their child may be emotionally distressed and is using drugs and/or alcohol to cope with her personal problems. Without friends who care about their welfare and parents who are sensitive to their everyday experiences, it becomes easy for teens to make that jump from experimental use to using drugs or alcohol to ease emotional stress and pain.

Clean & Sober

Daryl Poynter is a high-strung, successful Philadelphia commercial real estate agent, who also happens to be a drug addict and alcoholic. Two unfortunate circumstances force Daryl to enter rehab: he wakes up after a night of partying to find the woman in bed next to him unconscious, and he loses $92,000 in the stock market, money he had "borrowed" from his company's escrow account. The fact that he actually might be a drug addict is the last thing on Daryl's mind. The drug rehab clinic is his escape, but with the help of his coach, Craig, and his AA sponsor, Richard, he is forced to take moral inventory of his life, and he learns to accept the fact that he is and always will be an addict. This realization is the first step toward becoming "clean and sober." Once out of the clinic, Daryl tries to build a relationship with Charlie, a fellow addict he met in rehab, but unfortunately Charlie is still addicted to drugs and her abusive long-time boyfriend Lenny.

This film is one of the few to spend a great deal of time on the process of rehabilitation in a drug clinic. Daryl exemplifies the addict—his denial, the extreme and destructive circumstances that force him to finally deal with his problem, and the slow and laborious process of finally surrendering and admitting to addiction. Daryl thinks that he can help Charlie get out of her destructive relationships with Lenny and drugs, but this film shows us that it is impossible to help someone who does not want to help themselves. This film shows that drug and alcohol rehabilitation is a never-ending process. It also shows the process of detoxification, therapy, attending AA meetings, getting a sponsor, and reentering the community without ever walking away from the program.

Discussion Questions:

- Why does Daryl go to rehab? Does he really want help?
- Do you think Craig was too hard on Daryl? Was it fair for Craig to throw Daryl out of the program?
- What is your impression of the rehab experience? Should it be so tough and demanding?
- How does Richard help Daryl?
- How does Iris getting thrown out of the program affect Daryl?
- What is Charlie's problem? How does her relationship with Lenny prevent her recovery?
- What do Daryl and Charlie get from each other?
- Why does Charlie keep going back to Lenny?
- How does Charlie's death affect Daryl? Do you think that Daryl will stay "clean and sober" now?

Pointer:

Discuss the drug rehabilitation process. Do you know anybody who has been through rehab? Did it help him overcome his addiction? Do you know someone who has had an addiction to anything? How did that addiction interfere with his life? What kinds of things can you be addicted to? Can you be addicted to an abusive relationship like Charlie was to Lenny? To whom can you talk when you cross the line?

Basketball Diaries

Jim Carroll is a smart, talented, and athletic seventeen-year-old at a Catholic school in New York City. His promising future is threatened when he and his friends shift from recreationally smoking marijuana and taking pills and inhalants to snorting and eventually mainlining heroin. Jim is instantly addicted and soon his passion for writing and shooting hoops is replaced by his passion for shooting "smack." He gets kicked out of school and his mother's apartment, and becomes a full-fledged junkie, even going so far as to prostitute himself for drugs. When Jim's mom calls the cops, he goes to jail for six months, where he goes through detox and stays clean. In jail he writes *The Basketball Diaries,* the creative culmination of his experience as a junky and his first published work as a poet, writer, and artist.

This film shows that even the most promising and talented of children are not immune to the lure and danger of drugs. It shows how smoking and drinking can often serve as a gateway to using other more dangerous drugs, and that ultimately, the only thing that can save a person is himself. The pain that so many teens experience makes them susceptible to the mind-numbing, pain-erasing ways of drugs. This film is a harsh but effective way of illustrating the evils of drugs within a flashy, fast-paced, contemporary milieu to which many teens will relate. It also shows how one's suffering and pain can be translated into an inspiration for creating art, the way Jim used his experiences as the inspiration for his creative works.

Discussion Questions:

- What kind of circumstances led to Jim's addiction?
- What was Jim like before the drug addiction? What kind of person is Jim?
- What are these boys like as a group? As individuals? With which one do you most identify?

- What do you think of Jim taking his sick friend Bobby out of the hospital? Was it the right thing to do?
- What effect does Bobby's death have on Jim's drug problem?
- What role did playing basketball serve in these boys' lives?
- How did the addiction to heroin accelerate?
- What kinds of things did Jim do to "work" for his heroin addiction? What other kinds of things do addicts do to work for their drugs?
- What was the purpose of the Catholic confessional scene? Was it spiritually helpful to Jim in any way to confess his sins to the priest? What kind of comment is this film making about the role of Catholicism?
- Did Jim have any positive male role models?
- What is the significance of Jim's dream where he kills everyone in the classroom?
- What is right for Jim's mom to throw him out of the house? What do you think you would have done if you were a parent in that situation?
- Why does Reggie try to help Jim?
- What ultimately helped Jim overcome his drug addiction while he was in jail for six months?

Pointer:

Parents need to make sure they discuss the things that upset their children, because those things are what could escalate and serve as "stressors," which trigger the need to seek comfort in drugs or alcohol. Pain and suffering need to be shared with friends and family members so that they can be addressed on a healthier level and possibly prevent an addiction from forming. Who do you know who has been addicted to drugs, and what were the circumstances in her life that may have caused that addiction?

When a Man Loves a Woman

Alice and Michael Green are a happily married couple who live in San Francisco with their two daughters, Casey and Jess. For years, Alice has hidden her alcoholism—drinking in the closet and wrapping the empty vodka bottles in newspaper before throwing them away. Michael does a great job of taking care of her when she's had too much to drink, but then things get out of hand: she falls out of a boat; she comes home late and causes Michael, an airline pilot, to miss a trip; and she's impatient with and inattentive to her daughters. Her problem culminates when, after slapping Jess, she passes out in the shower. Michael is finally forced to face the severity of his wife's addiction, and Alice checks into rehab. She emerges from the clinic sober and independent, very different from the fun, spontaneous, flirtatious, and needy person she was before. Alice's sobriety and newfound self-awareness threaten Michael, who thrives as an enabler, enjoys cleaning up Alice's mess, fixing her problems, and taking care of his family. Michael refuses to accept responsibility for his role in their problems and has a hard time relating to his changed spouse, so the two decide to separate.

This film is about the challenge of how to keep a marriage together when everything you have known has changed. Michael, in his attempt to be the perfect, supportive husband and father, actually exacerbates Alice's problem, enabling her to function as an alcoholic and preventing her from full recovery. Part of getting over an addiction is learning to own up to mistakes and struggle through life's everyday challenges. But Alice's sobriety and change in attitude leave Michael feeling alone and useless. This film emphasizes the importance of communication and how a partner should be supportive without solving an addict's problems for him. This film shows the effect of alcoholism on a marriage, and how in order for the rehabilitation process to work, members of a family, especially spouses, must be willing to change.

Discussion Questions:

- What do you think of Alice's drinking in the beginning of the film? Does her drinking seem normal or does it seem like an addiction?
- What led Alice to hit Jess when she came home? What do you think it would be like to see your mother passed out in the shower?
- Why didn't Michael realize how severe his wife's problem was?

- Why is it so important for people in rehab to be completely isolated from their friends and family?
- Why did Jess and Casey seem so much more aware of Alice's alcoholism than Michael?
- Why is Alice so fearful of returning home? How has she changed? Why was Michael so uncomfortable at the rehab clinic?
- Why was Michael so angry when he came home and saw Alice talking with Gary? What was he really jealous of?
- Why was it so important for Alice to remain friends with the people she went through rehab with?
- How has Alice's sobriety affected their marital dynamic?
- How does the last scene resolve their issues? What do you think will happen to their marriage?
- Do you know any families who have had to deal with a family member's alcohol problem? How did they handle it?

Pointer:

Talk about people you know who have addictions and how that affects their family. Do you know any "enablers"? It is important to recognize that even families where drug use is not a problem can have unhealthy patterns or enablers who make it easier for destructive habits to thrive. Discuss with your child the way your family operates during a crisis. Is there someone who always tries to "fix" everything like Michael does in this film?

The Doors

This films feels like a documentary, as it follows the rise and fall of one of America's rock and roll icons, Jim Morrison. Morrison drops out of film school, writes music and poetry, forms a band called The Doors, and rises to early fame. Amidst the drugs and hippie culture of the sixties, it is still clear that Jim's desire for drugs is not about getting high, or even about becoming numb for that matter, it's about complete and absolute oblivion. Jim's obsession with death pervades his actions, his songs, and his poetry. He begins to self-destruct—gaining weight, ruining performances, betraying his wife and friends. His downward spiral is irreversible and concludes with his early death in Paris at the age of twenty-seven.

Set amidst a realistic backdrop of sixties pop culture, most teens, especially fans of Jim Morrison and The Doors, will enjoy the exposure to this era, and learning about the self-destructive behavior that ended this pop star's life. Like other musical greats such as Jimi Hendrix, Janis Joplin and more recently, Kurt Cobain, drugs and alcohol contributed to his self-destruction and ended the career and life of Jim Morrison. The film never glorifies this destructive lifestyle, and actually sets Jim in contrast to the other band members who may use drugs recreationally, but are sober for performances and taping sessions. *The Doors* only shows one scene from Jim's childhood, but the implications are that Jim never quite got over the feeling of rejection by his military father. There are a few references throughout the film that Jim may have been subconsciously trying to seek the love and acceptance he never got from his father and that he craved from his fans.

Discussion Questions:

- What is the significance of the car crash scene in the desert when Jim was little?
- Jim quotes a line from William Blake, via Aldous Huxley, "If the doors of perception were cleansed, everything would appear to man as it is." What does this mean?
- How do drugs connect the band to music? How do The Doors use drugs to bring them closer as a group?
- What is the significance of the American Indian who keeps appearing?
- Do you think they should have changed the lyrics of "Light My Fire" for *The Ed Sullivan Show*? How would you feel about changing your lyrics for a national television audience?
- How are the Federal Communications Commission's regulations different today? Could a band sing "girl we couldn't get much higher" on television today?
- What media outlet is today's equivalent of *The Ed Sullivan Show* (i.e. MTV, *The Tonight Show*, etc.)?
- Why do the band members start to distance themselves from Jim?

- What do you think about The Doors' decision to sell the rights to "Light My Fire" to a television commercial?
- How do drugs influence Morrison's performances?
- How does Pam affect Morrison's use of drugs? Is Pam addicted to drugs too?
- What is the significance of Morrison's being buried in Cimetiere du Pere Lachaise in Paris amongst some of the world's greatest musicians, writers, and poets?

Pointer:

What is it about fame that causes so many people to directly or indirectly end their own lives? Discuss actors, artists, and musicians who have experienced similar fates, like Elvis, Jimi Hendrix, Janis Joplin, or Marilyn Monroe. What about more current celebrities like Kurt Cobain? Compare and contrast famous celebrities of the past to those of the present. Is the lifestyle the same?

Chapter 22

"For as long as I can remember, I've been searching for something, some reason why we're here. What are we doing here? Who are we? If this is a chance to find out even just a little part of that answer ... I don't know, I think it's worth a human life. Don't you?"
— Ellie Arroway, Contact

Paranormal and the Unknown

As teens mature intellectually, they begin to see the world very differently from their younger peers, and ponder the possibilities of things beyond their own comprehension. Famous cognitive psychologist Jean Piaget believed that the highest form of intellect is the ability to think in terms of hypothetical possibilities—not in a haphazard, unrealistic, or wishful sense, but with a belief, based partly on reason and partly on intuition; in other words, taking logic and reasoning further than one can see in everyday reality. For example, as Ellie hypothesizes in *Contact*, if life can develop and flourish on earth, why shouldn't it be able to happen elsewhere in this vast universe? Or as Max obsesses in *Pi*, why shouldn't there be a mathematical pattern in the systems of nature? Anther question teens may start to explore is how much God plays a role in this process. What does the future hold? What happens to us when we die?

Teens' advanced reasoning abilities may provoke their curiosity about life and death as never before, wondering about an afterlife, and attempting to somehow comprehend the existence of things beyond their senses. The field of parapsychology, the study of unusual phenomena, has yet to prove through scientific methodology the existence of communication with the dead, reincarnation, and psychic healing. However, very controlled experiments at some well-respected universities have shown the possible existence of things beyond our ordinary sensation and perception. Because things happen in films that are beyond our everyday experiences, they provide a great opportunity for discussing these issues and gauging where you teen is intellectually.

Understanding Things Beyond our Current Understanding of Reality

When teens progress to the highest level of intellect, they'll have the ability to reason in abstraction or possibilities, and the world as they know it will forever be changed. It is very unsettling to suddenly realize that you may not exist beyond your own mortality, or that intelligent life from other worlds may not be benevolent, or that Mother Nature (as evidenced in natural catastrophes like earthquakes and tornadoes) does not discriminate. These are the realizations that make the protected, secure world of childhood truly come to an end.

Separating or Integrating Religion and Science

Often, research in science such as parapsychology (the study of extra-sensory perception) or the search for extra-terrestrial life crosses the realm of science into the realm of religion. The uncovering of nature's secrets may have religious overtones to it. Parents must keep in mind that while many of these films, like *The Sixth Sense, Defending Your Life,* and *Contact,* challenge the traditions and beliefs of organized religion, watching, questioning, or discussing the concepts do not make your teen anti-religious or take away from her religious upbringing in any way.

Our Need to Believe in Things Beyond Our Comprehension

Life's lessons can be painful and can leave us with a sense of being very alone. Therefore it can be comforting to believe that someone or something more powerful than ourselves is directing or influencing our world. To think that the universe has no order or that there is no purpose to our existence in the world is a thought so frightening for many people that we crave evidence of something beyond our own senses. Our own psychological needs (security, love, affirmation, and achievement) most likely dictate what we choose to believe in when it comes to the paranormal. The research of Abraham Maslow with self-actualized people indicates that the more secure, loved, and competent a person is, the less need they have for the traditional structure of religion, and what those faiths present in terms of a perception of what God is, heaven and hell, etc. According to Maslow, the healthiest people, psychologically, also believe in things beyond themselves but don't seem to follow the traditional image of the world and God which man has created. They appear to see beauty and wonder in the simple things in nature and life that the rest of us don't see.

Contact

Ellie Arroway is a scientist who studies extra-terrestrial messages through radio waves. Instilled with a passion for science by her father when she was young, Ellie is fascinated with the possibility of life on other planets. As an adult, Ellie works for the Search for Extra-Terrestrial Intelligence (SETI) institute that searches for extra-terrestrial life forms by monitoring radio waves, and she picks up a signal encrypted in a television transmission from Vega. The signal includes a set of instructions for some kind of transport vehicle. The government becomes involved, and suddenly the world is tracking the process of building the transport vehicle and selecting an individual to go meet the senders. There is a romantic subplot, as Ellie's ex-lover, a theologian, sits on the selection committee and publicly challenges her belief in God. Ellie eventually gets to go on the transport mission, and the controversy about what actually occurred forces Ellie to accept the occurrence of things beyond her own scientific explanation.

Contact may seem unrealistic as a big-budget Hollywood film, but it is based on a novel by astronomer Carl Sagan, and many of the hypotheses in this film are scientifically sound. It explores society's struggle between politics and science, the search for intelligent life on other planets, and our conflicting human need to both explore the unknown and protect ourselves from it. The film looks at far-fetched ideas through scientifically accurate theory, and poses the question as to the role and importance of having faith in God or some higher being in our quest for life on other planets or in other solar systems. This film tackles humanity's first contact with an extra-terrestrial life form, while also addressing an individual's personal search for meaning in life.

Discussion Questions:

- What's the significance of Ellie's fascination with using the radio when she was young?
- What's the conflict between Ellie and Dr. Drumlin? If they are both pro-science, then where do they differ?
- How do you distinguish what is and what is not worthy of scientific investigation?
- What do Ellie and Palmer Joss offer each other intellectually? How do they differ in their opinions and how do they agree?
- Why would aliens use prime numbers to communicate?
- Do you think it was fair for the government to take control of Ellie's privately funded project?
- Why does Kitz see the Nazi broadcast as a breach of security?
- What kind of effect does this "contact" have on sensitive and vulnerable people? Why do anti-science, extremely religious people get so upset?
- How much control should private industry have in affecting the economy and security of a government? How was S.R. Haddon a threat?
- Do you think it would be safe to build a transportation vehicle designed by aliens?
- What do you think about the selection process? Was it fair that Ellie was not chosen when it was her project that led to the initial contact?

- Was it fair to ask her if she believes in the existence of God? Should the first person to make contact with extra-terrestrial beings be a believer in God?

Pointer:

Use the ending of the film to get a sense of where your teen falls within the spectrum of fantasy versus science. Does your teen think Ellie really saw the alien or that it was just a dream? Discuss your beliefs regarding whether intelligent life exists in outer space.

Defending Your Life

Daniel Miller is a fortysomething advertising executive who dies in a car crash on his birthday while playing with the CD player in his new BMW. He arrives in Judgement City, a commercialized midway point where newly dead souls are put on trial. The question at hand: Did they overcome their fear? Did they take risks and live life to its fullest? He falls in love with Julia, whose "trial" seems to be going much better than his. Even in death, Daniel has not been able to triumph over his fear: fear of rejection, fear of embarrassment, and fear of being average. The judges determine that he is not ready to go on to the next level, which means that he will be sent back to earth for another chance; Julia's trial has a better conclusion, as she is allowed to move to the next level. As their trams depart on separate tracks, Daniel finally proves that the courage he lacked in life he has finally found in Judgement City.

This film is light and humorous, despite the fact that it deals with the very serious subject of what happens to us when we die. Though the two main characters in the story are dead, it really examines what we should do with our lives. *Defending Your Life* takes a somewhat practical approach to the Christian issues of judgement, purgatory, and getting through the gates of heaven. Here, what makes someone good is not their saintliness, but their ability to overcome fear. It's an interesting idea and can provide a great start to a discussion about what our purpose is in life, and by what standards we should be judged. It also explores the issues of reincarnation and past lives, heaven, and what happens when we die.

Discussion Questions:

- What do you think of Judgement City?
- What do you think of Daniel Miller's life before he died?
- What do you think of the concept of deciding the value of one's life based on overcoming fears?
- Do you think heaven and hell exist? Do you think there is a judgement period?
- What do you think about the idea that most humans only use a small percentage of their brain?
- Do you think eight-year-old Daniel did the right thing by not fighting back in the schoolyard? Was it fear or restraint?
- What do you think about the other examples from Daniel's life: when he took the blame for his friend at school, when he didn't invest in Casio even though he got an inside stock tip, when he didn't negotiate with his boss for a higher salary? Did these examples prove that he was still ruled by fear?
- What do you think about Daniel and Julia's relationship? What do they see in each other?
- What did you think about the Past Life Pavilion? Do you think you were somebody else in a past life? If so, is your past life tied to your own personality?
- What do you think of the initial verdict in Daniel's trial? Was it fair that he had to go back to Earth?
- How does Daniel's love for Julia make him overcome his fear?

Pointer:

Discuss what your biggest fear is. Parents should discuss fears they've had in their lives and how their fear of things (failure, rejection, change, etc.) has held them back. If you were in Judgement City, what video clips would the prosecuting and defending lawyers show as evidence to argue their points? Would you be allowed to move onward or would you be sent back to Earth?

Pi

Pi is a science fiction thriller about a young but tormented genius named Max Cohen who is obsessed with the idea that mathematics, if applied correctly, can unlock all the mysteries of the world and predict the chaos of nature. Max is prone to headaches, nosebleeds, and panic attacks; it is unclear whether these are symptoms of insanity or stress. He is aggressively pursued by a corporate Wall Street company that wants to hire him as a consultant to unlock the code of the stock market, and by an orthodox Jew who studies the Kabbala and believes that Max may be able to determine the true name of God.

Despite warnings from his elderly mentor and friend, Max continues his obsessive quest to crack the code until finally, like the huge computer in his apartment, he shuts down completely, and perhaps regains some sanity.

Pi explores one man's obsession with linking the structured world of mathematics to the chaotic world of nature. It examines the link between genius, obsession, and psychosis. But beyond all the interesting scientific and mathematical theories, it seems to have a message, one articulated simply by Max's mentor, to "take a break." Often when we are so consumed by a goal, the best thing we can do is step back and leave it alone. When our involvements become obsessions, we can almost guarantee failure. Max as an individual is sick, has no friends, and has very little enjoyment in life. Instead of seeing the beauty around him, he can only break it down into smaller mathematical statements. This movie provokes an interesting discussion about the connection between nature and mathematics.

Discussion Questions:

- Do you think Max is crazy? Why or why not?
- Do you think Max is a genius? Why or why not?
- What do you think of his hypothesis that there is a numerical pattern to everything? Was it crazy or delusional for him to see mathematics in everything and be obsessed with breaking the code?
- Do you think people are really out to get Max, or is it just his paranoia?
- What do you think about his seizures or attacks? What triggers them? Is it a real medical problem or is it in Max's head?

- What is the significance of this 216-digit number? Why does Max eventually want to destroy evidence of the numbers?
- What does Sol try to tell Max about searching for pi?
- Do you think it's possible for the stock market to have a pattern in it or to be predictable?
- What do you think the little girl, Jenna, and her questions represent to Max?
- Have you ever become obsessed with anything—art, business, a person, an idea? What is the value of obsession?
- How has Max changed now that he has drilled his head? What do you think he'll be like now?

Pointer:

Sol tells the story of how Archimedes was not able to solve the theory of displacement until he took a break and relaxed in a bathtub. The lesson here is that when you are too consumed by something, you lose perspective and you compromise the quality of your life. Max's life was compromised by his obsession with pi. Discuss what things you have been so consumed by that they prevented you from enjoying life. Have you ever found an answer by simply taking a break? What did the last scene in this film mean? Is Max's life going to be different now?

Total Recall

It is some time in the future when it has become scientifically possible to implant false memories in a person, wipe out his memories, and download new memories, thereby creating a whole new identity altogether. Douglas Quaid is fascinated by Mars, a planet threatened by terrorist activities. He buys a virtual vacation package at Total Recall, Inc., where you can purchase the "memory of your ideal vacation, cheaper, safer, and better than the real thing." But when the memories are being downloaded, a technical glitch occurs and suddenly Quaid isn't sure who he is, what's real and what's a memory. He travels to a colonized Mars where mutant rebels are fighting back against their oppressor. Every time he thinks he understands his role in everything, a new piece of information is uncovered and he is once again left questioning the authenticity of his own memories and life.

Total Recall presents a fun opportunity to discuss with your family what each other's vision for the future is. It explores, among other things, technological advancements like virtual vacations, holograms, interplanetary travel, the atmospheric problems on other planets, and the colonization of planets. On a psychological level, this film poses the question of how much of our identity is based on memories, and what would happen if those memories were altered.

Discussion Questions:

- What's different about earth in the future? What do you like and dislike about this vision of the future?
- What do you think of the idea of being able to implant someone with memories? Are memories of an event, vacation, or experience just as important as actually doing it?
- Do you think Quaid specifically chose to be a secret FBI agent, or is it because that's who he was as Houser?
- Do you think we will have programmable holograms like Lori's tennis instructor in the future?
- What do you think it would feel like to be told that your whole life is just a memory that was implanted in you?
- What do you think of the political structure of Mars? Was it believable at all? Do you think we'll ever have the capacity to colonize Mars and live there?
- Will vacationing to other planets ever be as common as vacationing to other countries is now?
- What was Cohaagen's motive?

Pointer:

How does the situation with Mars parallel current events? Discuss what your fears and concerns are about the future, as well as what technological advances you are looking forward to. Compare and contrast how things have changed from when you were a teen. What does your teenager think his children will have that he doesn't have now?

The Sixth Sense

After being shot by a mentally disturbed former patient, child psychologist Dr. Malcolm Crowe tries to rectify the failure of his past by helping a new young patient with similar characteristics. The patient is a troubled little boy named Cole Sear from a recently divorced family. Crowe becomes so focused on helping eight-year-old Cole that he barely has time for his wife. Cole is tormented by his dark secret, and Crowe eventually learns what that is: Cole sees dead people who don't know they are dead. He sees them all the time and they communicate to him, as if they want something from him. By searching to help Cole, Dr. Crowe finally has a breakthrough of his own.

This film, regarded as a smart psychological thriller, was praised for its shocking surprise ending. Most people at some point in their lives have had a feeling so strong it was more than just an intuition—seen something move when it shouldn't have, or have been able to predict an odd occurrence before it happened. This is the same sixth sense that terrorizes Cole Sear, and perhaps it exists to a lesser degree in all of us. This film is a wonderful opportunity for you and your teen to share your beliefs regarding paranormal phenomenon, the sixth sense, mind readers, fortune tellers, and people who claim to communicate with the dead.

Discussion Questions:

- What do you think happens when you die?
- Do you believe people have a sixth sense? If so, what is it? Do you know anyone who claims to have any special abilities like the sixth sense?
- Do you believe in poltergeists?
- Did you ever at any point in the film think that Dr. Crowe may have been dead?
- Do you think mental health professionals are at risk from angry, disturbed former patients?
- What were your first impressions of Cole Sear? Did you think he had psychiatric problems or was he just scared?
- What do you think was happening during the classroom scene? Did the dead possess Cole or was he simply communicating what they were telling him? How did he know his teacher used to

stutter when he was younger?
- Has anyone ever told you they heard voices? Would you believe them or would you think they were psychologically disturbed?
- What do you think happened during the scene when all the cabinets and drawers opened? How would you react to that situation if you were Cole's mom?
- What did you think about Dr. Crowe's marriage? Did you suspect anything was wrong?
- Why was it so important to Dr. Crowe to help Cole?
- Dr. Crowe tells Cole to listen to the dead people because they need to communicate something. If he listens, then perhaps they will go away. What do you think about this advice?
- Why would a mother ever purposely feed her daughter arsenic?
- Do you think deceased relatives could ever communicate to living ones?
- How does Cole come to accept his "sixth sense"? How does Dr. Crowe help Cole?
- How does Cole help Dr. Crowe?

Pointer:

Use the issues addressed in this film to lead a discussion about whether you can have a sixth sense. Is it related to the departed? Discuss what types of things you believe in—fortune tellers, mediums, palm readers, psychics, astrologists, etc. Share an experience where something happened to you that was beyond normal experience and explanation.

APPENDIX
Determining a Film's Appropriateness

Knowing Your Child

You are more of an expert on your child than any psychologist, movie rating system, or film guide. Use these tools to help you make decisions, but ultimately be prepared to make a decision that feels right to you. Just because it is rated R does not mean that your fourteen year old is not mature enough to watch a film like *Scent of a Woman,* which focuses on how a teenage boy learns to deals with honesty, integrity, courage, and life decisions in the midst of a prep school crisis. On the other hand, just because a film is rated G does not mean it is appropriate for your sensitive four year old, given the scene in *The Lion King* when Simba's daddy is killed, and he is made to believe it is his fault.

Rating System

The Motion Picture Association of America has developed the following rating system with the goal of offering parents some advanced information about movie content so that they can decide what movies they don't want their children to watch. Keep in mind that the voluntary rating system should be used as a guide but cannot, under any circumstances, replace the importance of parental decisions in family movie watching. You, not the Rating Board, know what your child is like, what will scare her, confuse her, or negatively influence her; therefore, use the rating system as a guide, but remember to trust yourselves as parents and ultimately make your own decision even when it goes against the rating system.

G

GENERAL AUDIENCES — "All ages admitted." This is a film that does not have any content—theme, language, nudity and sex, or violence—which would be offensive to parents whose younger children see this film. This does not mean that it is a children's film, simply that the content would not be inappropriate if they were to watch it.

PG

PARENTAL GUIDANCE SUGGESTED — "Some material may not be suitable for children." Parents should look into this film before they allow their younger children to see it. Some parents, depending on their views and the age of their children, may consider some content in this film unsuitable for children. The rating serves as a warning that parents should look into the film before making a determination as to whether or not it is appropriate for their children.

PG-13

PARENTS STRONGLY CAUTIONED — "Some materials may be inappropriate for children under 13." This stronger warning is for parents to decide whether it is appropriate for their children, particularly those under thirteen years old, to see this film. Any drug use, non-sexual nudity, or a single use of a harsher sexually-derived expletive will automatically require at least a PG-13, while more than one such use will give that film an R rating. Basically films that fall somewhere between PG and R will be given PG-13 ratings.

R

RESTRICTED — "Under 17 requires accompanying parent or adult guardian." This film definitely contains some adult material and parents are strongly encouraged to learn more about this film before they allow a child under seventeen to accompany them. R-rated films may include violence, sexually-oriented nudity, drug use or abuse, hard language, or some mix of the above.

NC-17

NO ONE 17 AND UNDER ADMITTED — Most parents would consider the material in these films inappropriate for their children who are seventeen or younger.

FILM INDEX

ARTHUR'S BABY
Length 30 minutes
Rating: Not rated
Recommended age group: 3 and up
Subjects: family issues, siblings, dealing with newborn sibling
Possible problems: None.

AUTHOR! AUTHOR!
Length 100 minutes
Rating: PG
Recommended age group: 9 and up
Year released: 1982
Director: Arthur Hiller
Cast: Al Pacino, Tuesday Weld, Dyan Cannon, Alan King, Andre Gregory
Subjects: divorce, remarriage, family relations, stepparents, stepsiblings
Possible problems: Some mature subjects like marital infidelity.

AVALON
Length 126 minutes
Rating: PG
Recommended age group: 13 and up
Year released: 1990
Director: Barry Levinson
Cast: Armin Mueller-Stahl, Elizabeth Perkins, Aidan Quinn, Joan Plowright, Elijah Wood
Subjects: immigrants, family relations, extended families, aging
Possible problems: None.

BABE
Length 94 minutes
Rating: G
Recommended age group: 5 and up
Year released: 1995
Director: Chris Noonan
Cast: Christine Cavanaugh, Miriam Margolyes, Danny Mann, Hugo Weaving (voices)
Subjects: stereotypes, animal hierarchy, friendship, individuality
Possible problems: An animal dies.

BAMBI
Length 69 minutes
Rating: G
Recommended age group: 3 and up
Year released: 1942
Director: David Hand
Cast: Bobby Stewart, Peter Behn, Stan Alexander, Cammie King, Donnie Dunagan, Hardie Albright, John Sutherland, Tim Davis, Sam Edwards (voices)
Subjects: growing up, learning independence, death, circle of life, animals, love, reproduction, hunting
Possible problems: Bambi's mother's death may present first exposure to death for some little ones.

THE BASKETBALL DIARIES
Length 1994
Rating: R
Recommended age group: 15 and up
Year released: 1995
Director: Scott Kalvert

Cast: Leonardo DiCaprio, Bruno Kirby, Lorraine Bracco, Mark Wahlberg
Subjects: drug use, drug addiction, sexual promiscuity, prostitution, violence, basketball
Possible problems: Graphic scenes of drug use; prostitution; violence; sexuality and profanity.

BEAUTY AND THE BEAST
Length 84 minutes
Rating: G
Recommended age group: 4 and up
Year released: 1991
Directors: Kirk Wise, Gary Trousdale
Cast: Paige O'Hara, Robby Benson, Rex Everhart, Richard White, Jesse Corti, Angela Landsbury, Jerry Orbach (voices)
Subjects: morality, individuality, values, stereotypes
Possible problems: None.

THE BERENSTAIN BEARS LEARN ABOUT STRANGERS
Length 36 minutes
Rating: Not rated
Recommended age group: 3 and up
Year released: 1982
Director: Buzz Potamkin
Subjects: fears, strangers, obeying rules
Possible problems: None.

THE BERENSTAIN BEARS PLAY BALL
Length 30 minutes
Rating: Not rated
Recommended age group: 3 and up
Year released: 1981
Directors: Mordecai Gerstein, Al Kouzel
Subjects: competition, gender differences
Possible problems: None.

THE BERENSTAIN BEARS & THE TROUBLE WITH FRIENDS
Length 30 minutes

Rating: Not rated
Recommended age group: 3 and up
Year released: 1986
Director: Buzz Potamkin
Subjects: friendship, resolving conflict, apologizing, personality differences
Possible problems: None.

THE BERENSTAIN BEARS IN THE DARK
Length 30 minutes
Rating: Not rated.
Recommended age group: 3 and up
Year released: 1983
Director: Buzz Potamkin
Subjects: fears, imagination
Possible problems: None.

THE BLACK STALLION
Length 120 minutes
Rating: PG
Recommended age group: 5 and up
Year released: 1979
Director: Carroll Ballard
Cast: Kelly Reno, Mickey Rooney, Teri Garr, Clarence Muse
Subjects: friendship, love, loss
Possible problems: The scene when the boat sinks, or the scene on the beach with a rattlesnake may scare some younger kids.

THE BOY WHO COULD FLY
Length 120 minutes
Rating: PG
Recommended age group: 8 and up
Year released: 1986
Director: Nick Castle
Cast: Lucy Deakins, Jay Underwood, Bonnie Bedelia, Collen Dewhurst, Fred Savage, Fred Gwynne, Louise Fletcher
Subjects: fantasy, death, autism, single-parent family
Possible problems: Mild profanity; alcohol use by a teen; scenes from a mental institution.

BOYZ N THE HOOD
Length 112 minutes
Rating: R
Recommended age group: 14 and up
Year released: 1991
Director: John Singleton
Cast: Laurence Fishburne, Ice Cube, Cuba Gooding, Jr., Angela Bassett
Subjects: father-son relationships, loss of virginity, crime and violence, drugs
Possible problems: Profanity; sex talk; drug talk; brutality in the streets of the ghetto.

THE BREAKFAST CLUB
Length 97 minutes
Rating: R
Recommended age group: 13 and up
Year released: 1985
Director: John Hughes
Cast: Emilio Estevez, Judd Nelson, Molly Ringwald, Anthony Michael Hall, Ally Sheedy
Subjects: friendship, social life, cliques, family life, sexual experiences
Possible problems: Scene of high-schoolers smoking marijuana; profanity; discussions about sex.

BYE BYE, LOVE
Length 106 minutes
Rating: PG-13
Recommended age group: 12 and up
Year released: 1995
Director: Sam Weisman
Cast: Paul Reiser, Matthew Modine, Randy Quaid, Janeane Garofalo, Amy Brenneman, Rob Reiner
Subjects: divorce, family relationships, blended families, marriage, custody arrangements
Possible problems: A child walks in on his dad in bed with a girlfriend.

CHARLOTTE'S WEB
Length 93 minutes
Rating: G
Recommended age group: 3 and up
Year released: 1973
Directors: Charles A. Nichols, Iwao Takamoto
Cast: Debbie Reynolds, Agnes Moorehead, Paul Lynde, Henry Gibson (voices)
Subjects: friendship, loyalty, compassion, farm life, rank
Possible problems: None.

CHILDREN OF A LESSER GOD
Length 119 minutes
Rating: R
Recommended age group: 15 and up
Year released: 1986
Director: Randa Haines
Cast: William Hurt, Marlee Matlin, Piper Laurie, Philip Bosco
Subjects: deafness, handicaps, romance
Possible problems: Sexual scenes; harsh language; mature subjects.

A CHRISTMAS STORY
Length 95 minutes
Rating: PG
Recommended age group: 8 and up
Year released: 1983
Director: Bob Clark
Cast: Peter Billingsley, Darren McGavin, Melinda Dillon, Ian Petrella
Subjects: family, siblings, neighborhood bullies, dares, Christmas, parental restrictions
Possible problems: None.

CLEAN & SOBER
Length 124 minutes
Rating: R
Recommended age group: 16 and up
Year released: 1988
Director: Glenn Gordon Caron
Cast: Michael Keaton, Kathy Baker, Morgan Freeman
Subjects: cocaine addiction, alcohol addiction, drug detoxification and

rehabilitation, AA meetings
Possible problems: Graphic depiction of drug addiction; sexuality.

CLUELESS
Length 105 minutes
Rating: PG-13
Recommended age group: 15 and up
Year released: 1995
Director: Amy Heckerling
Cast: Alicia Silverstone, Stacey Dash, Brittany Murphy, Paul Rudd, Dan Hedaya
Subjects: social life, friendship, cliques, sexual experiences
Possible problems: Shows three teens smoking marijuana, but lead character does not condone it. Many sexual references, although main character is a virgin.

CONTACT
Length 153 minutes
Rating: PG
Recommended age group: 12 and up
Year released: 1997
Director: Robert Zemeckis
Cast: Jodie Foster, Mathew McConaughey, James Woods
Subjects: extra-terrestrial life, astronomy, science, mathematics, religion, faith
Possible problems: None.

CORRINA, CORRINA
Length 114 minutes
Rating: PG
Recommended age group: 10 and up
Year released: 1994
Director: Jessie Nelson
Cast: Whoopi Goldberg, Ray Liotta, Tina Majorino, Don Ameche, Wendy Crewson, Larry Miller, Jenifer Lewis
Subjects: death, family relations, single-parent family, racism, interracial romance, grieving
Possible problems: Light profanity.

DANCES WITH WOLVES
Length 181 minutes
Rating: PG-13
Recommended age group: 13 and up
Year released: 1990
Director: Kevin Costner
Cast: Kevin Costner, Mary McDonnell, Graham Greene
Subjects: American Indians, Civil War, prejudice, civilization, American frontier
Possible problems: None.

DEAD MAN WALKING
Length 120 minutes
Rating: R
Recommended age group: 15 and up
Year released: 1995
Director: Tim Robbins
Cast: Sean Penn, Susan Sarandon
Subjects: capital punishment, morality, ethics, forgiveness, revenge, repentance
Possible problems: Harsh language; violence; brutal rape and murder scene.

DEFENDING YOUR LIFE
Length 112 minutes
Rating: PG
Recommended age group: 13 and up
Year released: 1991
Director: Albert Brooks
Cast: Albert Brooks, Meryl Streep, Rip Torn, Lee Grant, Buck Henry
Subjects: death, afterlife, overcoming fear, heaven
Possible problems: None.

DIARY OF ANNE FRANK
Length 150 minutes
Rating: Not rated
Recommended age group: 10 and up
Year released: 1959
Director: George Stevens
Cast: Millie Perkins, Joseph Schildkraut, Shelley Winters, Ed Wynn, Richard Beymer
Subjects: World War II, Nazis, holocaust, racism, Holland

Possible problems: Sophisticated theme; scenes where the families are almost discovered may be scary for younger children.

THE DOORS
Length 138 minutes
Rating: R
Recommended age group: 14 and up
Year released: 1991
Director: Oliver Stone
Cast: Val Kilmer, Meg Ryan, Kyle MacLachlan, Kevin Dillon
Subjects: 1960s, rock and roll, drug and alcohol abuse and addiction
Possible problems: Graphic depictions of drug and alcohol abuse and sex.

DO THE RIGHT THING
Length 120 minutes
Rating: R
Recommended age group: 15 and up
Year released: 1989
Director: Spike Lee
Cast: Danny Aiello, Spike lee, John Turturro, Rosie Perez
Subjects: racism, prejudice, hate crimes, violence
Possible problems: Violence; harsh language.

DUMBO
Length 63 minutes
Rating: G
Recommended age group: 3 and up
Year released: 1941
Director: Ben Sharpsteen
Cast: Sterling Holloway, Edward S. Brophy, Verna Felton, Herman Bing, Cliff Edwards (voices)
Subjects: prejudice, friendship, individuality, empathy, family
Possible problems: None.

ESCAPE TO WITCH MOUNTAIN
Length 105 minutes
Rating: G
Recommended age group: 6 and up
Year released: 1975
Director: John Hough
Cast: Kim Richards, Ike Eisenmann, Eddie Albert, Ray Milland, Donald Pleasence
Subjects: telekinesis, ESP, magic, aliens, searching for origin
Possible problems: None.

E.T.: THE EXTRA-TERRESTRIAL
Length 115 minutes
Rating: PG
Recommended age group: 6 and up
Year released: 1982
Director: Steven Spielberg
Cast: Dee Wallace Stone, Henry Thomas, Peter Coyote, Drew Barrymore
Subjects: friendship, aliens, loneliness, single-parent family, siblings, fears
Possible problems: None.

EVE'S BAYOU
Length 109 minutes
Rating: R
Recommended age group: 13 and up
Year released: 1997
Director: Kasi Lemmons
Cast: Jurnee Smollett, Meagan Good, Samuel L. Jackson, Lynn Whitfield, Debbi Morgan
Subjects: voodoo, siblings, marital infidelity, dysfunctional family, morality
Possible problems: A scene showing incestuous actions by the father; adultery; some violence.

FRIED GREEN TOMATOES
Length 130 minutes
Rating: PG-13
Recommended age group: 14 and up
Year released: 1991
Director: Jon Avnet
Cast: Kathy Bates, Jessica Tandy, Mary Stuart Masterson, Mary Louise Parker

Subjects: friendship, death, racism, sexism, aging, loyalty, spousal abuse
Possible problems: One scene shows domestic violence; mild profanity.

GOOD WILL HUNTING
Length 126 minutes
Rating: R
Recommended age group: 15 and up
Year released: 1997
Director: Gus Van Sant
Cast: Robin Williams, Matt Damon, Ben Affleck, Minnie Driver
Subjects: coming of age, friendship, therapy, romance, dealing with intelligence
Possible problems: Strong language, including some sex-related dialogue.

THE GREAT SANTINI
Length 118 minutes
Rating: PG
Recommended age group: 14 and up
Year released: 1980
Director: Lewis John Carlino
Cast: Robert Duvall, Blythe Danner, Michael O'Keefe
Subjects: father-son and family relationships, racism, military life
Possible problems: Father has outbursts of bad temper that result in physical abuse.

GUESS WHO'S COMING TO DINNER
Length 108 minutes
Rating: Not rated
Recommended age group: 13 and up
Year released: 1967
Director: Stanley Kramer
Cast: Spencer Tracy, Katherine Hepburn, Katherine Houghton, Sidney Poitier, Cecil Kellaway, Beah Richards
Subjects: interracial marriage, racism, prejudice, romance, family relations, gender differences
Possible problems: None.

HARRIET THE SPY
Length 101 minutes
Rating: PG
Recommended age group: 8 and up
Year released: 1996
Director: Bronwen Hughes
Cast: Michelle Trachtenberg, Rosie O'Donnell, Vanessa Lee Chester, Gregory Smith, Robert Joy, Eartha Kitt, J. Smith-Cameron
Subjects: friendships, arguments, individuality, social life, growing up, family issues
Possible problems: Harriet and her friends get pretty nasty when they get angry.

THE ICE STORM
Length 113 minutes
Rating: R
Recommended age group: 16 and over
Year released: 1997
Director: Ang Lee
Cast: Sigourney Weaver, Kevin Kline, Joan Allen, Christina Ricci, Jamey Sheridan, Elijah Wood, Tobey Maguire
Subjects: alcohol, extramarital affairs, teenage and adult sexuality, death
Possible problems: Promiscuous adolescents; distant, uninvolved parents; profanity.

IRRECONCILABLE DIFFERENCES
Length 114 minutes
Rating: PG
Recommended age group: 13 and up
Year released: 1984
Director: Charles Shyer
Cast: Drew Barrymore, Ryan O'Neal, Shelley Long
Subjects: marriage, divorce, parenting, remarriage, careers
Possible problems: Nudity; mature language.

THE JACKIE ROBINSON STORY
Length 76 minutes
Rating: Not rated

Recommended age group: 8 and up
Year released: 1950
Director: Alfred E. Green
Cast: Jackie Robinson, Ruby Dee, Minor Watson, Louise Beavers, Richard Lane, Harry Shannon, Ben Lessy
Subjects: racism, prejudice, segregation, civil rights, baseball, history
Possible problems: None.

KIDS

Length 90 minutes
Rating: Not rated
Recommended age group: 17 and up; mature high schoolers
Year released: 1995
Director: Larry Clark
Cast: Leo Fitzpatrick, Justin Pierce, Chloe Sevigny
Subjects: STDs, loss of virginity, friends, drugs, promiscuity
Possible problems: Graphic depictions of sex and drugs; sexually promiscuous young teens engaging in unprotected intercourse and recreational drug use.

KRAMER VS. KRAMER

Length 105 minutes
Rating: PG
Recommended age group: 15 and up
Year released: 1979
Director: Robert Benton
Cast: Dustin Hoffman, Meryl Streep, Jane Alexander, Justin Henry
Subjects: divorce, custody issues, marital relationships, father-son relationships
Possible problems: None.

LASSIE

Length 92 minutes
Rating: PG
Recommended age group: 6 and up
Year released: 1994
Director: Daniel Petrie
Cast: Helen Slater, Jon Tenney, Tom Guiry, Brittany Boyd, Richard Farnsworth
Subjects: family relations, stepparenting, death,

adjusting to new environments, morality
Possible problems: Mild profanity.

THE LION KING

Length 87 minutes
Rating: G
Recommended age group: 4 and up
Year released: 1994
Directors: Roger Allers, Robert Minkoff
Cast: James Earl Jones, Jeremy Irons, Matthew Broderick, Moira Kelly (voices)
Subjects: identity, coming of age, living up to parental expectations, family, jealousy
Possible problems: Death of Simba's father, Mufasa, is very scary and sad for kids.

THE LITTLE ENGINE THAT COULD

Length 30 minutes
Rating: Not rated
Recommended age group: 3 and up
Year released: 1991
Director: Dave Edwards
Subjects: determination, self-confidence, individual differences
Possible problems: None.

THE LITTLE MERMAID

Length 85 minutes
Rating: G
Recommended age group: 3 and up
Year released: 1989
Directors: John Musker, Ron Clements
Cast: Jodi Benson, Christopher Daniel Barnes, Pat Carroll, Rene Auberjonois, Samuel E. Wright, Buddy Hackett, Jason Marin
Subjects: identity, growing up, leaving family, resisting parental figures, first love
Possible problems: Sea witch may scare small children.

A LITTLE PRINCESS

Length 97 minutes
Rating: G
Recommended age group: 7 and up

Year released: 1995
Director: Alfonso Cuaron
Cast: Liesel Matthews, Eleanor Bron, Liam Cunningham
Subjects: friendship, fantasy, orphans, family, self-confidence, individuality
Possible problems: None.

LITTLE WOMEN
Length 118 minutes
Rating: PG
Recommended age group: 11 and up
Year released: 1994
Director: Gillian Armstrong
Cast: Winona Ryder, Trini Alvarado, Claire Danes, Kirsten Dunst, Christian Bale, Gabriel Byrne, Susan Sarandon, Samantha Mathis, Mary Wickes
Subjects: sisters, Civil War, coming of age, romance, marriage, sexism, gender issues, death
Possible problems: None.

LUCAS
Length 100 minutes
Rating: PG-13
Recommended age group: 11 and up
Year released: 1986
Directors: David Seltzer, Linda Sutton
Cast: Corey Haim, Kerri Green, Charlie Sheen, Winona Ryder
Subjects: first love, social life, high school, friendship
Possible problems: None.

MARY POPPINS
Length 139 minutes
Rating: G
Recommended age group: 5 and up
Year released: 1964
Director: Robert Stevenson
Cast: Julie Andrews, Dick Van Dyke, Glynis Johns
Subjects: family, fantasy, work versus family issues, caretakers
Possible problems: None.

MASK
Length 120 minutes
Rating: PG-13
Recommended age group: 12 and up
Year released: 1985
Director: Peter Bogdanovich
Cast: Cher, Sam Elliott, Eric Stoltz, Estelle Getty, Laura Dern
Subjects: physical handicap, sickness, death, drug abuse, mother-son relationship
Possible problems: Mother uses drugs; harsh language.

MATILDA
Length 93 minutes
Rating: PG
Recommended age group: 8 and up
Year released: 1996
Director: Danny DeVito
Cast: Danny DeVito, Rhea Perlman, Embeth Davidtz, Mara Wilson, Pam Ferris
Subjects: child abuse, magic, special powers, adoption, family
Possible problems: Depicts mean parents and teachers who mentally and physically abuse children.

MEN DON'T LEAVE
Length 120 minutes
Rating: PG-13
Recommended age group: 12 and up
Year released: 1989
Director: Paul Brickman
Cast: Jessica Lange, Chris O'Donnell, Joan Cusack, Arliss Howard, Charlie Korsmo
Subjects: death, grieving, single-parent family, loyalty, blended families
Possible problems: None.

A MIRACLE ON 34TH STREET
Length 97 minutes
Rating: Not rated
Recommended age group: 8 and up
Year released: 1947

Director: George Seaton
Cast: Maureen O'Hara, John Payne, Edmund Gwenn, Natalie Wood, William Frawley, Porter Hall
Subjects: Christmas, imagination, fantasy, miracles, family
Possible problems: None.

THE MIRACLE WORKER
Length 107 minutes
Rating: Not rated
Recommended age group: 8 and up
Year released: 1962
Director: Arthur Penn
Cast: Anne Bancroft, Patty Duke, Victor Jory, Inga Swenson, Andrew Prine, Beah Richards
Subjects: handicaps, deafness, blindness, teachers
Possible problems: Some of the teaching sessions may scare younger children.

MR. MOM
Length 92 minutes
Rating: PG
Recommended age group: 6 and up
Year released: 1983
Director: Stan Dragoti
Cast: Michael Keaton, Teri Garr, Christopher Lloyd, Martin Mull, Ann Jillian, Jeffrey Tambor, Edie McClurg
Subjects: family relations, gender roles, household responsibilities, unemployment, marital difficulties
Possible problems: Near-sexual situations.

MRS. DOUBTFIRE
Length 125 minutes
Rating: PG-13
Recommended age group: 9 and up
Year released: 1993
Director: Chris Columbus
Cast: Robin Williams, Sally Field, Pierce Brosnan, Mara Wilson
Subjects: divorce, families, custody issues, single parenting
Possible problems: None.

MY GIRL
Length 102 minutes
Rating: PG
Recommended age group: 10 and up
Year released: 1991
Director: Howard Zieff
Cast: Anna Chlumsky, Dan Aykroyd, Jamie Lee Curtis, Macaulay Culkin, Richard Masur
Subjects: coming of age, menstruation, first kiss, death, remarriage
Possible problems: None.

MY LIFE
Length 112 minutes
Rating: PG-13
Recommended age group: 13 and up
Year released: 1993
Director: Bruce Joel Rubin
Cast: Michael Keaton, Nicole Kidman, Bradley Whitford, Queen Latifah, Michael Constantine, Rebecca Schull
Subjects: sickness, death, forgiveness, birth, family relationships
Possible problems: None.

OCTOBER SKY
Length 108 minutes
Rating: PG
Recommended age group: 10 and up
Year released: 1999
Director: Joe Johnston
Cast: Jacob Gyllenhaal, Laura Dern, Chris Cooper, Natalie Canerday
Subjects: father-son issues, individuality, coming of age, rocketry, teachers, education
Possible problems: Brief teen sensuality; alcohol use.

ONE TRUE THING
Length 127 minutes
Rating: R
Recommended age group: 15 and up

Year released: 1998
Director: Carl Franklin
Cast: Meryl Streep, William Hurt, Renee Zellweger
Subjects: sickness, death, dying, family relationships, forgiveness, commitment
Possible problems: Profanity.

ORDINARY PEOPLE
Length 124 minutes
Rating: R
Recommended age group: 13 and up
Year released: 1980
Director: Robert Redford
Cast: Donald Sutherland, Mary Tyler Moore, Judd Hirsch, Timothy Hutton, Elizabeth McGovern
Subjects: death, suicide, therapy, mental illness, divorce
Possible problems: Mature subjects.

THE OUTSIDERS
Length 91 minutes
Rating: PG
Recommended age group: 10 and up
Year released: 1983
Director: Francis Ford Coppola
Cast: C. Thomas Howell, Matt Dillon, Ralph Macchio, Patrick Swayze, Rob Lowe, Diane Lane, Tom Cruise
Subjects: gangs, cliques, bullies, friends, death, heroes
Possible problems: Violent knife fights between gangs.

PARENTHOOD
Length 124 minutes
Rating: PG-13
Recommended age group: 12 and up
Year released: 1989
Director: Ron Howard
Cast: Steve Martin, Mary Steenburgen, Dianne Wiest, Jason Robards, Rick Moranis, Keanu Reeves
Subjects: parenthood, divorce, children's behavior, dating, marriage, grandparents
Possible problems: Implied teen sexuality; reference to parent smoking marijuana; joke about mother's vibrator.

THE PARENT TRAP
Length 127 minutes
Rating: PG
Recommended age group: 8 and up
Year released: 1998
Director: Nancy Meyers, Charles Shyer
Cast: Lindsay Lohan, Dennis Quaid, Natasha Richardson
Subjects: divorce, identical twins, camp, marriage, remarriage
Possible problems: Distraught mother is drunk in one scene; minor mischief by the twins.

PETER PAN
Length 76 minutes
Rating: G
Recommended age group: 3 and up
Year released: 1953
Directors: Hamilton Luske, Clyde Geronimi, Wilfred Jackson
Cast: Bobby Driscoll, Kathryn Beaumont, Hans Conried, Heather Angel, Candy Candido (voices)
Subjects: fantasy, fears, imagination, growing up, jealousy, parents
Possible problems: None.

PI
Length 85 minutes
Rating: R
Recommended age group: 16 and up
Year released: 1998
Director: Darren Aronofsky
Cast: Sean Gulette, Mark Margolis, Ben Shenkman, Pamela Hart, Stephen Pearlman
Subjects: mathematics, Jewish mysticism, stock market, chaos theory, numerology, paranoid schizophrenia
Possible problems: Bizarre scenes and disturbing images; harsh language.

PINOCCHIO
Length 87 minutes
Rating: G
Recommended age group: 3 an up
Year released: 1940
Director: Ben Sharpsteen
Cast: Dick Jones, Cliff Edwards, Evelyn Venable, Walter Catlett, Frankie Darro (voices)
Subjects: conscience, honesty, bravery, obeying parents, adventure
Possible problems: Scary scenes include Pleasure Island, where boys are turned into donkeys, and inside the mouth of Monstro the Whale.

POCAHONTAS
Length 90 minutes
Rating: G
Recommended age group: 5 and up
Year released: 1995
Directors: Mike Gabriel, Eric Goldberg
Cast: Irene Bedard, Mel Gibson, Judy Kuhn, David Odgen Stiers, Russell Means, Linda Hunt (voices)
Subjects: stereotypes, American Indians, English settlers, racism, romance
Possible problems: None.

POLLYANNA
Length 134 minutes
Rating: G
Recommended age group: 7 and up
Year released: 1960
Director: David Swift
Cast: Hayley Mills, Jane Wyman, Richard Egan, Karl Malden, Adolphe Menjou, Agnes Moorehead
Subjects: orphans, being positive, small town community, selflessness, parenting issues, wealth
Possible problems: None.

QUIZ SHOW
Length 130 minutes
Rating: PG-13
Recommended age group: 12 and up
Year released: 1994
Director: Robert Redford
Cast: John Turturro, Ralph Fiennes, Rob Morrow, David Paymer
Subjects: ethics, morals, media, television, 1950s, racism, game shows
Possible problems: Mature language.

REALITY BITES
Length 98 minutes
Rating: PG-13
Recommended age group: 15 and up
Year released: 1994
Director: Ben Stiller
Cast: Winona Ryder, Ben Stiller, Ethan Hawke, Janeane Garofalo, Swoosie Kurtz, Steve Zahn
Subjects: jobs, dating, love, sex, STDs, homosexuality
Possible problems: Sexually promiscuous character; depiction of recreational drug use; profanity.

REBEL WITHOUT A CAUSE
Length 111 minutes
Rating: Not rated
Recommended age group: 13 and up
Year released: 1955
Director: Nicholas Ray
Cast: James Dean, Natalie Wood, Sal Mineo, Jim Backus, Corey Allen, Edward Platt, Dennis Hopper
Subjects: alienated teenagers, parental problems, social life, gangs, police
Possible problems: None.

SCENT OF A WOMAN
Length 149 minutes
Rating: R
Recommended age group: 12 and up
Year released: 1992
Director: Martin Brest
Cast: Al Pacino, Chris O'Donnell, James Rebhorn, Gabrielle Anwar, Phillip S. Hoffman

Subjects: preparatory schools, morality, lying, suicide, honor, integrity, class
Possible problems: Profanity; main character drinks.

SCHOOL TIES
Length 110 minutes
Rating: PG-13
Recommended age group: 13 and up
Year released: 1992
Director: Robert Mandel
Cast: Brendan Fraser, Matt Damon, Chris O'Donnell, Andrew Lowery
Subjects: anti-Semitism, cheating, academic and parental pressure
Possible problems: Harsh language.

SEARCHING FOR BOBBY FISCHER
Length 110 minutes
Rating: PG
Recommended age group: 10 and up
Year released: 1993
Director: Steven Zaillian
Cast: Joe Mantegna, Max Pomeranc, Joan Allen, Ben Kingsley, Laurence Fishburne, Michael Nirenburg
Subjects: competition, individuality, parenting, teachers, chess, achievement
Possible problems: None.

THE SECRET GARDEN
Length 101 minutes
Rating: G
Recommended age group: 8 and up
Year released: 1993
Director: Agnieszka Holland
Cast: Maggie Smith, Kate Maberly
Subjects: handicaps, death, grieving, friendship, healing, garden, nurturing
Possible problems: None.

SIMON BIRCH
Length 113 minutes
Rating: PG
Recommended age group: 9 and up

Year released: 1998
Director: Mark Steven Johnson
Cast: Ian Michael Smith, Joseph Mazello, Ashley Judd, Oliver Platt, David Straithairn
Subjects: friendship, handicaps, sickness, death
Possible problems: Some harsh language; a scary accident.

THE SIXTH SENSE
Length 105 minutes
Rating: PG-13
Recommended age group: 13 and up
Year released: 1999
Director: M. Night Shyamalan
Cast: Bruce Willis, Haley Joel Osment, Toni Collette
Subjects: death, ghosts, paranormal, fear, psychology, single parenting
Possible problems: Very scary, gory scenes and depictions of dead people may scare children under 13.

SLUMS OF BEVERLY HILLS
Length 90 minutes
Rating: R
Recommended age group: 15 and up
Year released: 1998
Director: Tamara Jenkins
Cast: Natasha Lyonne, Alan Arkin, Marisa Tomei, Kevin Corrigan
Subjects: coming of age, loss of virginity, family life, 1970s
Possible problems: Nudity; sexuality; profanity.

THE SNEETCHES (in **Dr. Seuss'** *Sing-a-long with Green Eggs & Ham, and The Zax*)
Length 50 minutes
Rating: Not rated
Recommended age group: 3 and up
Year released: 1960
Subjects: diversity, prejudice, racism, equality
Possible problems: None.

SOUNDER
Length 105 minutes
Rating: G
Recommended age group: 7 and up
Year released: 1972
Director: Martin Ritt
Cast: Paul Winfield, Cicely Tyson, Kevin Hooks, Taj Mahal, Carmen Mathews, James Best, Janet MacLachlan
Subjects: family issues, poverty, education, racism
Possible problems: A racist man shoots the family dog.

SPLENDOR IN THE GRASS
Length 124 minutes
Rating: Not rated
Recommended age group: 12 and up
Year released: 1961
Director: Elia Kazan
Cast: Natalie Wood, Warren Beatty, Pat Hingle, Audrey Christie, Sandy Dennis, Barbara Loden
Subjects: first love, sexual awakening, mental illness, loss of virginity, parental pressures
Possible problems: None.

STAND AND DELIVER
Length 105 minutes
Rating: PG
Recommended age group: 13 and up
Year released: 1988
Director: Ramon Menendez
Cast: Edward James Olmos, Lou Diamond Phillips, Rosanna de Soto, Andy Garcia
Subjects: education, racism, morality, ethics, minorities, mentors
Possible problems: None.

STAND BY ME
Length 87 minutes
Rating: R
Recommended age group: 8 and up
Year released: 1986

Director: Rob Reiner
Cast: River Phoenix, Wil Wheaton, Jerry O'Connell, Corey Feldman, Kiefer Sutherland, Richard Dreyfuss, Casey Siemaszko, John Cusack
Subjects: friendship, growing up, social life, bullies, death, family
Possible problems: Profanity; physical fighting.

STEPMOM
Length 150 minutes
Rating: PG-13
Recommended age group: 11 and up
Year released: 1998
Director: Chris Columbus
Cast: Susan Sarandon, Julia Roberts, Ed Harris
Subjects: divorce, stepparenting, family relationships, blended families
Possible problems: None.

SUMMER OF '42
Length 102 minutes
Rating: R
Recommended age group: 12 and up
Year released: 1971
Director: Robert Mulligan
Cast: Jennifer O'Neill, Gary Grimes, Jerry Houser, Oliver Conant
Subjects: coming of age, loss of virginity, first love, sexual awakening
Possible problems: None.

THE SWISS FAMILY ROBINSON
Length 126 minutes
Rating: G
Recommended age group: 4 and up
Year released: 1960
Director: Ken Annakin
Cast: John Mills, Dorothy McGuire, James MacArthur, Tommy Kirk, Janet Munro
Subjects: family, gender roles, dealing with crisis, nature, civilization, adventure, danger
Possible problems: None.

To Kill A Mockingbird
Length 129 minutes
Rating: Not rated
Recommended age group: 9 and up
Year released: 1962
Director: Robert Mulligan
Cast: Gregory Peck, Robert Duvall, Brock Peters
Subjects: prejudice, mortality, ethics, values, racism
Possible problems: Plot includes scenes from a rape trial; threatened lynching.

Tom and Huck
Length 92 minutes
Rating: PG
Recommended age group: 8 and up
Year released: 1996
Director: Peter Hewitt
Cast: Jonathan Taylor Thomas, Brad Renfro, Eric Schweig, Charles Rocket, Amy Wright, Michael McShane
Subjects: friendship, loyalty, honesty, morality, rules
Possible problems: Stabbings; a near drowning; skeletons in a scary cave.

Torch Song Trilogy
Length 126 minutes
Rating: R
Recommended age group: 16 and up
Year released: 1988
Director: Paul Bogart
Cast: Harvey Fierstein, Anne Bancroft, Matthew Broderick, Brian Kerwin
Subjects: homosexuality, relationships, prejudice, bisexuality, infidelity, death
Possible problems: Scenes of gay life in New York, including gay bashing and gay bars; mature language.

Total Recall
Length 113 minutes
Rating: R
Recommended age group: 13 and up
Year released: 1990
Director: Paul Verhoeven
Cast: Arnold Schwarzenegger, Rachel Ticotin, Sharon Stone, Ronny Cox
Subjects: the future, Mars, mutants, interplanetary travel and colonization
Possible problems: Violence; mature language.

Toy Story
Length 80 minutes
Rating: G
Recommended age group: 3 and up
Year released: 1995
Director: John Lasseter
Cast: Tom Hanks, Tim Allen, Annie Potts, Don Rickles, John Ratzenberger, Wallace Shawn (voices)
Subjects: friendship, jealousy, empathy
Possible problems: None.

A Tree Grows in Brooklyn
Length 128 minutes
Rating: G
Recommended age group: 8 and up
Year released: 1945
Director: Elia Kazan
Cast: Peggy Ann Garner, James Dunn, Dorothy McGuire, Joan Blondell, Lloyd Nolan, Ted Donaldson, James Gleason, John Alexander
Subjects: family, poverty, education
Possible problems: Alcoholism.

Truly, Madly, Deeply
Length 107 minutes
Rating: PG-13
Recommended age group: 12 and up
Year released: 1991
Director: Anthony Minghella
Cast: Juliet Stevenson, Alan Rickman, Bill Paterson
Subjects: death, grieving, relationships
Possible problems: None.

WHEN A MAN LOVES A WOMAN
Length 124 minutes
Rating: R
Recommended age group: 15 and up
Year released: 1994
Director: Luis Mandoki
Cast: Andy Garcia, Meg Ryan, Lauren Tom, Mae Whitman, Ellen Burstyn
Subjects: alcoholism, addiction, enablers, marriage, rehabilitation process
Possible problems: Depiction of adult alcoholism; one scene shows physical abuse of child; mature language.

WILLY WONKA & THE CHOCOLATE FACTORY
Length 98 minutes
Rating: G
Recommended age group: 7 and up
Year released: 1971
Director: Mel Stuart
Cast: Gene Wilder, Jack Albertson, Peter Ostrum
Subjects: manners, greed, morality, parenting, rules, social class, integrity
Possible problems: Some scenes may scare children under 7.

THE WIZARD OF OZ
Length 101 minutes
Rating: G
Recommended age group: 6 and up
Year released: 1939
Director: Victor Fleming
Cast: Judy Garland, Margaret Hamilton, Ray Bolger, Jack Haley, Bert Lahr, Frank Morgan, Charles Grapewin
Subjects: identity, dreams, homesickness, facing fear, believing in oneself
Possible problems: Some scenes may be scary for children under 6.

YENTL
Length 134 minutes
Rating: PG
Recommended age group: 8 and up
Year released: 1983
Director: Barbra Steisand
Cast: Barbra Steisand, Mandy Patinkin, Amy Irving, Nehemiah Persoff
Subjects: gender roles, identity, sexuality, romance, stereotypes, Eastern Europe, Judaism
Possible problems: Boys 8-12 may not be able to handle this film; the confused gender issue may make them silly or uncomfortable.

AUTHORS' NOTES

Having worked with children and parents as a psychologist for over twenty-five years, I have always tried to find more creative and effective ways for families to talk over important issues without sounding like it's gospel from Mount Sinai. On a personal level, some of my own family's best exchanges of ideas, where everyone shared or learned something from everyone else, have taken place after seeing a good movie. Films made surviving adolescence with our now-twenty-year-old college student somewhat easier. We'd frequently talk over the ideas of drugs, sex, friendships, and other issues that if brought up in another context (i.e. around the dinner table), would not have been heard as readily. Likewise, movies provide concrete examples of various issues that we discuss with our eight-year-old twins.

Discussing movies has also helped me illustrate concepts in my twenty years of teaching undergraduate and graduate college students in psychology. What better way to describe the pressures and stereo-types teens struggle with today than by showing clips from *The Breakfast Club,* which just about every young person has seen at one time or another.

Corey and I saw an opportunity to take critical developmental issues and apply them to the many wonderful movies available to parents, and help them have more fun, learn a little more, and maybe even help a family interact a little better after having used our discussion questions and pointers. We also try to warn parents where some of the sensitivities may be in asking certain questions, and try to open the lines of communication about topics that can be so difficult to discuss.

Here is a book where families, education, and important issues are brought together to enrich family lives. We hope you enjoyed it.

—Ronald Madison, Ed.D.

I grew up in a household where it was required by my father to watch classic films. A sports filmmaker himself, he always appreciated quality films from various genres. Films served as a bridge between my dad and me, and continued to play that role throughout our life changes. Regardless of the sensitivities and difficulties we were struggling with in our personal relationship, movies provided a common ground on which we'd inevitably connect. Today, my father and I still come together on our mutual love of watching films, and discuss them both from cinematic and psychological perspectives afterwards.

Sometime after receiving an undergraduate degree in psychology from the University of Pennsylvania and working in public relations, I began to think about how the very process that worked so well for my father and I might work for other families. The idea for *Talking Pictures* grew out of my natural life experiences—therein laid the beauty of the concept: *Everyone* watches movies, but clearly not everyone has such an easy time communicating with their families. *Talking Pictures* had been alive and well not only in my life, but in the lives of families throughout the world, though perhaps they just didn't know it. Ron and I designed this book as a guide to help other families do what's been working so well for ours for so many years. We hope you got as much out of these films and this process as we have.

—Corey Schmidt

INDEX